INDO-NEPAL TRADE RELATIONS

Indo–Nepal Trade Relations

A Historical Analysis of Nepal's Trade with the British India

Shreeram Prasad Upadhyaya

Nirala Series-20

Nirala Publications
Jaipur New Delhi

Nirala Publications
G. P. O. Box 394
Nawab Ka Chauraha, Ghat Gate
Jaipur—302 001 (India)

2525, Kuch Challan
Darya Ganj, New Delhi—110002

First Edition 1992

Printed at
Rajendra Printers
S-2, Shopping Centre, Tilak Nagar
Jaipur—302 004
and
Shalimar Offset Printers
Darya Ganj, New Delhi—110002

Nirala Series

A Series of Contemporary Writing

1. *The British and the Brave*
   Kamal Raj Singh Rathaur
2. *The Khasa Kingdom*
   Surya Mani Adhikary
3. *Sources of Inflation in Asia*
   Raghab D. Pant
4. *Fire of Himal : The Sherpas*
   Ramesh Raj Kunwar
5. *Nepalese Plan Performance*
   Gunanidhi Sharma
6. *Folk Culture of Nepal*
   Ram Dayal Rakesh
7. *Fundamentals of Library and Information Science*
   Madhusudan Sharma Subedi
8. *Transit of Land-locked Countries and Nepal*
   Gajendra Mani Pradhan
9. *The Gurungs : Thunder of Himal*
   Murari P. Regmi
10. *Folk Tales of Sherpa and Yeti*
    Shiva Dhakal
11. *Gods and Mountains : The Folk Culture of a Himalayan Kingdom, Nepal*
    Kesar Lall
12. *Art and Culture of Nepal*
    Saphalya Amatya

13. *The Dhimals : Miraculous Migrants of Himal*
Rishikeshab Raj Regmi
14. *Sales Promotion in Nepal : Policies and Practices*
Parashar Prasad Koirala
15. *Glimpses of Tourism, Airlines and Management in Nepal*
B. R. Singh
16. *The Taming of Tibet*
Tirtha Prasad Mishra
17. *Dolpo : The Hidden Paradise*
Karna Sakya
18. *Secrets of Shangri-la*
Nagendra Sharma
19. *Transportation Systems in Nepal*
Mukund R. Satyal
20. *Indo-Nepal Trade Relations*
Shri Ram Upadhyaya
21. *Politics and Development in Nepal*
Narayan Khadka
22. *The Gorkha Connection*
Purushotam Baskota
23. *Lore and Legend of the Kathmandu Valley*
Shiva Dhakal
24. *Recent Nepal : The Analysis of Recent Democratic Upsurge and its Aftermath*
Laxman Bahadur K. C.
25. *Popular Emblems and Images of Nepal*
Dhrub K. Deep
26. *The Cultural Heritage of Nepal Terai*
Ram Dayal Rakesh

Born at Siraha, District Siraha, Sagarmatha zone Dr. Shreeram Prasad Upadhyaya, is Nepal's prominent historian. He was educated first at Tribhuvan University, Kathmandu where he received his Master Degree in two different subjects : M.A. in History and M.Ed. in Social Studies. Later, he received his doctoral degree from the University of Delhi, Delhi for his research "Indo-Nepal Trade Relations 1858-1914".

Since then Dr. Upadhyaya has been writing articles for the leading journals. He is the author and co-author of two important books titled, *Modern History of Eastern Asia* and *History of Europe*. He has done research both on History and Education. Tribhuvan University has published his thesis on Education.

Dr. Upadhyaya is Associate Professor of History in Tribhuvan University, Kathmandu. He is also chairman of History Instruction Committee and Subject Committee and a member of the Faculty Board.

Acknowledgments

The present thesis seeks to analyse the nature and extent of Indo-Nepal trade relations during 1858-1914 and to explain the causes of its fluctuations from time to time. The political and cultural relations between the two countries have been covered in numerous books by foreign and Nepalese scholars. But economic and trade relations have not received adequate attention from historians. This study is a modest attempt to fill this gap during a major part of the long Rana regime, when the pattern of Nepal's commercial relations with British India underwent a significant change. I have tried here to indicate the process of this change and analyse the circumstances under which it took place.

In his book titled *Indo-Nepal Trade in the Nineteenth Century* Dr Jahar Sen has discussed some aspects of Indo-Nepal trade. It is the first attempt in this field. In it he has not dealt with some of the most important aspects of Indo-Nepal trade, such as commercial policies, rates of customs duties, taxes, transaction of commodities, smuggling, growth of market and trade centres and the impact of this trade on Nepal. The major thrust of Dr Sen's work is British interest in Nepal. Consequently his treatment of Indo-Nepal trade remains lopsided. Another limitation of his work stems from his inability to have access to the documents of the Foreign and Finance Ministries of Nepal which are a rich source of information.

Political and diplomatic aspects of Indo-Nepal relations

have been dealt with in numerous monographs. I have therefore only briefly touched on such political and diplomatic aspects as had some bearing on the commerical contacts between the two countries. The main area of my investigation has throughout remained trade and commerce between the two countries. As far as possible I have tried to check and correlate evidence culled from the National Archives of India with that from Nepalese sources. Reports on Indo-Nepal trade published by Regmi Research Centre, Kathmandu, the Bengal and North Western Provinces Governments and the Gazetteers edited by W.W. Hunter and P.C. Roychaudhury are extremely useful and I have used them extensively. Sifting and selecting documents and private papers kept in the record section of the Foreign Ministry of Nepal and the Charkhal Adda record section and Kaushitosakhana under the Ministry of Finance in Nepal took a lot of my time because no catalogue or index has been prepared for consulting them for research purposes. Apart from official records and private papers, newspapers and journals in Nepali and English have helped me considerably in understanding Indo-Nepal trade relations properly, and in reconstructing its history during the period under study.

I have had to face numerous difficulties in collecting relevant materials, which are neither classified nor kept systematically and properly in the Nepalese Ministries. But even more difficult was to get permission for access to the documents available in the Foreign Ministry of Nepal.

The present thesis shows that the British India's relations with Nepal in the 19th and early 20th centuries started and developed with trade and commerce. The British were greatly interested in expanding their trade in Nepal. But the Nepalese were always suspicious of British motives and were unwilling to allow unrestricted expansion of British trade and economic enterprise in their country. None of the Rana Prime Ministers, including even those who were most amenable to British advice and overtures, were willing to let the British treat Nepal as no man's land in their economic interests, for they genuinely feared that it would ultimately undermine the freedom of their country. Nevertheless, despite these handicaps, Indo-Nepal trade during the period made notable progress.

I would like to express my deep sense of gratitude to Dr R.L. Shukla, Professor in the Department of History, University of Delhi, under whose able guidance the present study was completed. In spite of his busy schedule he has helped me in many ways throughout the entire period of my research. I express my gratitude to Shri Sita Ram Singh, Professor and former Head of the Department of History, Bihar University, Muzaffarpur, for his nicely written "Foreword' to this book. I also wish to express my gratitude to Mrs Kumud Shukla for inspiring and consoling me when the sudden death of my respected father Shri B. Krishna Prasad Upadhyaya in the course of this study upset me. I remember the days when she would express anxiety about the progress of my research.

I acknowledge with thanks the help and support which many individuals and institutions extended to me in course of my work. I am especially grateful to Mr P.K. Shukla of the Indian Council of Historical Research, New Delhi, to Dr. and Mrs Pushkar Reejal, Triratna Manandhar, Mr and Mrs Shyam Prasad Kharel and Mr Deepak Prasad Kharel for the kindness they showed to me. I would also like to express my affection to my younger brother Pradhuman Prasad Upadhyaya who made my stay in Delhi possible by taking the burden of the family on his shoulders after the death of my father. The love of my small daughter Pranita was also a constant source of encouragement to me.

I would be failing in my duty if I do not thank my wife Mrs Bhagawati who suffered a breakdown of her health while helping me in my research work. I am grateful to her for supplying me with material used in the thesis for geographical locations and for suggesting the inclusion of maps.

During the course of my study I visited several ministries, institutions and libraries in Nepal as well as in India. I wish to express my thanks to the staff of the Ministry of Foreign Affairs and Ministry of Finance, His Majesty's Government of Nepal, the National Archives of India, New Delhi; Central Library, University of Delhi; Pattan Tata Library, University of Delhi; Library of the Indian Council of World Affairs, Sapru House New Delhi; Library of ICHR, New Delhi; I.C.S.S.R. Library, New Delhi; Central Library, Tribhuvan University, Kathmandu and Kaiser Library Kathmandu. The staff of the Department of History, University of Delhi, were always helpful to me.

Finally, I am very much thankful to my friend Mr. Yuyutsu R.D. Sharma, for undertaking the publication of this book.

Delhi —**Shreeram Prasad Upadhyaya**

Foreword

The British occupation of India was a classical example of imperialism gradually spreading its tentacles over the entire life of an ancient, culture. Beginning as a trading company in the era of mercantilism, the British dragged India through the period of industrial capitalism and ultimately converted it into the exporter of raw materials and importer of finished goods in the age of finance capitalism.

It was this colonial India whose trade relations with Nepal (1858—1914) Dr Upadhyaya proposes to examine in this book. Secure in their mountainous vastness, extremely proud of their freedom in their land-locked country, the Nepalese were very suspicious of the motives of the British. They had already had a foretaste of British diplomacy and armed might in 1816. They had also perceived how India had been pulverised in course of the preceding hundred years morally as well as materially. They had seen the Nepalese proverb—'The tradesman brings the Bible, the Bible brings the bayonet'—fully exemplified in India. So there was in this respect remarkable continuity and consistency in the attitude of the Rana Prime Ministers that they were always suspicious of British motives. Aware of the Indian precedent, they were extremely reluctant to allow the free entry of colonial Indian traders into Nepal. The Nepalese Government never permitted the penetration of British capital and enterprise in Nepal. Even commercial activities were to remain within specified limits prescribed through mutual agreements arrived at from time to time between the contracting parties. To keep trade within reasonable limits, the Nepalese

Government pursued a carefully worked out policy of monopolies especially in case of timber which covered a sizable percentage of Nepalese exports. This policy was also favoured because of the high profits derived from the lucrative Indo-Nepalese trade in which senior civil and military officers of Nepal were engaged. Rulers sold monopoly rights to merchants who remitted a share of their profit to the Prime Minister. Monopoly also served to divert the attention of the elite (Sardars, notables, officers intellectuals, etc.) from politics to commerce, which brought them handsome profits. Apprehensive of political and territorial designs characteristic of British imperialism, the rulers of Nepal refused to be beguiled by the prospects of material prosperity dangled before them by the colonialists.

The writer has made an in-depth study of the commercial transactions between Nepal and British India round which political and cultural relations between the two revolved. Fluctuations in trade relations were there from time to time, but these ups and downs were not always due to economic and commercial causes; often non-commercial factors interceded to alter its pattern and the commodities involved in transactions between the two countries. There were fluctuations due to the changing politics and attitudes of the governments of the two countries, particularly in the case of the Nepalese Prime Ministers. Their attitude towards this trade reflected change rather than continuity. The Prime Ministers were often dictated by the motives of personal gains and occasionally by their whims and caprices.

For example, Jang Bahadur Rana had very friendly relations with the British and had rendered them valuable service in the Revolt of 1857, and so the sluggish Indo-Nepal trade had a remarkable boost during his rule. It continued to grow during the entire period of the political supremacy of the Ranas which may be called the golden age in the commercial annals of Nepal. She had a favourable balance of trade by virtue of her exports which far exceeded her imports. The policy of different Rana Prims Ministers never made a sharp break with the traditional policy of isolation and of opposition to free trade and to unrestricted economic and commercial penetration into Nepal which had ominous political implications. Whatever relaxation, flexibility or liberalisation was allowed was dictated by the motives of expediency which in the case of Ranodip Singh and Bir Shamsher was to seek British support to strengthen the autocratic stronghold of the Ranas. But even this was not free from suspicion. Even repeated British denials of any annexationist motive could not disabuse the Nepalese mind. So their persistent policy was to keep the British at a safe distance.

During the time of Chandra Shamsher the British were able to enjoy an upper hand in Indo-Nepalese trade under changed circumstances. The British now suspected Franco-Russian designs on the Himalayan regions. There was also the necessity of recruiting Gorkha soldiers to the Indian army in view of the growing nationalist movement in India. Thus the two countries were drawn together and commerce between Nepal and India followed.

Towards the close of the 19th century certain other factors also encouraged trade between the two countries. Development of transport and communication, proximity of the Terai to British India and opening of Indian railways in the districts bordering Nepal encouraged trade and commerce. Now there was a growth of towns and markets on the Nepalese side as well, for example, Nepalganj, Birganj, Biratnagar. Newar merchants from Kathmandu and Muslim merchants from India flocked to the places. Rivers and rivulets flowing from Nepal into the bordering districts of Purnea, Bhagalpur, Darbhanga, Muzaffarpur, Champaran, Gorakhpur, Basti, Pilibhit, etc. also served as waterways and encouraged trade between the two countries. But the Nepalese were not enthusiastic in developing the roads which would break the hills. The Nepalese were opposed to it as they regarded the hills as their natural fortifications. But this did not seriously hamper the Indo-Nepalese Trade.

Equally unwilling was Nepal to allow the British to trade with Tibet through its territory. From Jang Bahadur onwards they were jealous of opening up Tibet for trade fearing damage to Nepalese commercial interests in that country. There was also intense competition between Nepal and British India on the entrepot trade with Tibet through Nepal. But Nepal never submitted to British pressure and maintained her privileged position in Lhasa where she enjoyed extra-territorial rights since 1856.

The writer also throws light on the nature of Indo-Nepalese trade. Nepal had a very favourable balance of trade. Her exports were forest products, food grains (particularly rice). The imports to Nepal were salt, sugar, tobacco, cloth and luxury goods for the use of the Rana family and the elite groups.

An important feature of the Indo-Nepalese trade was slave traffic. Slavery had been abolished in colonial India long back, but it was still legal in Nepal. Poor people from North India sold their children in Nepal to officials and the gentry.

Dr Upadhyaya has also discussed the impact of Nepal's trade relations with colonial India on the social and political life of the country. There was some sort of westernisation and some progress of science and technology, and stately buildings of western style came up at places. But this prosperity was confined to the classes rather than the masses. It was the ruling Ranocracy and the insignificant elite which utilised this wealth derived from trade and commerce to purchase foreign goods of luxury for its worthless life. It was not put to the production of useful goods to build up a modern industrial society which would have cleared the way for the rise of a prosperous Nepal. Colonial India also bolstered up a reactionary ruling class in Nepal which would help it in maintaing a decadent colonial system in India. It was no accident that the year of the adoption of a republican democratic, egalitarian and secular constitution by India also witnessed the emergence of a democratic Nepal and the end of the Ranocracy.

Dr Upadhyaya's book should be of great interest to both Indian and Nepalese citizens. They will realize that the fate of the two countries is inextricably linked up. A colonial India was a menace to Nepal; a free, democratic and socialist India will be a helpful partner in common prosperity. Sincere cooperation between the two countries on the basis of liberty, equality and fraternity will usber in an era of unprecedented development to the mutual benefit of both the countries. Geography and history have destined India and Nepal to work together for their common development and for the welfare of the world.

I wish this book a wide circulation.

—Sita Ram Singh
Former Professor and Head
Department of History
Bihar University

List of Tables

Dedicated to my late Father
Shri **B. Krishna Prasad Upadhyaya**

Contents

Background

CHAPTER ONE

1.1 Introduction

The intimacy of India and Nepal developed with the growth of trade and commerce between these two countries. Nothing but trade helped the people of both the countries to come closer and to understand each other. But with the establishment of British power in Bengal after 1757 British trade policy came to be looked upon with great suspicion in Nepal. There is a Nepalese proverb, "A trader brings the Bible, the Bible brings the bayonet." Even the Malla Kings of the Kathmadu Valley did not have good opinion about the British, but it was the question of survival which compelled Jaya Prakash, the last Malla King, to accept British help against Gorkha[1]. Gorkha soldiers under the leadership of Prithvi Narayan Shah blockaded the Kathmandu Valley to deprive the Malla ruler from the revenue derived from the Tibetan trade.[2] The impact of this economic blockade was felt in Tibet, in the Kathmandu Valley as well as in the territories of the East India Company. The first to react were the British, who were determined on military intervention in Nepal in favour or Jaya Prakash.[3] Prithvi Narayan Shah defeated the East India Company soldiers sent under the command of Captain Kinlock at Sindhuli in 1767.[4] After this defeat the East India Company realised the strength of Gorkha soldiers and the weakness of the British army. From that time until the mid-nineteenth century, relationship between Nepal and the Company remained unhappy and often got engulfed in misunderstanding, hostilities and enmity.[5] Prithvi Narayan Shah was quite annoyed with the British. But the British lost no time in changing their policy in favour of friendship. A British mission headed by James Logan was sent to strengthen the tie of friendship and to improve trade relations[6] with Nepal. He carried two letters from Governor Verelst to Prithvi Narayan Shah. In his letter to the King, the Governor was apologetic and he conveyed that his Government helped Jaya Prakash Malla against Gorkha on account of ignorance. But it had no effect upon the mind of Prithvi Narayan Shah. The Logan Mission failed to achieve its purpose.[7]

Even after the failure of Logan Mission the British followed a policy of conciliation. They sent envoys and residents; they proposed treaties and agreements. but Nepal remained firmly shut. Not only were the markets of Nepal closed to the direct exploitation of the British traders, but the lucrative markets of Tibet as well.[8] The result of this policy brought Nepal in the line of direct confrontation with the British in 1814.[9] Nepal was badly defeated in the war and she had to lose vast area of her territory. Altogether some forty thousand square miles were given up.[10] She was compelled to receive British Resident permanently. The Resident was a constant reminder of their defeat. The attitude of the Nepal Darbar towards the Resident was 'suspicious and haughty". After the war of 1814-16, Nepal not only remained a mere centre for their commercial transaction, but also acquired an important position in their 'strategic calculations'.[12] It was for the first time that the British realised that any further hostility with Nepal would be a costly affair for them and to avoid that risk peace was to be maintained.[13]

With the coming of Jang Bahadur Rana to power in 1846, Indo-Nepal Relations entered a new phase. The British got a stable, friendly and co-operative Government. He mobilized his army to protect the British during the dark days of the Mutiny of 1857.[14] As a reward for his services Nepal received back from the British Government the whole of the lowlands between the river Kali and Rapti, and the whole of the lowlands between the river Rapti and the district of Gorakhpur which were in the possession of Nepal in the year 1815, and were ceded to the British Government by Article III of the treaty concluded at Sugauli on 2 December in that year.[15]

Jang Bahadur maintained friendly and cooperative but not close relations with the British Government of India. He never allowed tee door of Nepal to be opened to Europeans in any field whether commercial, social or political.[16] There was constant tug of war between the British and Nepalese Governments for getting more privileges in Nepal in the matter of trade and commerce. In spite of all these obstacles Indo-Nepal trade flourished. Annual value of trade which appropriately trebled in the fifty years from 1835 trebled again by the end of the century, with the value of Nepalese exports being double that of imports.[17] However, the First World War of 1914-18, affected the Indo-Nepalese trade. The volume of commodities exported from and imported into Nepal declined considerably as a result of the war.[18]

Geography: Nepal, a beautiful and small country,[19] is land-locked by highly populated countries of Asia, China in the north and India in the south. It lies between 80° 15'-88°10' east longitude and 26°20-30°10' north latitudes, along the southern slopes of the Himalayas. It has an area of 147,181 sq. km[20] with a population of 15, 022, 839.[21] Its rectangular shape covers a length of roughly 800 kilometres and a width varying from 130-240 kilometres.[22] Its northern border touches Tibet of the Peoples Republic of China and the rest of the three sides are covered by the Indian States of Sikkim, North Bengal, Bihar and Uttar Pradesh. All varieties of climate and topography, ranging from the subtropical to the Alpine, are found within the short span of its area.[23] The nearest sea coast is about 127 kilometres.[24]

The country can be divided into three geographic regions extending from north to south—the high Mountains, the Hills and the Tarai. The high Mountain or Himalayan region lies at an altitude of 4, 877[25] to 8, 848[26] metres above the sea level with the snow line running at 4877 metres. In this region the world's famous peaks of Mount Everest (8,848 m), Kanchanjungha (8598 m), Makalu (8470 m), Dhaulagiri (8172 m) and Annapurna (8078 m) are located.[27] This is an entirely mountainous tract with climate too cold for human settlement.[28]

The Hill region is formed by the Mahabharat range that soars up to 4877 m above the sea level. It is also called Mid-Himalayas.[29]

This region covers 68 per cent of the total land area of Nepal. To the south of it lies the Churia range whose altitude varies from 610 to 1524 m.[30] This region includes the capital city of Kathmandu along with other small and big valleys.

The flat land south of the Churia range is called Tarai or 'Madesha'. It slopes gently towards the south. It covers 15 per cent of Nepal's land area. It is approximately 500 miles long from its western boundary, the Mahakali river, to its eastern boundary, the Mechi river. The actual boundary line between the Nepal tarai and the Indian States of Uttar Pradesh, Bihar and West Bengal follows a circuitous route of more than 500 miles. At its widest point, the tarai has a span of 33 miles and at its narrowest, 2 or 3 miles. The total average width of the tarai along its entire east-west axis is 20 miles. The eastern Tarai is wider and spreads continuously while the Western Tarai is narrow and irregular.[31] The elevation of the tarai is average 300 metres above the sea level.[32]

Nepal has a composite population stemming from various racial groups. The inhabitants of high Mountain or Himalaya region are Sherpas, Tamang, Kirantis, Limbu and Bhotiyas and have descended from Mongoloid stock. This region is largely an arctic waste land and has been a marginal area of human settlement. Population is still sparse and the main economic activities are barter trade, pastoralism and shifting agriculture.[33] The density of this area rarely exceeds 25 persons per square mile.[34]

The majority of the population of Nepal has been packed in Hill region or 'Pahar'. It is a traditional zone of Nepalese settlement, and places of origin of political power in the country. This sector is inhabited by Magars, Gurung, Thakali, Sunwars, Newars, Brahmans and Chhatriyas. It has an average density of 125 persons per square mile. Regional variations in density here range from 80 persons per square mile in west Nepal to 157 persons per square mile in Central Nepal to 168 persons per square mile in East Nepal. The Kathmandu valley has a high density of over 2,000 persons per square mile and the urban density of Kathmandu city even exceeds 50,000 persons per square mile.[35] Subsistance agriculture is the basis for the hill economy.[36]

Thirty one per cent of the total population of Nepal with an average density of 300 persons per square mile, is found in the Tarai or 'Madesh'. The Tarai is the backbone of Nepalese economy. It produces about 59 per cent of the nation's gross domestic product and about 76 per cent of the Government revenue for agricultural and industrial productivity of the region. The Tarai produces rice for the hill region and for the neighbouring states of India. Large amounts of rice is exported to India every year.[37] In the inner Tarai region, Tharu, Danuwar. Chepang, and Magar Indian immigrants hold a dominant position. The development of means of transport has enabled the people to move from the hill to the Tarai. Hence, there is mixture of different races in the region.[38]

The most important economic resources of Nepal are forests which cover about 29 per cent of the total land area. The principal products of the forests are timber, beams and faggots. Herbs, drugs, fruits, bamboo are the minor products of the forest.[39]

Nepalese Society is predominantly agricultural. About 91 per cent of the total population derives its livelihood from agriculture and allied activities. Main crops are paddy, maize, millet, barley, wheat, potato, jute, sugarcane and oil seeds. Cash crops of Nepal include tobacco and tea [40] Cottage industries also played significant role in the growth of Nepalese economy.

1.2 Historical Background

The history of Indo-Nepal trade relations is as old as history itself. Mulasarvativadavinayasangraha, one of the ancient texts, clearly mentions that Gautam Buddha[41] visited Nepal along with a group of merchants from India. Similarly Kautilya's Arthashastra, describes the popularity of Nepalese blanket called 'Bhingise' and 'Apasarak' in the Indian markets.[42] Therefore, on the basis of these two texts, it can be assumed that the commercial relations between Nepal and India had existed more than five hundred years before the Christian era.[43] In the first half of the seventh century A.D. Nepal was the centre of transit trade between India and Tibet. The Tang annal indicates that the merchants were numerous and cultivators rare in Nepal. It clearly shows that trade must have developee greatly in those days.[44] There was little prospect of a large scale agricultural development in Nepal owing to the hilly nature of the rocky soil in most places. Sarthabaha Ratnasangha was the prominent merchant community in fifth century Nepal. Trade between Nepal and outside world was flourishing under the guidance of this community. Guhyamitra was the leader of the merchant community who sent caravans to distant places within Nepal and to neighbouring countries. The caravans of traders were enterprising, courageous and resourceful. They controlled export and import trade of the country. They had contracts in Tibet and in India with their agents.[45]

Hiuen Tsang, the great Chinese pilgrim who was in north Bihar in 637 A.D. heard that trade was in a flourishing condition in Nepal.[46] He disclosed that Nepal exported corn, fruits, copper and yak to Tibet and India. The yak Nepal got from the areas bordering on Tibet formed an important article of commerce and it was exported to India in the form of Chamars (fly-whisk). The merchandise was carried by itinerary merchants and handed over to marketing organizations stationed in Tibet and India, who did the disposal business amongst the consumers.[47] Amsuvarma, one of the enlightened rulers of that period, inspired the people for the development of trade. For example, all the articles such as iron, flywhisk, musk and copper utensils, which were otherwise prohibited for export, were allowed to be exported by the people of Tistung Village. They could go without obstruction through the customs with these articles for sale and return with other articles purchased in return. They were exempted from paying customs duty (sulka) which were payable also while returnin.[48]

Indo-Nepal trade continued to develop in the Medieval period also.[49] Some of the Indian texts[50] mention the prosperity of Indo-Nepal trade. Some of the Christian missionaries and travellers have also praised the growth of Nepalese trade in their accounts. Ralph Fitch, a traveller who visited India in 1583, heard that there was regular commercial transaction between India and Tibet through the passes of Nepal and Bhutan.[51] Hovhannes Joughayetsi, an Armenian merchant, wrote in the closing decades of the seventeenth century that the merchants from India, who carried on trade with Nepal and Tibet, used to derive net profits ranging from 70 to 130 per cent from their transactions.[52] Father Horace Della Penna who visited Nepal in the ear y eighteenth century also mentions some of the articles exported from and imported into Nepal. The trade was free and unrestricted and also protected by the Newar Kings of Nepal.[53]

The merchants of India and Nepal had good commercial contact with each other and had commercial depots in each others country. The Nepalese dealers had their own sale depots in Patna and Banaras. Similarly some Muslim and Kashmiri merchants from India lived permanently in the trade marts of Kathmandu, Bhaktapur and Patan. Father Ippolito Desideri who arrived at Kathmandu in December 1721 on his way back from Lhasa, wrote that there was much commerce in Nepal and many merchants from India and Tibet used to come for trade and merchants from Kashmir had offices and shops in the town.[54] In 1766 Padre Tranquille, a Christain missionary, saw Muslim merchants from Bettiah carrying some articles for trade in Tanahu in Western Nepal.[55]

Till the eighteenth century Nepal was the trade link between China and India. The imports to Nepal from Tibet included mainly herbs, salt, yaktail, silver, gold and from India spices, salt, embroidery and silk cloth; India obtained herbs, hides, wooden frame and certain metal goods from Nepal.[56]

Indo-Nepal trade sharply declined as a result of Gorkha conquest of Kathmandu Valley in 1769.[57] The East India Company tried to revive the trade relations by sending their representatives and trade missions. The British Governor-General, Warren-Hastings was eager to develop this relation. He sent several missions to Tibet and Bhutan to explore the possibilities of Indo-Tibet trade through Nepal.[58] In 1784 he also sent the Foxcroft mission with his letter to the King of Nepal, expressing his desire to open trade relations with the latter.[59] Prithvinarayan Shah was not unfriendly towards the British.[60] But he wanted to keep them out of the reach of the mountain "Keeping them at arms length."[61] He believed that foreign merchants would impoverish the people if they were allowed into the country. He directed the people of Nepal. "The use of foreign cloth shall be prohibited. Local weavers shall be provided with samples and trained to weave (similar fabrics). If this is done, money will not be flow outside. Herbs and drugs and other indigenous products shall be sent to foreign countries and money thus attracted."[62]

However, Nepal signed a commercial treaty with the East India Company on 1 March 1792. The treaty provided unrestricted trade between the two countries subject only to a reciprocal collection of customs duties at 2½% ad valorem.[63] The treaty was signed by the British largely with an eye to the Tibetan market,[64] although it was silent on all trade matters with that country.[65] Even then the English traders complained that the Government of Nepal was not letting their goods pass through its territory to Tibet.[66] On the other hand, the Nepalese Government was desirous of utilizing the treaty to encourage its own exports to India rather than movement of goods from India to Tibet through its territory. The permission was granted to English merchants to export wax, timber and other indigenous commodities to India, often even on a tax free basis. Local officials who tried to prevent them from purchasing such commodities were scolded and ordered not to create trouble with the agents of English merchants on minor matters.[67]

The treaty of 1792 was never actually implemented. The urgency of British assistance against China in the Sino-Nepal war of 1790–92, led the Nepalese Government to sign the first trade treaty with India. But its utility disappeared when the war ended and the Chinese army withdrew from Nepalese territory in November 1792.[68] After the failure of the treaty the trade mission led by Captain Kirkpatrick returned from Nepal. But this did not mean that commercial contacts between Nepal and India were entirely cut off. In 1795, Sir John Shore, the Governor-General of India, sent another mission headed by Maulvi Abdul Qadir to Nepal. He thought that Nepalese would be less apprehensive of an Indian Muslim than of a Firanghee.[69] He did not produce any new treaty with Nepal but communicated some valuable information regarding trade possibilities. He reported that the Nepalese acted as the medium between the Indian and Tibetan merchants. He estimated the total annual exports from the Company's territories to Nepal at Rs 4 or 5 lakhs.[70] He also suggested to the Company to link up the Tibetan and China trade through Nepal. From this time till 1800, the British inter course with Nepal was restricted to occasional friendly letters.[71]

In 1801 the Nepalese Government signed another treaty with East India Company, with the object of improving trade relations, giving full effect to the treaty of 1792 which had become a dead letter and procuring a suitable settlement for the deposed king Ran Bahadur Shah of Nepal. Captain W.O. Knox was sent to Nepal as the first British Resident at Kathmandu.[72] He was directed to send information regarding the demand of European and Indian manufacturers in the Nepaleses market and the possibilities of opening trade with Tibet and Bhutan either directly or through Nepal. When Knox found that the affairs in Nepal were hopelessly bad and that trade relations could not be revived he left Kathmandu on 19 March 1803 without achieving his goal.[73]

The Nepalese policy of excluding foreign traders and controlling all trade between Tibet and the plains prevented the British merchants from the commercial exploitation of the hill markets. From 1767 to 1801 the British policy towards Nepal was to reopen Nepalese market for trade. In pursuit of their objective the British had followed a policy of conciliation towards Nepal. But when this policy failed with the failure of the 1792 and 1801 treaties, the East India Company declared war against Nepal in 1814-16. This war ended military activity of Gorkhali for ever. After the treaty of Sugauli in 1816, Gardiner, the British Resident in Nepal, was instructed to remove all future causes of misunderstanding and maintain a friendly attitude towards the Nepalese Darbar with the idea of strengthening the confidence of the Nepalese in the British Government.[74] But in fact for twenty years after the war there was no cordiality between the two governments.[75] The Nepalese policy towards the British changed when Bhimsen Thapa, the iron man in Nepalese history,[76] was deposed from Prime Ministership in August 1837.[77] The British Resident Brain Houghton Hodgson got an opportunity to exploit the situation of Nepal in his favour. He wanted to divert warlike mentality of the Nepalese towards commerce and trade. He argued: "I would reach the Government through the people, commerce should be my instrument."[78] In his voluminous work he elaborately discussed the future possibilities of improving Indo-Nepal trade and its prevailing condition. He reported that there were 52 natives and 34 Indian merchants in Kathmandu Valley, engaged in foreign commerce. The trading capital of the former was considered to be not less than Rs 5,018,000 and of the latter Rs 2,305,000. He estimated that the total value of exports and imports of Nepal was more than thirty lakh rupees in 1831.[79] Hodgson was a strong advocate of Indo-Tibetan trade through Nepal. Dr A. Cambell, an officiating Assistant to the Resident from 1830 to 1838 also favoured the necessity for developing Indo-Nepal trade.[80] In March 1835 Hodgson presented a draft of proposed treaty with Nepal for the Governor General's consideration. According to this proposal the products and maaufactured goods of Nepal and Tibet were to be charged a duty of 4 per cent Kuldar ad valorem in India and the British and Indian products an import duty in Nepal of 5 per cent Mahendra Malli rupees ad valorem according to the market rate of exchange in Nepal. It was suggested that there should be 17 customs Houses in India and 21 in Nepal.[81] Duty was to be levied once and at one of the specified places in India.[82] The Board of Customs, salt and opium in India did not accept these proposals on the ground that a duty of mere 4 per cent on all Nepalese goods was too low as compared to the normal rate of import duties levied by the British in India.[83] The Government of India thereafter exempted all the Nepalese goods from the Customs duties in June 1836 and expressed the hope that the Nepalese Government should follow suit but the Nepalese Government declined to do so.[84]

On 6 November 1839, an engagement with British India was signed by the Nepalese Government. The articles 4 and 5 mention, "British subjects shall hereafter be regarded as her own subjects in regard to access to the courts of law, and the cause of the former shall be heard and decided without denial or delay, according to the usages of Nepal." The fifth paragraph of this engagement reads, "The Nepal Government engages that an authentic statement of all the duties leviable in Nepal shall be delivered to the

Resident, and that hereafter unauthorized imports not entered in this list shall not be levied on British subjects."[85] This engagement was an imperfect document. The traffic was not applicable to the whole of Nepal.

With the rise of Jang Bahadur Rana in 1846, the Nepalese adopted the policy of cooperation with the British. But like Prithvinarayan Shah he too was extremely opposed to a closer commercial intercourse with British India. He wanted to monopolise Indo-Nepalese trade. He set up trading marts in the same fashion as Prithvinarayan Shah wanted. The main objective behind the establishment of such markets in southern border areas was to capture the trade which the Tibetans used to conduct directly with the English. The Government of Nepal felt that, "If Tibetans and Firangis (Englishmen) meet and trade with each other, our ryots and traders will lose their employment and the result will not be good."[86] Traders were prohibited to deal directly with the English. In spite of all these hindrances Indo-Nepal trade con tinued to grow rapidly with the passage of time.[87]

REFERENCES

1. S. K. Jha, "British Indias policy towards Nepal'. *Journal of Bihar Research Society*. Vol. IX Pts 1-4, p. 194.
2. Ludwig F. Stiller, S. J. "A Note on Himalayan Trade". *Journal of Tribhuvan University*, Kirtipur, Nepal, Vol. VII, November 1972, No. 1, p. 7.
3. Ibid., p. 8.
4. Rishikesh Shaha, *An Introduction to Nepal.* Kathmandu, 1975, p. 91.
5. Asad Husain, *British India's Relations with the Kingdom of Nepal. 1857-1947*, London, 1971, p. 32.
6. Ibid.
7. S. K. Jha, *op. cit.*
8. Ludwig F. Stiller S. J., *The Rise of the House of Gorkha* : A Study on the Unification of Nepal 1768-86. Kathmandu, 1975, p. 327.

9. *Ibid*, p. 367.
10. John Premble, *The Invasion of Nepal*, Oxford, 1971, p. 86.
11. S. K. Jha, *op. cit.* p. 205.
12. Ibid.
13. Ibid.
14. Rishikesh Shaha, *Essays in the Practice of Government in Nepal.* Delhi, 1982, pp. 79–81.
15. C. U. Aitcheson, *A Collection of Treaties, Engagements and Sunnuds Relating to India and Neighbouring Countries.* Vol. II. Calcutta, 1863, p. 224.
16. Asad Husain, *op. cit.*, p. 109.
17. Piers Blaike, John Cameron, David Seddon, *Nepal in Crisis; Growth and Stagnation at the Periphery.* Delhi, 1980, p. 37.
18. N. P. Banskota, *Indo-Nepal Trade and Economic Relations*, Delhi, 1981, p. 24.
19. India is twenty two times bigger in size and forty-four times larger in population and China is seventyfive times bigger in size and seventy times larger in population than Nepal. But it is as big as Bangladesh and twice the size of Sri Lanka. See Harka Gurung, "Geographic Foundations of Nepal". *The Himalayan Review.* Nepal Geographic Society. Kathmandu, 1968, p. 1.
20. Central Bureau of Statistics, *Population Census Report of Nepal.* Kathmandu, 1984, p. 1.
21. *Ibid*, p. 11.
22. His Majesty's Government and Asian Development Bank, *Nepal Agriculture Sector Strategy Study.* Vol. II, Kathmandu, December, 1982, p. 1.
23. *Ibid.*
24. Central Bureau of Statistics, *op. cit.*
25. Ibid.
26. His Majesty's Government of Nepal and Asian Development Bank, *op. cit.*
27. Central Bureau of Statistics, *op. cit.*
28. Sharanhari Shrestha, *Modern Geography of Nepal.* Kathmandu, 1972, p. 8.
29. Central Bureau of Statistics, *op. cit.*
30. Ibid.
31. Frederick H. Gaige, *Regionalism and National Unity of Nepal*, Delhi, 1975. p. 3.

32. Chandra B. Shrestha and Pitamber Sharma, "Physical Setting and Natural Resources, Availability and Prospect". *Nepal's Economy-An Overview.* Centre for Economic Development and Administration, Tribhuban University, Kirtipur, Kathmandu, April 1980, p. 2.
33. B S. Bhoosan, *The Development Experience of Nepal.* New Delhi, 1979, p. 20.
34. Gurung, *op. cit.* p. 6.
35. *Ibid.*
36. B. S. Bhooshan, *op. cit.*
37. Frederick H. Gaige, *op. cit.*
38. Central Bureau of Statistics. *op. cit.* p. 5.
39. *Ibid.*
40. *Ibid.*
41. Sylvain Levi, *Le Nepal.* Paris, 1905, Vol. III, pp. 181–85.

    In fact, Gautam Buddha never visited Nepal. One of the Buddha's disciples, Anand had travelled to Nepal and was warned by the Lord about risks involved in the journey. See, D. R. Regmi, *Ancient Nepal.* Calcutta, 1969, p. 59.
42. Kangle (11, p. 119) translated the passage of Kautilya's text as follows"

    "The black bhingisi, made out of a collection of eight woven strands (and) the apsarak which keeps of rain that is woollen cloth from Nepal." Cited in Ibid, *Inscriptions of ancient Nepal.* New Delhi, p. 19.
43. Balchandra Sharma, *Nepal Ko Aitihasik Rup Rekha.* Banaras, 1976, pp. 71–72.
44. D. R. Regmi. *Ancient Nepal.* p. 262.
45. *Ibid*, p. 263.
46. *Ibid*, Inscription of ancient Nepal, p. 19.
47. *Ibid*, Ancient Nepal p. 262.
48. *Ibld*,
49. Roughly extending one thousand years from the middle of the eighth century to that of the eighteenth century.
50. Yuktikalpataru of Bhoja mentions that sword making industry of Nepal was quite well known in India. Rasaratnasamuchchaya describes the superior quality of copper brought to India from Nepal. Dhatumanjari, a part of Rudrayamalatantra, mentions the location of copper found in Nepal. See, B. P. Majumdar, *The Socio-Economic History of Northern India.* Calcutta, 1960, pp. 199-201.

51. Clement R. Markham, *Narrative of the Mission of George Bogle to Tibet and of Journey of Thomas Manning to Lhasa.* London, 1876, p. I iv.
52. Levon Khaceikian,"The Ledger of the Merchant Hovhannes Joughayetsi". *Journal of Asiatic Society.* Calcutta, 1966, Vol. VIII No. 3. pp. 153-86.
53. Markham, *op. cit.* p. IX.
54. Filippo De Fillippi (ed.) *An Account of Tibet : The Travel of Ippolito Desideri of Pirtorea S.J. 1712-1727.* London, 1973, pp. 317-18.
55. D.R. Regmi, *Modern Nepal.* Calcutta, 1960, p. 34.
56. *Ibid, Ancient and Medieval Nepal.* Kathmandu, 1952, p. 176.
57. Leo E. Rose, *Nepal strategy for survival.* Bombay, 1971, p. 25.
58. George Bogle mission of 1774 to 1779. Turner 1783, Purangir Gossain 1785 to Tibet and Hamilton mission to Blutak in 1775, were planned by Warren Hastings. See, Jahar Sen, *Indo-Nepal Trade in the Nineteenth Century.* Calcutta, 1977, p. 20.
59. K. C. Chaudhuri, *Anglo-Nepalese Relations from the Earliest Times of the British Rule in India Till the Gorkha War*, Calcutta, 1960, pp. 59–60.
60. When Raja Chait Singh of the State of Bejaygarh revolted against the Company, Prithvi Narayan Shah came to the latter's aid. But before the Nepalese army arrived, Bejaygarh was captured. Asad Husain, *op. cit.* p. 33.
61. *Ibid.*
62. Ludwig F. Stiller S. J., *Prithvi Narayan Shah in the light of Dibya Upadesh.* Kathmandu, 1968, p. 18.
63. Aitchison, *op. cit.*, p. 197.
64. M. C. Regmi, *A. Study in Nepali Economic History.* New Delhi, 1978, p. 148.
65. Jahar Sen, *op. cit.*, p. 22.
66. Regmi, *op. cit.*, p. 149.
67. *Ibid.*
68. *Ibid.*
69. Hussain, *op. cit.* p. 34.
70. Chaudhari, *op. cit.* pp. 90–91.
71. Aitchlson, *op. eit.* p. 44.
72. *Ibid.*
73. B. D. Sanwal, *Nepal and the East India Company*, Bombay, 1965, p. 112.
74. Husain, *op. cit.* p. 40.

75. Kanchanmoy Mojumdar, *Anglo-Nepalese Relations In the Nineteenth Century*. Calcutta, 1973, p. 6.

76. Chittaranjan Nepali, *General Bhimsen Thapa Ra Tatkalin Nepal*-Kathmandu, (2013 V. S.), 1956, p. 111.

77. Baburam Acharya, "Rajendra Vikram Shah Ko Shasan" *Purnima*. Vol. 27. Kathmandu, 1977, p. 174.

78. Foreign Consultant, 12 June 1834 No. 140. Cited in M. S. Jain, *The Emergence of New Aristocracy in Nepal*. Agra, 1973, Fn. p. 9.

79. B. H. Hodgson, *Essay on the Languages, Literature and Religion of Nepal and Tibet*. London, 1874, Reprint. New Delhi, 1972, p. 92.

80. A. Campbell, *Notes on the Agriculture and Rural Economy of the Valley of Nepal*. Kathmandu, 1837.

81. W. W. Hunter, *Brain Haughton Hodgson*. London, 1896. pp. 141–42.

82. N. K. Sinha, *The Economic History of Bengal*. Calcutta, 1970, Vol. III, p. 53.

83. Ramakant, *Indo-Nepalese Relations 1816-1877*. Delhi, 1968, p. 125.

84. Ambrose H. Oldfield, *Sketches from Nepal*. London, 1880, Delhi (reprinted). p. 281, Aitchison, *op. cit*. p. 83.

85. Aitchison, *op. cit*., pp. 212–13.

86. Shankarman Rajvamsi, *Shahkalin Aitihasik Chittipatra Sangraha* (A Collection of Historical Documents of the Shah period). Department of Archaeology, Kathmandu, Vol. I 2023 V. S. (1966), p. 33.

87. Regmi, *op. cit*. p. 153.

Transport and Communications

CHAPTER TWO

Different routes and means of communications were used by the traders during their transaction between India and Nepal. The trade routes used by the traders under review may be classified into three parts : (1) Land routes, (2) Railways, and (3) Water communications.

2.1. Land routes

The land routes usually used by the traders on the Indo-Nepal border may be divided into three main channels. These channels were trade passing between (1) Oudh and North Western provinces and Western Nepal, (2) trade passing between the British Indian district of Champaran, Muzaffarpur, Darbhanga, Bhagalpur and Purnea (all in Bihar) and adjoining Nepalese districts, and finally (3) trade passing between the British Indian district of Darjeeling and the Nepalese district of Ilam (on the border of Darjeeling).

The main places in British India in the North Western provinces and Oudh from where trade was carried on with the neighbouring districts were Kumaun, Bareilly, Kheri, Bahraich, Gonda, Basti and Gorakhpur. The Nepalese districts near these places were Doti and Silgarhi in the western part of the hill, and various places in the Western Tarai region which included Butwal, Banke, Bardia, Kailali, Kanchanpur, Banke, Bardia, Kailali and Kanchanpur were called "Naya Muluk" (new country). These four districts which were captured by the British after the war of 1814-6, were restored to Nepal in 1860. The territory ceded was two hundred miles in extents.[1]

Ranodip Singh, the second Rana Prime Minister

Jang Bahadur Rana, the First Rana Prime M

who monopolised Nepalese trade with British India.

Prime Minister Ranodip Singh with his second wife,
Hari Priya Devi (c. 1880).

Kumaun to Doti : The trade routes between Kumaun in India and Doti district in Nepal were Barmdeo. Jhulaghat, Gurjia Ghat, Darchula and Boondee. The route connected with Barmdeo was considered to be more important than all others put together.[2]

Bareilly to Western Tarai : The routes for the trade between Bareilly and the Western Tarai of Nepal were Doknabagh, Ghurrighat, Belauri, Nanda, Simara, Doti and Pooryna. Pilibheet, Madho Tanda and Purunpur were the main places in Bareilly district from where trade passed between the above men tioned Nepalese routes and Bareilly.[3]

Kheri to Western Tarai : The trade between Kheri district in India, and Western Tarai of Nepal, was conducted through Pullea to Pallian. Via Satyana and Chandi Ghat, through Khyraghur to Putda via Puchperwa, through Singahi and Simri to Golamandi via Bunberpur and Kakrowli Ghat and via Ramnagar Ghat. There were other roads via Mohna to Golamandi viz. Hallona and Kalaupur. These roads were usually cut off in the rains and repaired by the traders themselves. The Nepalese Government did not make any repair.[4]

Baharaich to Western Tarai : The trade between Baharaich district in India and the Western Tarai of Nepal was conducted through Sujauli to Golamandi via Kalania Ghat, through Sujauli to Dubra, through Motipur to Golamandi via Dharmapur and Kalania Ghat, through Motipur, Nanpara, Kutra Bazar via Golaria and Sidhanee Ghat to Banke.[5]

Gonda to Western Tarai : The trade between Gonda district in India and Nepalese districts of Deokhur passed over the Danduwa range. There were altogether eleven passes which served as trade routes. These passes were Garia, Barchwa, Patali, Goron, Khabu, Bais Mata, Bhambhur, Jarva Byrat, Khangra, Sirya and Jarwa. The communications in Nepal connected by these passes with routes in India were also mere tracks.[6]

According to Girdlestone, the British Resident in Nepal, Dara pass which was omitted in the list was one of the best routes across the hills.[7] The roads were made on the Indian side of the range during the famine years 1873-74. A metalled road was constructed from Nawabganj to Bahramghat. About a mile eastward of Nawabganj, the high road sent an offshoot to Bahramghat. This was a direct route from Lucknow to Bahraich and Gonda.[8]

Basti and Gorakhpur to Butwal : The trade that passed between the North Western Provinces and Western Nepalese Tarai was carried on between Basti in India and Butwal in Nepal. The trade suffered during the rainy season, as considerable amount of business was transacted during the cold weather. There was trade traffic also from Gorakhpur into Butwal which passed through 19 routes, the most important on the Nepalese side being Palhi. Nineteen routes in Gorakhpur district were Bagohi, Bataidiha, Kurhwa, Kaulahi, Bhundi, Persia, Naikat, Nautanwa, Pipra Bazar, Ranjita, Deo Ghat, Mirchahva, Nichloul via Thun thibaria via Chetteach, via Sitapur, Rengahia, Baknar, Baitamya Bazar via Amra, Baitambya. Similarly, nineteen routes connecting these routes in the Nepalese territory were Punchmara, Makundghar, Piprahwa, Bagauli, Tirlokpur, Majharia Bilarawa Ghat, Kadhmahwa, Belahia, Golapur, Rajbari, Sudri, Palhi, Bhujahwa, Khairatwa, Dharmuli, Sunauli, Khairatwa and Tribeni Ghat. Nichloul via Thunthibari was the best road in the Gorakhpur district. It was linked through Nichloul by a series of roads and other important local marts. This route carried the highest amount of traffic. Nautanwa, Pipra Bazar, Deoghat and Mirchawa road in Gorakhpur and Kadamahwa, Balakia, Rajabari, Sundri in Butwal carried considerable amount of trade. Bagohi, Kurha and Bahnar routes were only fit for foot passengers. Their continuations in Nepal were confusing.[9]

There were three routes from Uska to Butwal. These routes were via Chillea, via Birpur and via Bulka. An other route passed through Lotan.[10] Other relevant roads of the Basti district were Basti to Nepal via Domriaganj, Uska to Naugarh, Birpur and Nepal frontier, Jharna to Nepal frontier, Alidapur to Nepal frontier, Lotan to Nepal frontier.[11] An important route in the Nepal-Basti trade started from Sirsewa, Bahadurganj and

Captainganj by way of Marui in the northwest corner of the district of Kakrahighat on the Banganga above that rivers junction with Rapti. The principal roads in the Bansi parganah from Domariaganj to Nepal by way of Intwa and Basti to Nepal by way of Bansi, Dumdumwa and Birdpur were unmetalled in 1881. But after a lapse of two decades the Bansi roads connected with Basti were metalled. The same road was extended by way of Uska to the Nepal frontier. It was crossed at Birdpur by a road which traversed the north of Bansi passing through Chillea and continued eastward to Karkrahwa bazar in Nepal.[12]

Bengal to Kathmandu and Eastern Tarai : The trade between Bengal and Kathmandu and Eastern Tarai was conducted via Champaran, Muzaffarpur, Darbhanga, Bhagalpur and Purnea in India and Nepalese districts of Chitwan, Bara, Rautahat, Sarlahi, Mahottari, Janakpur, Morang etc. The trade which passed between these districts is sometime referred to as Bengal trade in British records. It was this trade which gained importance in the Kathmandu valley and eastern Nepal, from where it passed to Tibet. In other words the products of Kathmandu valley along with the principal items of export from the eastern Nepalese Tarai, passed along these routes. Likewise, British goods that were imported into Nepal from Bengal and Bihar, passed through the border districts of Nepal. Before 1875 no attempt was made even by the British Government to register the amount of the trade traffic passing through this sector.[13]

The trade between Champaran district in India and Chitwan district in Nepal was carried through Bettiah via Tribeni, via Thori, via Raxaul, Sugauli via Raxaul, Motihari via Kutkonwa and Gorasahan in Champaran and Chitwan, Semrabassa, Bareywali and Simrounghur in Chitwan district.[14]

Before 1800, there was no good road in Champaran except one in Saran. Good roads were constructed for the passage of troops during Anglo-Nepalese war 1814-16. The lines of communication were between the frontier of Nepal and India.[15]

The trade route of Champaran Led direct to Kathmandu and were also chosen for direct traffic with Calcutta and Patna.

The principal route started from Patna and proceeded nearly due north through Champaran district to the Capital of Nepal.[16]

There was no great traffic through Bettiah via Tribeni, except at the time of the annual fair in February and March, held on the Indian side of the border. The road was fit for driving to Tribeni. The Chitawan route led along the valley of the Chota Rapti to Netauda, where it joined the main road to Kathmandu.[17]

The traffic on route Bettiah via Thori was insignificant. The trade routes of Bettiah and Sugauli via Raxaul and Motihari via Katkenwa in Champaran in Semrabasa and Barewah in Chitwan were in good condition. All these routes met at or before Semrabasa which was about 30 miles from Sugauli by the direct route through Raxaul. The onward road was the main route to Kathmandu. In dry weather it could be traversed by lightly laden carts through the low pass in the Chiriaghata hills and also through Hetauda to Bhimphedi, a distance of about 60 miles from Sugauli. The distance between Bhimphedi and Thankot is nearly 15 miles with two steep passes intervening. The traffic was moderate on the route going through Motihari via Ghorasahan to Semrounghur in Nepal. The road passed through Mukwanpur into Hetauda where it merged in the main road to Kathmandu. The most important routes were those which led from the Nepal border to the railway and the bank of Gandak.[18]

The trade routes from Muzaffarpur to Nepalese districts of Bara, Rauthat, Mahottari were approached through Bairgania, Majorganj, Sonbarsa, Bela Muchpakauni, Sursand and Madhwapur in Muzaffarpur district and Semrounghur, Sangrampur, Adamara, Muggurthana, Jalaswar and Janekpur in above mentioned Nepalese districts. Roads were made along all these routes to the border. Numerous village tracks also intervened.[19]

The trade routes from Darbhanga to Nepalese district of Saptari passed through Basupatti to Janakpur, two roads from Darbhanga via Jayanagar to Siraha, Madhubani via Jayanagar to Siraha, Darbhanga via Lawkoha to Hanumannagar. There was a considerable volume of trade between Darbhanga and Saptari in Nepal. The roads were good in India, but degenerated into tracks across the border.[20]

In 1872-73 a road from Darbhanga to Narah and Jayanagar on the Nepal frontier was constructed at the cost of Darbhanga Raj.[21] Roads from Darbhanga to Sitamarhi as well as roads to the frontier and to Simri passed through Kantaul, about 15 miles north west of Darbhanga. A considerable portion of the road with Nepal passed by this route.[22] There were also several roads proceeding from Darbhanga, Pandaul and Madhubani to the Nepal frontier.[23]

The trade routes from Bhagalpur to Saptari passed through Kundauli to Hanumannagar and Birpur to Ameerpur. Girdlestone, British resident in Nepal, reported that new roads had been constructed in Kaundauli and Birpur in the Bhagalpur district. The continuation of these two roads to Hanumannagar and Ameerpur in sub-tarai area of Nepal were no more than tracks.[24]

In Bhagalpur district there was a good road leaving the South Emigration Road at Balha near Sukhpur through Supaul, Chandipipra and Dagmara. It ended at Kundauli on the Nepal frontier.[25] Another road passed from Inampati to Birpur on the Nepal frontier. The North Emigration Road entered the Bhagalpur district from Darbhanga, a few miles South of the Nepal frontier.[26] It ran eastward via Pratabganj to Nathpur (on the east bank of the Koshi) and entered Purnea. A road also ran to the north via Mauliganj and Muddehpur to Singheshwar. From this point one route turned to Sapaul and another via Pipra Pratabganj to Birpur on the Nepal frontier. A branch of South Emigration Road ran via Supaul to Kundauli on the Nepal frontier. Another road moved southward via Banganj to Khagaria in Monghyr. A branch from North Emigration Road ran into Nepal via Panchparamia.[27]

The trade route from Indian border district of Purnea to the Nepalese district of Morang ran through (1) Nawabganj to Dewanganj, (2) Amona (via Sahibganj) to Dewanganj, (3) Mirganj to

Sahibganj, (4) Kusambha to Pathardewa, (5) Rajola (via Dhobi) to Gogra, (6) Megha (via Harecha) to Jhontiaki, (7) Kosakhatta to Rangeli, (8) Sikti to Raugeli, (8) Dhubeli (via Kochaba) to Chailghazi, (10) Phulwari (via Teragach) Chailghazi, (11) Khania-bad to Athmauza or Athgon in Nepal, (12) Bairia to Ultabari in Nepal, (13) Karabari (via Pulsa) to Mohabari to Baniani, (14) Digulbank (via Tanganduba) to Jhilmilya, (15) Gandharbdanga (via Khudabhita) to Pautapara, (16) Tatpoa Market to Lodhabari, (17) Simalbari (via Ambari) to Khatamani, (18) Bhawaniganj (via Changhati) to Khariobhita, (19) Kalughat to Panthamari, (20) Bhatgaon (via Dhobagachi to Dholabari) to Dohnagiri. These routes could be traversed with ease in the dry weather but they were difficult for travel during rainy season. Some of the trade routes in British territory in India were improved from local funds.[28]

Hunter has mentioned three other routes connecting Purnea with Nepal. One of the routes mentioned was from Sahibganj to Bhopla-Tajpur started from the frontier of Nepal in the north west corner of the district. This route was 78 miles long. It crossed the North Emigration Road near Matiyari and then ran through Basantpur, the headquarters of Arariya sub-division. After that, it passed through Dalmalpur market, Ameer-Kasba Police Station across the Ganges, Darjeeling road, and the river Mahananda at Dengra ferry. It passed on through Raniganj Police outpost and market, crossing the river Sadanu to the river Nagar on the Dinajpur frontier. This was the main line of communication from the north-west of the district to the eastern division. The people of Nepal sub-Tarai used this route during their journey to the Nekmard and other fairs of the Rajshahi division.[29] A 16 miles long road from Arariya to Sikti and another 15 miles long road from Araria to Kursakata connected the headquarter of Arariya sub-division with the Police outpost on the Nepal frontier.[30]

Darjeeling to Ilam : There were three main routes frequented by Nepalese traders to Darjeeling. The first route via Ilam Garhi in Nepal to a place called Nagree across the river Mechi. The second route was via Mayoong in Nepal to Goong, on the other side of the border. The last route was via Toonglong and Fulaloong in Nepal, to Samaboong across the border.[31]

British resident in Nepal, Charles Girdlestone reported on 19 September 1876 that there were various hill paths between Eastern Nepal and Darjeeling, of which the best known was from Ilam across the Mechi near Thapalia. The trade was very insignificant. He remarked, "with the greater facilities of access from Purneah, it is not to be expected that any great result should be achieved from the direction of Darjeeling."[32]

In 1874 the construction of the road from Little Ranjit to the Nepal frontier was started. In 1876 it was completed as far as Tongloo and extended northward along the frontier to Phalut where the frontier of Sikkim, Darjeeling and Nepal meet. This road was also extended to a southward direction along the Nepal frontier to a point near Singhali Tea Garden. It was proposed to take it across Balasan river to the projected terminus of the North Bengal railway.[33] J.W. Edgar, the Deputy Commissioner of Darjeeling, reported to the Commissioner of Rajshahi and Coochbehar on 11 December 1878 that the condition of the Northern Nepal Road and the South Nepal Road was in fair order and an inspection bungalow was put up at Tongloo.[34].

The Deputy Commissioner of Darjeeling reported in 1886 that flourishing marts were situated at convenient point along these roads and the system only wanted the completion of the road from Siliguri to Naxalbari and Nepal frontier being constructed on a proper scale.[35] After seven years, it was informed that the road from Matigara to Naxalbari was completed.[36]

2.2.1. Important routes

The above mentioned routes were classified[37] into ten important routes in North Western Provinces and Oudh[38] and six routes in Bengal and Bihar adjoining Nepalese districts.[39] Ten routes in North-Western Provinces and Oudh on Indo-Nepal border were as follows :

(1) The route between Nepal and Almora, crossing the Kali river at Jhulaghat.

(2) The route across the Sarda river from the Nepalese mart Barmdeo into Kumaun.

(3) The route between Pilibhit and Nepal across the Sarda by a number of ghats which vary from year to year with the condition of river. Most of this trade ran between Pilibhit and the Sarda in two lines via Neuriyaghat and via Madho Tanda.

(4) The route between the Nepalese mart of Golamandi and the Kheri district (a) via Ramnagar on the Kauriala river, (b) via Singhaii.

(5) The route between Golamandi and the Bahraich district (a) via Sujauli, (b) via Katgarh.

(6) The routes between the Nepalese mart of Banke (Nepalganj) and the Bahraich and Gonda districts : (a) via the mart Nanpara, (b) crossing the Rapti at Gularia, (c) via Gobapur.

(7) The route between the valley of Deokhar and Dang and Gonda district via the Dora pass.

(8) The route between the Nepalese mart of Sirsewa, Bahadur ganj and Captainganj (in the province of Sheuraj) and the Basti district, via Marni or Kakrahighat.

(9) The route between the Nepalese mart of Butwal and Basti district (a) via Uska (b) via Lotan.

(10) The route between Butwal and Gorakhpur district by several tracks, the chief of which were Bahuar and Thunthibare.

Another report[40] of North Western Provinces and Oudh mentioned nine important routes adjoining Nepalese districts. These routes were as follows :

(1) The route between Kumaun and Western Nepal via Jhulaghat and Barmdeo.

(2) The route between the western part of Nepal Tarai and Town of Pilibhit via Nuria Husainpur and Sangadhi.

(3) The route between the Nepalese mart of Golamandi and its vicinity and Kheri and Bahraich district via Palia via Singhai, Kamnagar and Sujauli.

(4) The route between the Nepalese mart of Nepalganj (or Banke) and the Bahraich district via Katgarh and Babganj.

(5) The route between Deokhar and Gonda district.

(6) The route between the Nepalese marts of Bahadurganj, Captainganj Sirsewa and the Basti and Gonda districts via Marni, Materighat and Kakrahighat.

(7) The route between the Nepal Tarai or Nepalese mart of Butwal and the Tarai around it and the Gorakhpur district via Jogiabari, via Nautanwa via Thunthibari.

(8) The route between Nepal Tarai and the marts of Uska, Lotan and Sohas.

(9) The Gandak river.

Six important routes in Bengal and Bihar adjoining Nepalese districts were as follows :

(1) The route entering the Nepal territory near Kutkenwa in Champaran.

(2) The route via Sitamarhi entering Nepal near Sonbarsa.

(·) The route via Madhubani in Darbhanga entering Nepal near Lowkahi.

(4) The route entering Nepal near Kuhauli in Bhagalpur.

(5) The route entering Darjeeling near Naxalbari from Dhulabari in Nepal.

(6) The route from Ilam to Darjeeling entering Darjeeling near Ghumpahar.

2.2.2. Commodities passing through these routes

Different commodities were transacted through these routes. Rice and timber were the principal articles exported to India through most of the routes on Indo-Nepal border.

Rice and timber constituted more than two-thirds of total export to India through the route between Kumaun and Western Nepal via Jhulaghat and Barmdeo and Pilibhit via Neuria Husainpur and Sangadhi.[41]

Timber formed one third of the total export to India through the route between the Nepalese mart of Golamandi and its vicinity and Kheri and Bahraich district via Palia and via Singhai, Kamnagar and Sujauli. Nepal imported cotton goods through these routes. Besides timber, other articles of export were rice and oilseeds.[42]

Ghee, spices, timber, rice and oilseeds were exported to India through the route between the Nepalese mart of Nepalganj (or Banke) and the Bahraich district via Katgarh and Babaganj. Nepal imported cotton goods, salt, sugar and tobacco from India through this route in return. More ghee, oilseeds and spices were exported by this route than by any other.[43]

Rice was the principal article of export from Nepal through the route between Deokhari and Gonda district. Two important lines of traffic merged in this route. Both ran between Gonda and Basti and the Nepal's district of Sheoraj, bounded on the west by Arrahnala. One line started from the villages and forest of Sheoraj and then travelled by a number of district roads which converged at Materiaghat on the Rapti. This route was famous for the export of timber and rice. The second line via Marvi carried on trade with the town of Sheoraj. It was by this route that most of the cotton and sugar were imported from India.[44]

Nepal imported cotton goods and salt through the route between Nepal Tarai and the marts of Uska, Lotan and Sohas. The large portion of the cotton-goods were of European manufacture and reached Uska and Lotan by road from Zamniah on the East Indian Railway. The salt was principally Liverpool salt, brought up by Gogra from Calcutta, Patna and other marts in Bengal. The cotton goods formed 76% of the imports. This route carried the large importation of non-intoxicating drugs and manufactured fibrous products. Nepal exported rice and oilseeds through this route.[45]

Nepal exported major part of the rice through the route between the Nepal Tarai or Nepalese mart of Butwal and the Tarai around it and the Gorakhpur district via Jogiabari, Nautanwa, Deoghat, Baitaulia and Thunthibari. More cotton goods imported by these routes than by any other into Nepal. Nearly half the whole supply consisted of European piece-goods. Only timber was exported through the Gandak river.[46]

E. C. Buck, Esq., Director of Agriculture and Commerce of North Western Provinces and Oudh reported total value of traffic which passed in 1878–79 through the different routes as follows.[47]

District	Description of routes	Total value of traffic passed in 1878-79 (in Rupees)
Bahraich	Via Sujauli between Golamandi (Nepalese marts) and Motipur	2,50,028
	Via Ratgarhi between Nepalese mart of Banke and Motipur	3,43,725
	Via Babaganj between Nepalese mart of Banke and Nanpara	11,33,413
Basti	Via Marni between Nepal marts of Bahadurganj and Sirswa and the Basti and Gonda district	3,33,170
	Via Uska / Via Lotan } between the British marts and Nepal Tarai	5,04,475
Gorakhpur	Via Jogiabari between Nepal marts of Batiwal and Gorakhpur district	5,12,248
	Via Bartaulia between Gorakhpur district and Nepal Tarai and mart of Butwal	2,90,178
	Via Thunthibari between Gorakhpur district and Nepal Tarai and mart of Butwal	3,22,442

Similarly, various articles passed through the different routes in Bihar and Bengal adjoining Nepalese districts. Among them the following were the important routes and articles. Nepal exported principally rice and paddy and imported cotton piece-goods, salt, sugar and kerosene oil through the route entering the Nepal territory near Kutkenwa in Champaran.[48] The statistical report showed that Patna despatched to Nepal, during the six months ending March 1876, 168 tons (4587 maunds) of spices and condiments which formed 26 per cent of the total export. Copper and brass manufacturers and betel nuts constituted 16 per cent and 11 per cent respectively. European cotton goods exported to Nepal amounted to Rs 87,025 or 78 per cent and miscellaneous native goods to Rs 10,935 or 10 per cent. These exports were mostly registered at Katkenwa in Champaran district. During the same six months these were received at Patna from Nepal only 574 maunds or 21 tons of which tobacco formed 84 per cent.[49]

Rice, Sakuwa wood, oilseeds and hides were mainly exported and cotton piece goods, salt, sugar and kerosene oil were received by Nepal in return through the route via Sitamarhi entering Nepal near Sonbarsa.[50]

In 1888–90 the subdivisional officer of Madhubani sub-division mentioned in his tour diaries that salt, cotton, castor, sugar, tobacco, English cloth, silk, etc. were the principal imports of Nepal and she exported paddy, rice linseed, saltpetre, timber, mustard seed through the route via Madhubani in Darbhanga. Similar articles were exported and imported through the route entering Nepal near Kunauli in Bhagalpur.[51]

Trade passing between Darjeeling and the border of Ilam in Nepal was not so encouraging. According to the information given by H.C. Wake, the Deputy Commissioner of Darjeeling in 1864, the trade return between Nepal and Darjeeling for four years (1860–63) amounted to Rs 96,960. This resulted mainly from the sale of Nepalese goods. Out of this figure the total export to Nepal from Darjeeling in the four years was Rs 4,000. The main items of export from Nepal to Darjeeling were blankets and cattle, which found a ready market in Darjeeling. The articles imported from Darjeeling through Darjeeling Ilam routes, were various kinds of chintz.[52] Nepal exported rice, paddy, potato seeds and cardamum through the different routes connecting Nepal with Darjeeling. The movement of rice and paddy in and out of Nepal was partly due to the superiority of the transportation system of Darjeeling over that in Nepal. Imports of Cardamom took place from Nepal through the Tista Valley and Nepal frontier bazars. Potatoes imported from Nepal were despatched to the districts of West Bengal, Bhagalpur, South Bihar and Orissa.[53]

2.2.3. Means of conveyance

Common country cart (Garis), pack animals such as ponies, donkeys, buffaloes, bullock, etc. and porters were the main conveyances used for transporting merchandise on Indo-Nepal border.

Carts driven by the oxen and buffaloes were the traditional mode of transport in the low land of Nepal viz. Tarai. The common country carts of northern India were generally used up to the foot of the hill in Nepal. Pack animals and porters were used in the hill.

The cart had an average carrying capacity of ten maunds (one maund is equal to 82 lb). Pack animals such as ponies and bullocks carried the load of three and half maunds. But the former carried less than the latter. The traders knowing they would get no rebate for half laden animals, took care to make up full loads. Porters generally used to carry two maunds. There was no lack of porters, but their employment constituted an expensive form of transport. The high cost of carriage was due to the inherent difficulties of the road and limited number of porters. In the hill the porters always carried loads on their back supported by a strap across the forehead. Newars carried their load in the baskets with a pole balance on the shoulders.[54] It is said that the hill coolies carry heavier weight than the Hindustani.

The following were the means of conveyance used on the different routes from the Western to the Eastern part of Nepal adjoining Indian districts.

The roads in Doti in Western Nepal were mere jungle paths unfit for carts. All the carrying was done by coolies.

From Bareilly to Western Tarai of Nepal, there were numerous tracks (road) of timber carts in the Nepalese Tarai. But except timber everything was carried on ponies, and for the hills coolies were substituted. In the opinion of the Joint Magistrate at Pilibhit more ponies would be forthcoming at present rate if trade increased. No traffic was borne by water.[55]

On the route from Kheree to Western Nepal Tarai, carts were the usual means of conveyance. Pack animals such as buffalloes, ponies and bullocks were often seen to carry salt, grain and tobacco.[56] The conservator of forest, Oudh, was of the opinion that the more the transport there, the cheaper it would become.[57] But the Deputy Commissioner of Kheri added that a gradual expansion of trade would be attended by competition amongst the owners of carriage so that the rate would be kept down. According to him there were two usual modes of conveying goods namely garis and pack animals, mostly ponies. Traders from British territories should not expect to find means of transport in Nepal. Therefore he suggested that the traders must carry conveyances with them.[58]

There was a gari track from Singhai to Korea, about 8 miles, and from the latter place to Hellono on the Mohana.[59]

On the routes from Bahraich to Western Nepal Tarai, carts and ponies were principally used.[60] All the routes were practicable for carts in dry season upto Golamandi, Dubra and Banke in Nepal. But the routes going from Sujauli to Dubra, Nanpara to Banke and Bhinga via Bhagoura and Balapur to Banke were useful for carts in all season. All the routes were fit for carts in British territory. Rice was carted everywhere by land route through Nepalganj in Banke district in Nepal. This route reached the junction of the Sarda and the Koerala rivers. Carts were the usual means of conveyance. But salt, grain and tobacco were transported on the back of buffaloes, bullocks and ponies. There were cart tracks to the east of Bhagouratal up to the foot of the hill. Timbers had to be cut in small pieces and carried down by men when it grew on the hill.[61]

The Officiating Deputy Conservator of Oudh Forest, Bahraich division was of the opinion that the amount of conveyances was regulated by the last season's crops. For example, if the cost of the grain was cheaper as 64 seers for one rupee, carts would be obtained with difficulty but when the grain was dear the carts could be easily obtained.[62]

Only foot passengers with or without headload could cross the eight passes viz. Garia, Barchwa, Patali, Goran, Khahu, Bais

Mata, Bhambhur and Jarva Byrat. Among the passes across the Dhundwa Range the last three passes were practicable for laden animals. None could be traversed by carts. Cart tracks led up to the passes in India. On the arrival at the foot of the hills, the load was transferred to either pack animals or coolies. The communications in Nepal connected by these passes with routes in India were also mere tracks.[63]

Carts, pack animals, such as ponies and bullocks, were the usual means of carriage on the route from Basti to the Butwal district of Nepal. Large numbers of carriages were available on this route. Therefore, the increased trade would not involve a greater relative expenditure for transport.[64]

On the route from Gorakhpur to Butwal, carts, ponies and bullocks were the common means of transport. The carts did not hold more than 10 maunds and their rate was $1\frac{1}{2}$ pie per maund per mile. The rates of pack animals were a little over one pie per maund per mile. Increased trade did not add to the cost of carriage. Any grain exported from Nepal by the Gandak river would be carried on carts to Narkulia or some other depots.[65]

On the route from Champaran to Chitwan, carts, bullock, ponies and porters were used as the means of conveyance. According to the officiating Magistrate and Collector of Champaran, "During the cold season the roads leading from the Ghauts on the Gandak into the Champaran district and Nepal were busy with up and down movements of carts, ponies and donkeys". The road through Bettaih via Tribeni to Chitwan was fit for driving up to Tribeni. From there, communication across the Gandak by cart track led to Butwal in the west and to Chitwan in the east. The bulk of traffic was carried on bullock cart.[66]

On the route from Raxaul in Champaran district to Kathmandu carts, bullocks, ponies and porters were used for transporting commodities. The cart could be used from Raxaul up to the foot of the hill called Churiya and through Hetauda to Bhimphedi. From Bhimphedi to Thankot the traffic was conveyed by porters. The road for the ten miles between Thankot and Kathmandu was fit for driving, but as there was hardly a cart in the valley, the coolies engaged at Bhimphedi used to carry their load on to the capital of Nepal. As far as Bhimphedi much of the traffic was conveyed by pack bullocks and ponies.[67]

On the route from the Muzaffarpur and Darbhanga districts to the Nepalese districts of Tarai, carts and pack animals were the usual means of conveyance. Coolies were employed for the hills.[68] In December 1889, the subdivisional officer of Madhubani mentioned that he could say with certainty that at least two hundred carts laden with grain passed along one road only through Paduma, Mahulia, etc. from Nepal.[69]

The continuation of Bhagalpur road to Hanumannagar and Ameerpur in the sub-tarai area of Nepal were no more than tracks, but carts moved freely. Bullocks were used for valuable articles like spices and salt. There was no reason to suppose that an increased trade would involve a greater relative cost for transport.[70]

The routes from the Purnea to the Morang district of Nepal, consisted of cart tracks carried for the most part along high ground. Carts were the commonest means of conveyance. Ponies and bullocks were less used, because they were more expensive. The district of Purnea could supply more transport without perceptible increase of cost.[71]

There were various hill paths between Eastern Nepal and Darjeeling.[72] Hence coolies were mostly used as a means of transport. Transportation up to Bejanbari was by coolie and thence to Darjeeling by ropeway or via Palbazar by briddle path. In the Tarai via Sanicharia in Nepal to Naxalbari via Bhadrapur in Nepal to Adhikari and via Galgalia was served by rail and Naxalbari by both cart and rail. Trade through Galgalic from Nepal was railed to Siliguri and other stations on the main Darjeeling-Himalayan Railway.[73] The communication system of Darjeeling had its growth in response to the commercial needs of the district. With the completion of the chains of roads surrounding the southern part of the district and facilitating trade with Nepal, the Tarai also emerged as a promising economic unit, having a distinct character of its own.[74]

2.2.4. Rope tram way and postal service

In 1902, Chandra Shamsher tried to establish a rope tram way from Bhimphedi to Thankot. These two places were separated by two high mountain ranges. The route between Bhimphedi and Thankot[75] was very bad. Goods were carried on man's back, and the transport was very slow and expensive. The Prime Minister requested the British Government for material and technical assistance for the construction of rope tram way. He needed the services of one or two European engineers to make the preliminary survey etc. The Prime Minister, Chandra Shamsher wished to erect the rope way on a similar model as existed in Cherrapunji.[76] In 1903, a survey was carried out by the firm of Martin and Company, Calcutta. But later on the firm of Messers R.S. Underhill and Company of London took the charge of surveying.[77] The Ropeway was supplied by Messrs Keymer, Son & Co., of London with Messrs R. Pearson and A.J. Knight as consulting Engineers. Mr Underhill was the incharge of the project. It was expected to be completed by mid summer 1925.[78]

Postal arrangement

Before 1881, there was no postal arrangement between India and Nepal except one line from Barewa to the capital of Nepal.[79] Barewa connected the postal service with the Motihari in Champaran district. It passed through Hetauda via Chitlang to Kathmandu. It followed the same route as the Resident's post which started from Sujauli. For the rest of the country there was no means of forwarding a letter, even for the Darbar himself, except by putting the cover in a cleft stick with the order that it was to be conveyed from village to village by whatever men were available en route. The result of this slow and uncertain procedure was that the Darbar more often than not communicated through British territory, and by the British post with its outlying stations on the West, South and East.[80]

In 1861, the Nepal Government complained to the Birtish Indian Government about the serious loss of revenue, owing to the constant receipt from, and delivery to Merchants at Kathmandu of Baughy Parcels containing articles of value which had paid no duty at the frontier. The Governor-General in Council informed the

Nepal Darbar through the Resident that Indian post office was not bound to deliver any letters or parcels in Nepal beyond the limits of the Residency. He instructed the Resident that he should refuse to receive any dispatch by the Post or any Baughy parcel from any persons living outside the residency limits, unless it be accompanied by a customs house pass. Again, he reminded that if this plan be adopted, he would have no difficulty in making arrangements which would be satisfactory to the Nepalese Government.[81]

In 1879, Charles Girdlestone, the British Resident in Nepal, reported about the loss of revenue of the Nepalese Government owing to the prevailing system of money order which operated within the Residency. "If the system of money orders be extended to the post-office of this Residency which is included in the Indian Postal Guides list, it is likely to be often recorded for the sake of evading the payment of duty. In proportion to the receipts for money order issued would be the loss of the Darbar by non-payment of its duty. Under these circumstances I submit the case for consideration whether the Nepal Post office should be exempted from the new system just as the Residency Treasury has hitherto been from the system in regard to money order".[82]

In 1880, the Government of Nepal organised internal postal line in the Nepalese districts adjoining Indian territory. Ilam near Darjeeling, Doti near Kumaun, Kerung and Kuti on Tibetan frontier were the main lines opened for postal services. The branch line of these lines were connected with the outlying towns and military posts of importance. Regular runners were appointed on the main lines to carry the despatches. The Prime Minister of Nepal informed the British Resident that the despatch reached Ilam in nine or ten days and it reached Silgarhi in the Doti district in ten or eleven days. The headmen of the villages en route were always to have one or more men ready for the conveyance of a mail received. The British Resident doubted whether there was or would be daily despatch. The facilities introduced were opened for general public and stamps were available for purchase. Stamps were manufactured locally.[83]

The Railway, telegraph and postal services had helped to transform the independent states of India into British dominion.

It was for this reason that much pressure was put on Nepal. She refused the extension of British telegraphic services, lest these appurtenances of civilization would affect their status as an independent country.[84] The Nepalese Government did not want to pursue a liberal policy regarding the extension of the railway or telegraphic system into its country as that would have necessitated the employment of Europeans in their territories.

2.2. Impact of Indian Railways

With the opening of the Indian railway in the districts bordering Nepal, the Indo-Nepal trade relations entered a new phase. The railway system had great impact upon the markets and trade centres in the border districts of Nepal and India. The branch lines of the railways were extended to the convenient points at the frontier with a view to encouraging and facilitating trade with Nepal. The new lines pushed up the growth of trade or affected its traditional passage.[85]

By the end of the nineteenth century, railway lines were built to connect a number of towns on the Nepal-India border situated along important centres of trade in Nepal.[86] In 1885, the Bengal and North Western Railway Company opened a branch line to Nepalgung Road on the Indian side of the border near Nepalgunj in Banke district of Nepal. Gorakhpur was the headquarter of the Bengal and North-Western Railway. A branch line from Gorakhpur to the Uska bazar was opened and it was extended from Uska to Tulsipur in Gonda. Formerly, rice from the Nepal tarai and Binayakpur was carried to Dhani bazar on the Dharmela. It was then delivered by boat along the Rapti and the Gogra to the markets of Bengal. These routes were superseded by the railways.[87] The Bengal and North Western Railway was extended in order to capture the large grain trade from Nepal. A branch line of this railway was extended from Gonda to Tulsipur. The line ran from Uska through the Centre of Bansi East and the north west portion of Bansi West. The section of the railway from Uska to Bahni near the Nepal frontier attracted the trade of large Nepalese market at Taulihawa, Sirsewa and Bahadurganj.[88] The extension of the railway to Uska diverted the grain trade from Mindehwal. Markets of Naugarh and Shohratgunj sprang up along the line of the railway. Biskohar, one of the important centres for Nepal trade declined as a market. The extension of the railway caused diversion of traffic to Naugarh and Uska. The importance of Lotan as store house of grain also declined on account of the diversion of traffic. The Gonda-Tulsipur Railway was extended to Panshperwa and Uskabazar in Basti with a branch from Gaisauri to Jharwa in the forest near the Nepal frontier.[89] Formerly, Bahramghat was one of the most important centres of trade between Nepal, Gonda and Bahraich on the north and the districts south of the Gogra. But after the construction of great Elgin Bridge at Chaukaghat in 1890, the importance of Bahramghat as a trade centre declined. This bridge carried over the Gogra the main line of the Bengal and North-Western Railway. Gram, Oilseeds and spices from Nepal to Bahraich and piece-goods, metals, salt, tobacco and sugar from Bahraich to Nepal were carried by the railway which terminated on the frontier close to Nepalgunj. The main line of the Bengal and North-Western Railway passed through the extreme corner of this district. The branch line from Gonda terminated at Katarnian Ghat on the Girwa with a branch from Nanpara to the Nepalgunj road on the frontier. A large trade with Nepal passed through this railway. The opening of the railway gave strong stimulus to the increase of trade in Bahraich. In Pilibhit, the railway acted as distributing centre for the products of the tarai and Nepal.[90]

Because of the extension of the Indian railway system, Nepalgunj, in the far western tarai region of Nepal developed into a bustling town with a brisk building activity, a growing population and even a rudimentary street-lighting system. There was a heavy influx of Indian traders, both seasonal and permanent, into Nepalgunj. By the end of the 19th century, the town accommodated nearly 45 permanent commercial establishments, in addition to more than 100 temporary stalls during November to May every year, operated by Marwaris and other traders from India.[91]

In 1890, the Assam-Bihar State Railway opened its Purnea section from Kasba to Forbesganj, adjoining the market town of Rangeli in Morang district of Nepal (nucleus of the modern town of Biratnagar).[92] It changed the trade-routes of the western and northern parts of the Araria and Sadar sub-divisions. Products were brought from Nepal to Forbesganj and then taken to Maniharight, where it was shipped and carried westward by river to Revilganj. The opening of the new railway stations at Anchraghat and Debiganj had given additional facilities for the trade of Purnea district. Debiganj attracted a good deal of traffic from Nawabganj which was an important trade centre near the Nepal frontier.[93]

The metre gauge Tirhut State Railway was started in 1874 by the construction of a line from Muzaffarpur to the left bank of the Ganga opposite Mokama Ghat. In 1890 the line was leased by the government to the Bengal and North-Western Railway Company. At the end of June 1905, the system consisted of 1,468 miles occupying the whole country north of the Ganga between the Gogra and the Koshi rivers.[94]

The extension of the Tirhut State Railway across the north of the Supaul sub-division to Pertapganj altered the course of the trade in the Bhagalpur district to a considerable extent and diminished the importance of the river-borne traffic. The effect of the construction of Tirhut State Railway was excellently summed up by the Collector of Champaran in one of his reports in 1882-83, 'Since the opening of the railway for traffic, piece goods have been imported exclusively, and salt and hardware to a very great extent by rail. Before the opening of the railway, piece-goods were brought from Muzaffarpur by cart, and salt and hardware generally by boat from Patna. Since the line has been opened, it has been fully utilised for the export of sugar, indigo, saltpetre, hides and makai. The goladars have it in contemplation to adopt for the future the railway route for the export of the more bulky commodities, such as grain and oilseeds with the view of avoiding the risk and delays upon export by boat.[95]

The Muzaffarpur branch of the Tirhut state Railway was opened on 24 February 1877. A survey regarding the proposed railway from Muzaffarpur through Motihari and Sugauli to Bettiah was completed in 1878. This project was regarded as a financial success because it was a thoroughfare for all the trade between

Nepal and the districts lying south of it. F.M. Halliday, the Commissioner of the Patna Division, hopefully reported, "Very great traffic exists between Nepal and the adjoining districts of Muzaffarpur and Darbhanga. There is undoubtedly a very extensive trade in timber with Nepal and the grain traffic is not inconsiderable. All this well, of course, be enormously developed when we have the railway extension from Muzaffarpur via Motihari to Battiah—a line which is in course of construction."[96] The extension of the Tirhut State Railway from Muzaffarpur to Bettiah (75 miles) and from Darbhanga to Peepraghat (28 miles) was sanctioned in July 1880. These extensions passed through highly cultivated and populous districts and were expected to tap the products of Nepal and north Bihar.[97]

The branch line of Tirhut State Railway from Muzaffarpur to Sitamarhi was opened in September 1890. Regarding the value of this line J.F.K. Hewitt, the officiating Commissioner of the Patna Division, reported in 1885. "The completion of this portion of the line will bring the railway communication into close connection with the Nepal Frontier." He was so much confident about the expansion of trade through this route that he further added, 'when the work will be completed, it will render it more than ever desirable that some understanding should be arrived at with the Nepal Darbar to induce it to abolish or at least systematize the frontier export and import duties and to put a stop to the illegal and vexatious exactions which interfere so much with the trade between the two countries.[98]

In 1896 arrangements were made to construct the Hajipur Begusarai-Katihar and the Sugauli-Raxaul lines in connection with the Bengal and North-Western Railway system. The construction of a feeder line from Raxaul on the Nepal frontier to the Tirhut State Railway was completed during the year 1898-99.[99]

The earth work of the Bengal North-Western Railway line running from Sakri to Jayanagar on the Nepal frontier was completed as a relief work during the famine of 1897. This line linked up the areas far removed from the railway. It passed through Madhubani, an important trading centre in Darbhanga district. Madhubani tapped large grain supply from Nepal. Another important centre for trade was Narahia. It was connected by road with the railway. Narahia also acquired large grain traffic from Nepal. Road communications from Darbhanga town and the Sakri, Jhanjharpur and Nirmali Railway were also extended to the Nepal frontier.[100]

The extension of the Indian railway system to market towns on the Indian side of the border gave a fillip to the growth of towns on the Nepal side of the border as well. Nepalgunj Birgunj and Birtanagar, all in Nepalese tarai were the examples of such growth. The emergence of a new market-town named Birgunj in the adjoining area of Nepal owes its growth to the extension of the Indian railway system to Raxaul in 1898. This town was named after the then Prime Minister Bir Shumshere. Goods exported to India from that area were channelled through Birgunj. The government constructed a number of buildings in the town which were leased to traders. A state trading agency, known as the Birgunj Mahajani Adda, was established, and through it trade was conducted in the state sector in raw silk and other commodities.[101]

The Tirhut State Railway was extended into Champaran from Muzaffarpur in the year 1883. It was the first railway line in the district. During the famine of 1897 this was the only railway line to serve the district. Since that time the management of this line was taken over by the Bengal and North Western Railway Company. It was extended beyond Bettiah to Bhikhna Thori on the Nepal border. In this way this railway line traversed the district from south to north. There was also a short line running due north from Sugauli to Raxaul with one intermediate station at Ramgarhwa. This railway line was connected with the Nepalese light railway at Raxaul in February, 1927. Before that there was no railway line in Nepal.[102] On the eve of the final stage of the extension of the Tirhut State Railway in Champaran district F.M. Halliday expressed his hope in 1882—in this way." In Champaran, the railway has not yet been completed and it is too early to say what its full effect will be. It may, however, be safely said that it will enormously develop trade. A great deal of grain comes down from Nepal which does not generally find a good sale. With the railway at Bettiah and improved communication between the line of rail and Nepal passes, there can be no doubt that an extensive trade in grain is likely to spring up and benefit the district generally."[103] Two years later he again reported, "The Magistrate of Champaran writes that although the railway has been opened for the traffic in his district for little over a year, its effects are already beginning to be felt. It has brought about a reduction of about 20 per cent in cart-here-hire in and around Bettiah and Motihari. It has attached to itself a fair share of the export and import traffic of the district. It has made Bettiah the highway for travellers from Gorukpore, Segowli and Motihari and for those from Nepal. It attracts light traffic from Goruckpore, Saran and Nepal. It may absorb a portion of the traffic now borne on the Gunduk."[104]

Champaran was traversed from south to north by the Muzaffarpur-Bikhna Thori branch of the Bengal and North Western Railway. It started from Muzaffapur, entered Champaran a few miles south of Mehsi, ran south of and parallel to the Sikrana river as far as Bettiah and reached its terminus at Bhikhna Thori on the Nepal frontier. The branch line of the railway from Sugauli to Raxaul was 18 miles long. It was reported in 1907 that the third line of Bengal and North-western Railway from Bagha to Bairagnia would convey the grain traffic of Nepal and the north of Champaran direct to Gorakhpur and the United Provinces without the present long detour through Muzaffarpur and Saran.

The North Gangetic State Railway connected the eastern and western limits of the Indian provinces adjoining Nepalese districts in Tarai, brought the districts of Muzaffarpur, Darbhanga and Champaran into closer connection with the rest of India and served as a distinct link in the chain of Indo-Nepalese trade.

The main trade route from Nepal to India was through Champaran. The bulk of trade passed through Raxaul, the terminus of the Sugauli-Raxaul branch railway. The railways were the main arteries of commerce but the Gandak and the Burhi Gandak also carried much traffic.[105]

The construction of a wooden bridge over the Sikrana river at Chainpatia, helped to improve the traffic in Indo-Nepal border. The bridge was constructed by the District Road Committee at the cost of the nearly Rs. 28,000—and it was 400 ft long. This bridge was 10 miles north of Bettiah. A road was constructed from this place via Hurdi to Bhikna Thori. The whole of Nepal traffic north and east of the Someswar range entered India through this route. After the completion of Sikrana bridge this route proved as a feeder of the Indian railway system. It ran through the fertile country north of Sikrano and also carried grain coming in from the Chitwan and other villages of the Nepal tarai to the north of Bettiah sub-division.[106]

The local authorities in India near the Nepal border realized the importance of the construction and extension of the railway in specific directions to increase the volume of Nepal trade. They expressed their satisfaction over the construction of a new railway line in the adjoining districts of Nepal. They were fully aware of the utility of the railway for the effective trade across the frontier. For example, the Sub-divisional officer in Supaul suggested the construction of a railway from the west to Pertapganj on the Koshi river to catch the traffic in grain and oilseeds from Nepal. The collector of Basti suggested a railway line connecting the Oudh and Rohilkhand line from the neighbourhood of Butwal in Nepal through Midnahwal and Basti to Faizabad. He stated that this line would be remunerative on account of the flow of merchandise and traffic of pilgrims to the holy shrines of Ajodhya on the Ghaghra.[107] In 1897 Fuller, Assistant Director, Department of Agriculture and Commerce, North-Western Provinces and Oudh, suggested that Nanpara should be made a terminus of a light railway, because it was "the collection and distributing centre" for a great portion of the Nepal trade. The railway might also be extended from Nawabganj to Basti and Gorakhpur. He was confident that such a line would probably serve the interests of the Nepal trade better than any other. He argued, "For a portion of this traffic the railway would act as a feeder to the Gogra, if the river export traffic kept to its present figure. But the completion of the Benares bridge would in all probability attract a very large portion of the present river traffic to the Oudh and Rohilkhand

Railway."[108] Major de Montmorency, the Deputy Commissioner of Bahraich, advocated the adoption of the route to Bahramghat. His main argument was that Nepal would thereby be connected with Kanpur, the commercial centre of the North Western Provinces. F.N. Wright, the officiating Director, Department of Agriculture and Commerce, North-West Provinces and Oudh in his report dated 6 September 1880 to the Secretary to Government North West Provinces and Oudh remarked, "considered commercially, there is every reason to believe that the proposed line from Nanpara through Bahraich and Gonda to Faizabad would prove a success....if river traffic is maintained, the proposed line would act as a feeder to it, but it is more than probable, it is almost absolutely certain, that the whole trade of Nepal which crosses on the Bahraich and Gonda frontiers, as well as that of the Bahraich and Gonda districts themselves, will use the rail for through booking to Howrah."[109]

The utility of the construction and extension of the railway system in the adjoining districts of Nepal was fully discussed in Faizabad Conference on 26 January 1880. Regarding the improvement of the Indo-Nepal trade through the Indian railway system the conference concluded. "It was considered that the experiment should be tried of stimulating traffic by a nearer apprcach of the railway system to the Nepal border. The direction in which a first experiment could be most easily made appeared to be in the extension of a railway line from Bahramghat to, or towards, the mart of Banke or Nepalganj. The line as far as Bahraich forms part of the present government scheme and would tend to bring into closer connection, with the two marts of Cawnpor (the great collection centre of North India) and Nepalganj (the most rising market on the Nepal side). The line has the further advantages of being a short one of not coming into competition with the river or with the Oudh and Rohilkhand Railway to which it could act as a feeder. It was considered that it might be proved by this one experiment whether it would be advantageous at other points along the frontier to bring railway carriage within nearer reach of the frontier marts, and in this view the construction of the railway might be desirable even though the initial profits were not to reach the Government standard."[110] The Department of Agriculture and Commerce was requested to place this recommendation before the Government of North-Western Provinces and Oudh in a separate communication, with such statistics and information as his Department might be able to provide with a view to its early consideration. The question was raised whether the Nepalese Government would be likely to assist any railway tending to increase Nepalese traffic by concessions in timber or otherwise. Charles Girdlestone, the Resident of Nepal, was of the opinion that the Darbar would require to make profit on material supplied. But the supply of sleepers and fuel for the railway would be in preferential rates as compared with those required in its ordinary dealings.[111]

The Government of India decided that the project of the railway from Bahramghat in the direction of Nepalgunj as suggested by the Faizabad Conference need not be considered till some more definite proposals were received from the Government of North-Western Provinces.[112]

On 1 November 1877 E. Buck, the Director of Agriculture and Commerce, North Western Provinces, had suggested that the light railway feeders might be extended from the main lines of rail through the North-Western Provinces and Oudh, either to the boundary of Nepal or if the Nepal Darbar would permit it, to the marts on the other side of the boundary. He pointed out that the most important of the two railway lines would be (1) from Bareilly to Pilibhit, to be extended possibly to Barmdeo, which would meet the requirements of Kumaun and Tibet trade as well as the Western portion of Nepal. However, if a railway would be constructed to Ramnagar or any other place at the foot of the hills, and western Kumaun, the extension of a railway to Barmdeo would perhaps not pay because this line would absorb the greater part of Kumaun and Tibet traffic. (2) The second important line would be a line through the Gorakhpur district parallel to the series of routes converging towards Butwal in Nepal. The railway through Gorakhpur would be fed largely by the tracks through which its route passes. The advantage of the railway was felt even by the Nepalese within their territory.[113]

The traffic by a line connecting Nanpara, Bahraich and Gonda with Nawabganj was estimated at 20 lakh of maunds. The greater portion of the Ghaghra traffic consisted in grain and oilseeds. The Nepal trade could be brought into contact with the existing railway system two points via Bahramghat and Faizabad. The stations of both of the places were on the Oudh and Rohilkhand railway. Bahramghat was connected with the main line by an extension from Nawabganj. Faizabad was on the main line itself. The route for Bahramghat would be through Nanpara and Bahraich. In the same way the route for Faizabad would be through Nanpara, Bahraich and Gonda.[114]

There were five recognised leading lines from which export traffic found its way through and from the North-western Provinces and Oudh to Nepal.

(1) From Pilibhit to Barmdeo, fed by the Oudh and Rohilkhand Railway which supplied merchandise from Bareilly.

(2) From Bahraich to Nepalganj, fed from Bahramghat on the Oudh and Rohilkhand Railway.

(3) From Gonda and Basti, via Marni to Bahadurganj, fed from Faizabad on the Oudh and Rohilkhand Railway.

(4) The Lotan and Uska routes from Gorakhpur and the Rapti Butwal.

(5) The Gorakhpur and Thunthbari route via Nichlal.[115]

For the second time on 20 October 1892, Franklin Prestages presented a scheme for the extension of the Darjeeling Himalayan Railway into Nepal. Regarding the advantages of the proposed railway line Prestage was of the opinion that line would help to reduce the rate of transport by 2/3 and would give cheaper and quicker transit. In case of scarcity or famine in Nepal it would give the most certain and cheap means by which food grains could be poured into the valley direct from the most productive district in Bengal.[116] But the proposal for the extension of the railway was rejected by the Nepalase Government.

The installation of branch lines connecting towns on the Nepal border with major centres of trade and commerce in the sub-continent was dictated by the need to expand and cheapen supplies of primary produce from the Tarai region of Nepal, particularly foodgrains and timber. Indeed, scarcity of firewood in the Gangetic Valley had been cited by British officials as early as the 1850s as a justification for constructing branch lines into the sub-Himalayan plains. Commercial links between the Tarai region of Nepal and the adjoining areas of India, traditionally close because of the absence of natural boundaries and the proximity of populous settlements on the Indian side of the border, were further cemented by the extension of India's railway system.[117]

The Northern Indian Railway system played a vital role in the development of Indo-Nepal trade in the closing years of the 19th century and in the beginning of the 20th century. However, there is no evidence to show that the railways entirely displaced river navigation in the traffic of goods. For example, Farbesgunj in Purnea district was connected by railway in 1890, but timber, cardamom, and other commodities were still being exported from eastern Nepal to Patna by boat at the end of the 19th century. Similarly, the bulk of Nepal's trade in the Central sector passed through Raxaul, the terminus of the Sugauli-Raxaul branch railway, but the Gandak and the Burhi Gandak also carried much traffic. River transport continued to play an important role in the movement of commodities from the interior areas to railheads on the Nepal-India border. Timber, foodgrains and other commodities were transported by river to the nearest Indian railhead, where they were transhipped to wagons and despatched to different destinations in India.[118]

In north Bihar, railway facilities were inadequate, and in the Koshi affected areas of Saharsa and Darbhanga the transport system had become disorganized by recurrent floods and changes in the course of the river. In north Bihar railway ran mostly parallal to the courses of the rivers, mainly because of the difficulty of constructing bridge and the danger of interference with riverine drainage by railway embankments. As a result, communication between important towns viz. Motihari to Chapra, Muzaffarpur to Darbhanga was long and tedious.[119]

2.3. River Communication

A series of rivers each with many tributaries are found in Nepal from West to east. The principal of these are the Karnali in Western Nepal, the Gandaki in Central Nepal and the Koshi in Eastern Nepal. These major rivers have seven tributaries each and are called the Sapta (seven) Karnali, the Sapta Gandaki and the Sapta Koshi. These rivers and estuaries carried the bulk of the country trade, and road was little used, especially in the rainy season.[120]

The Karnali—The seven tributaries of the Karnali river are the Seti, the Burhi Ganga, the Humla Karnali, the Mugu Karnali, the Tila, the Thuli Bheri and the Sani Bheri.[121]

The river Karnali rises in Tibet (30.4'N and 80.48'E) and flows through Nepal under the name of Karnali or Kauriala. The Karnali, the Seti and Bheri follow the independent courses through the lower Himalayas. The Karnali is reinforced by the Seti river after piercing through the Mahabharat range and is also joined by the Dun (Inner Tarai). The combined waters of the Karnali, the Seti and the Bheri penetrate the Siwalik range and enter India between Kheri and Bahraich and form the boundary of these two districts.[122]

The river Karnali is called Gogra (Ghagra, Gher-ghara, Sarju, Saryu, Decha, Dehwa) in India. It meets the Girwa near the border just below the Saheli, one of the three branches of the Sarda. Two rivulets known as Kuthi-yankti and Kalapani rise in the Panch Chuli mountains in the north-east corner of Kumaun. After travelling a few miles they combine and form the Kali or Kali Ganga. This separates Nepal from Kumaun. At a distance of one hundred and six miles from the source, the Kali meets the Sarju or Sarda at Pancheswar. It descends, on the plains at Barmdeo. The name Kali is lost after it flows through Pancheswar. The river is called the Sarju or Sarda. It comes down on the plains at Barmdeo. From Mundiaghat the river forms the boundary of Nepal and Pilibhit. It then enters Kheri. In Pilibhit it is joined on the rinht bank by the Chanka river. The Sarda has four district channels from south to north-the Ui, the

Sarda or Chauko, the Dahawar, the Suheli. The first of these is a small stream which joins the Chauka again.[123]

The main branch of the Sarda called Dahawar joins the Karnali at Mallanpur, a few miles below Kataighat. At Bahramghat another branch of the Sarda named Chauka meets it. From this point the united stream is called Gogra or Sarju. The Gogra turns east and divides Gonda on its north bank from Bara Banki and Faizabad on the south. It also divides Basti and Gorakhpur from Faizabad. It meets the Rapti and the little Gandak from the north. East of Gorakhpur the Gogra forms the boundary between Saran district of Bihar and Ballia district of the United Provinces for about forty miles. It falls into the Ganga in 26°44'N and 84°42'E.[124]

The Karnali and Girwa rivers were both navigable for a short distance before entering Indian territory. Until the opcning of the Bengal and North-Western Railway, traffic on the Gogra was considerable and was of great importauce. Large quantities of timber, grain and spices came down from Nepal through the Gogra. The most important place on the bank of the river is Faizabad, with Ajodhya, the sacred birthplace of Rama adjoining it.[125]

The Gandaki—The Mayangdi, the Kali, the Modi, the Seti, the Marsyangdi, the Burhi Gandaki and Trisuli are the seven tributaries of the Gandaki river.[126]

The Gandaki river rises in the Central mountain basin of Nepal, in 27°27 W. and 83°56 E. It drains the central regions of Nepal. The most important of its contributory stream is Trisuli or Trisulganga.[127]

The Gandaki river is called Saligram in Nepal and Narayani in the United Provinces. It enters India at Tribeni. It forms the boundary between Champaran and Gorakhapur districts for about twenty miles and also between Saran on the South-West and Champaran and Muzaffarpur on the north-east. It flows forty miles in Champaran. It finally joins the Ganga opposite Patna in

25°41'N and 85°12' E after a course of one hundred and ninety two miles.[128]

Soon after its entry into Indian territory the river acquires the character of a deltaic river. It was navigable throghout the year by country boat below Bagaha in Champaran district.

Rafts of timber passed down from Nepal and Gorakhpur forests and grain and sugar were exported by the same route. Navigation was however difficult as the channel during the dry season was narrow and winding, while in the rains it became a torrent. In the dry season the river was rarely more than a quarter of a mile across, but in the rains it winded to two or three miles.[129]

The Little Gandak rises in the lower hills of Nepal. It flows from North to South through the whole length of Gorakhpur. It then joins the Gogra within Saran district.[130] In dry season, little Gandak was generally forbidable. A good deal of trade was carried on by the little Gandak, If slightly improved, it would admit boats weighing 500 maunds coming up all the year round.[131]

The river Gandaki was used for the floating of timber from Nepal. Grains exported from Nepal through this river was carried on by carts to Narkulia and other depots on the right bank of the river. Boats of 800 maunds (between 26 and 29 tons) could navigate it throughout the year.[132]

Koshi—The seven tributaries of the Koshi river are the Indrawati, the Sun Koshi, the Tama Koshi, the Likhu Khola, the Dudha Koshi, the Arun Koshi and the Tamere or Tamur.[133]

In southern Nepal the Tamur joins the Arun a few miles downstream of the junction of the Arun and Sun Koshi. Then the waters of the three move through the Mahabharat range of the outer HImalaya and turn into the Koshi river of the Indian plains. It first touches India in the extreme north-west of the Bhagalpur district. It has a course of a few miles along the boundary between it and Purnea. It enters Purnea a few miles north of Anchraghat. Within Purnea it is a large river nearly a mile wide. After a course

General Jit Jang, second legitimate son of Jang Bahadur.

Dhir Shamsher, the brother of the Prime Minister Jan

r, with his seventeen sons, and four of his grandchildren.

Bir Shamsher, the third Prime Minister, who strengthened Nepalese relations with British India.

of about 84 miles within Bengal, it falls into the Ganga a few miles before it joins the Ganga. It meets the Gogra from North Monghyr and Tilijuga and Bagmati from North Bhagalpur.[134]

The Koshi was navigable all the year round for boats of 750 maunds or about 27 tons burden. It was navigable as far as the Nepal frontier for boats of 250 maunds or about 9 tons burden.[135]

The three Nepal basins of the Karnali, the Gandaki and the Koshi drain the Indian slopes of the Himalayas, for a distance of 300 miles.[136]

In addition to the above major river systems, there are other streams which originate only from the southern slopes of the Mahabharat Lekh (Lesser Himalayas) in their volume and length as compared to the mighty Himalaya rivers. These minor streams are quite small, but they can be quite dangerous and devastating during rainy season, Some of these streams from Western Nepal to eastward are the Mohana, the Babai, the Rapti, the Ban Ganga, the Tinau, the Bagmati, the Kamala, the Trijuga, the Bakra and the Kankar.[137]

Scores of rills and rivulets also rise in the Churiya zone to flow, south, but except in rainy season, many of them have very little or no water on the surface because of the porosity of the region.[138]

These rivers and rivulets carried bulk of the traffic from Nepal to the adjoining districts of India. These districts from east to west were Purnea, Bhagalpur, Darbhanga, Muzaffarpur, Champaran, Gorakhpur, Basti and Pilibhit.

The Koshi, the Buckra or Panar, the Kankai and the Mechi were the main waterways used for floating down timber from Nepal to the Purnea district of Bihar. The Panar had its origin in the Matiyari Police division on the junction of a number of hill streams coming down from Nepal. It first moves sout-east through Sultanpur parganas passing by Araria and also through Haveli Purnea about ten miles to the east of the headquarters town. Then it turns southward through Kada and Hatanda to the Ganga. It was navigable for boats of 250 maunds or about 9 tons in the neighbourhood of Purnea and above that stage for boats of 100 maunds (about $3\frac{1}{2}$ tons) almost to the Nepal frontier.[139] The Bakra rises in the Madhubani taluk of the Morang or lower Himalayan range of Nepal. It joins the Panar river at Rampur five miles north of Araria. A great deal of timber was brought down the Bakra from Nepal.[140]

Bhagalpur is drained mainly by the Trijuga and Dimra rivers. The Trejuga rises in the hills in the sub-tarai of Nepal. It enters Bhagalpur at the most northern point of paragana Naridigar. Then it marks the western boundary between Bhagalpur, Nepal and Darbhanga. Near Tilkeswar, it receives a great quantity of water from the Dimra. It also gets through the Katna, the united waters of the Talabas, Parwan, Dhusan and Loran. Trijuga was navigable for boats of two thousand maunds or seventy tons burden upto Tilkeswar and beyond that for boats of a quarter of that tonnage upto Dighia within ten miles of the Nepal frontier. Dimra rises in Nepal. It divides the Parganas of Dhapar and Naridigar for the first ten miles of its course in Bhagalpur. It meets the Trijuga at Tilkeswar. It was navigable during the rains within six miles of the Nepal frontier for boats of 100 maunds ($3\frac{1}{2}$ tons).[141]

The Kamala and Trijuga were the only streams that were navigable in Darbhanga district. During the rains timber was floated down the former to Darbhanga. The Bagmati, the Bakaya, the Shorum, the Lakhandyi, the Hurdee rivers were navigable in Muzaffarpur district only during the rains.

In the Champaran district, the river Gandak was used for floating timber in the rains. It was navigable for boats of 1000 to 1500 maunds (36 to 55 tons) burden throughout the year. It was navigable to a place called Nilpur in Nepal, twenty miles above Tribeni, but large boats rarely went beyond the shoals and rapids near Bagha.[142]

The river Gandak or Narayani was navigable in the Gorakhpur district. So far as it moved through Nepalese territory it was only used for floating timber. The Deputy Collector of

Gorakhpur was of the opinion that it was navigable all through the year for boats up to 350 maunds beyond the frontier of Nepal. Charles Girdlestone, however, did not agree with this view. He argued that there was water enough for such boats during the rains. But when the snow started melting the navigation became dangerous on account of the rapid currents or the mass of the large timber in the stream. In the dry season a boat of 100 maunds faced difficulty over the shallow between Tribeni and Narkulia. The boats of any size did not go above Narkulia. Grains exported from Nepal through this river was carried on by carts to Narkulia and other depots on the right bank of the river.[143] The river Rapti also used to flow through the Gorakhpur district. After wandering through Bahraich, Gonda and Basti, it enters Gorakhpur at Magalaha in pargana Haveli. A brisk trade was transacted in boats of 100 tons burden. The Rapti had great importance as a means of carrying cheaply, safely and quickly the large export trade in grain and wood from Nepal. Timber as will as grain were conveyed from Nepal to this district by the Rapti and its tributaries—the Dhamela and the Rohini. The greater portion of this traffic was absorbed by the Ghagra.[144] The Dhamela, an old channel of the Rapti, once bore a large traffic from Uska and the important grain market of Dhani.[145]

The waterways in Basti district were the Rapti, the Banganga and the Kunra or the Dhamela otherwise known as Tenavi on the Nepalese side of the border. The Rapti was less used than the Banganga and the Kunra. Much timber was floated down from Nepal through Banganga and Kunra. The grain traffic by the Kunra river was also shipped to the local mart of Uska. The mart of Uska collected and distributed rice from the surrounding country and the Nepalese terai. Throughout its course in Basti, the Rapti was navigable by boats of 100 maunds. The Kunra and its continuation the Dhamela in months of flood bore country boats of any size.[146]

There were no river routes in Gonda, Bahraich, Kheri and Bareilly districts. But the link of Bahraich with Nepal was maintained through ferries.[147]

The river Sarda enters Pilibhit in the extreme north of Pargana Puranpur, one mile above Mundiaghat. The latter was the ferry point between Pilibhit and Nepal and formed the principal line of traffic between the two countries.[148]

2.3.1. Bridges and Ferries

There were several wooden and rope bridges across different rivers on Indo-Nepal border. In the beginning most of the streams were spanned by rope and wooden cantilever bridges. Later on some of them were replaced by suspension and masonry bridges.

There were three main approaches into western Nepal from British India. Among these two could be crossed through the bridge over Kali (Sarda) river at Jhulaghat and the one[149] at Darchulo[150] in Nepal. "The Piers of these bridges were made of rough basket work weighted within and without with stone, which enable them to resist the ordinary force of the stream."[151]

There were four routes from Pilibhit to Mandiaghat and Nepal. These routes could be crossed through the wooden bridges over the Chanka river.[152]

The most important bridge near Indo-Nepal border was the masonary bridge across the Sariswa river with the frontier between Raxaul and Birganj. The construction of the bridge was finally completed in 1903.[153] Besides this, there were several other bridges across different rivers on the way to the capital of Nepal. The Rapti river on the way to Kathmandu could be crossed about twenty times by temporary bridges "composed of heaps of loose stones as piers, with a flooring of brushwood and sods."[154]

The Teesta Suspension bridge had great importance in the development of trade through the route going from Eastern Nepal to Darjeeling. According to the Deputy Commissioner of Darjeeling the Teesta suspension bridge and the road leading to Darjeeling and Siliguri and the road from the Nepal frontier at Naxalbari to Garidhura at the foot of the hills were "two great works of the district". He added, "These works may be said to consist of two systems (i) that dependent on the Teesta Suspension Bridge for opening up trade with Tibet and (ii) the lower part of Darjeeling cart road and the Naksabari—Garidura Road for opening up trade between the hills and plains and Nepal. The latter system has been completely successful. The roads are crowded with carts and pack animals."[155]

Regarding the construction of the road, Percival Landon writes, "The roads of Nepal have been improved rather by bridges than by a reconstruction of their surface.[156] Bridges on the larger rivers were rare. The passengers, carts, cattle and other commodities could be crossed in ferry boats. These ferries were leased annually at auction for a considerable sum.[157]

Tanakpur, the larger frontier town of British India on the West bank of the Kali, had no bridge to cross the border. The primitive boats which were nothing more than hollow tree trunks convey one to the further side.[158] The river Gogra in Oudh near the Nepal border was navigable by light draught streamers.[159]

The link of Bahraich with Nepal was maintained through ferries on the Ghaghra-Kamnagarghat, on the Rapti-Gangapur and Gulra. The Ghaghra-Kamnagarghat was connected with a cart track from Nepal through Kates to Khairigarh. The Rapti Gangapur was linked with a cart track from the north of the Chardo pargana to Nepal. Gulra was connected with the Nepal line at the meeting of the boundaries of the Bhingor and Charda pargana. All these rivers were crossed by small boats.[160]

During the rainy season, when the rivers were high, a considerable quantity of traffic was carried in country boats along the Gandak, little Gandak and Bagmati rivers. This traffic was carried between Muzaffarpur and the adjoining districts of Nepal. Sal logs and large quantity of bamboos from Nepal were floated down to the little Gandak and Bagmati.[161]

Some of the rivers in the Nepalese territory were not navigable because of the swift-current. These were used for the floating of timbers. These rivers were navigable only in the Indian plain. Goods were sent direct to Calcutta by the little Gandak, the Bagmati and the Ganga in the rainy season. But in the dry weather months, the Great Gandak alone was open for navigation by large craft. The main stream of trade followed its course to Patna and thence to Calcutta.[162]

The Indian Railway system did not entirely diminish the river borne traffic in Nepal. Even during the 1940s, goods were transported between Hanumannagar in the Saptari district and the Indian Railway station at Nirmali by boat through the Koshi river. In 1896, the Nepal Government requisitioned the services of an engineer from the British Indian Government to dredge the Karnali river in order to facilitate transportation of timber through the river.[163] On 15 October 1912, Chandra Shamshere, the Prime Minister of Nepal, accepted the proposal of the British Indian Government to construct boom on the Sarda river near Barmdeo for the purpose of catching the timber. But he wanted to discuss the project before its implementation.[164]

Water communication was cheaper[165] in comparison with the road. The cost of construction, maintenance and replacement of the original road bed would be higher than former.[166] The conservator of Forest, Oudh was of the opinion that if the river Mohan in Nepal were cleared as they (British Government) have cleared Soheli, a great deal of rice might be brought down to Bahramghat.[167] It was for this reason that the traders of India and Nepal followed this route from the beginning of their commercial relations. It is the best means of communication for the poor and hilly countries like Nepal which have plenty of water resources.

2.4. The road policy

There was a contradiction in the policy followed by the British Indian Government and that by the Nepalese in connection with the construction and opening of the new routes in the Nepalese districts adjoining British Indian territory. The British government was determined to compel the Nepalese government to construct good roads whereas the Nepalese were not ready to open all the roads for British merchandise.

The Nepalese were desirous of having only a few routes open for fear of British imperialist penetration. The British had long felt need for constructing new roads for military movement after the defeat of captain Kinlock in 1767. But the Anglo-Nepal war of 1814–16 was the first landmark in the recent history of development of roads and communications in Northern India. Some good military roads had to be made during the Nepal wars and lines of communication were established along the frontier. The next landmark in the history of development of roads and communications was the revolt of 1857 in India. "The military movements and particularly the march of the Nepalese army to suppress the revolt must have been hampered considerably by the existing bad communication."[168] The military road afterward served the need of commerce. The principal land routes were as much the creation of military requirements as of merchantile demands.

The Nepalese were fully aware of this fact. They regarded the hills as "their fortifications, and a good road over them would be a breach in his walls to a besieged General."[169] The Nepalese wanted to block the roads in Nepal which were extended beyond the frontier by the Britisher. They thought that in a few years the neglected routes would be either altogether forgotten or overgrown with woods as to prevent access, and a few remaining roads would be easily guarded by a small force. Besides the military reason the Nepalese government also intended to open only a few roads for customs purpose. They would have to employ more officials and construct more customs houses if they opened several routes near the frontier.

Moreover, the policy of isolation pursued by the Nepalese Government was also aimed at frustrating every British move to obtain the transit route to Tibet through Nepal. The British were interested in getting into Tibet through Nepal because the Nepalese passes were considered to be more suitable and lower than those of Kashmir, Lahaul, and Karakoram and the main routes from Punjab to enter Turkistan. The British India government had realised that the transit facilities in Nepal would open a new trade avenue with all the territories north of the Himalayas.[170] However, the Nepalese government refused to provide any such transit passage to the British as it threatened the special trading privileges enjoyed by Nepal in Tibet. The British claim for a rightful free passage to the Tibetan frontier for their merchants and goods in return for the full and free access enjoyed by Nepalese in British territories had no effect upon the Nepalese authorities.[171]

In 1875, when free passage to Tibet through Nepal still remained a remote prospect, the British India Government approached London "to sanction the survey to be undertaken to ascertain the estimated cost of making a tolerable bridle path throughout that portion of the route from Darjeeling to Tibet which lies within British territory." A few years later the construction of this road started which was to open Tibet ultimately in 1905. The British Government had no alternative but to accept to open this route.[172]

There was a great deal of conversation between the Nepalese Prime Minister Ranadip Singh and the British Resident Charles Girdlestone, regarding the improvement of roads on the Nepalese territory. The conversation was conducted on the basis of the instruction given by the Government of India to the British Resident in Nepal in 1879. It was directed that the Resident should bring "carefully" to the notice of the Nepal Darbar the matters regarding the improvement of communication on the Nepalese side of the border as one of the measures to increase trade between India and Nepal.[173] In the same way the Government of India also asked the commissioners of the divisions bordering on the frontier between Bengal and Nepal to enquire and report on the possibility of bridging at cheap cost the forest roads through which the traffic passed between these two countries.[174]

According to the instruction of the Government of India, the British Resident Charles Girdlestone requested the Nepalese Government to maintain better communication on the Nepal side of the border. The conversation between the Prime Minister and the British Resident was put in writing on 18 July 1879 at the request of the former. It was mentioned that the border roads in India were numerous and well cared. The laden carts were able to travel along the border with comfort. But from the border onwards in Nepalese territory, there was either no continuation of them, or the continuation was so bad that laden carts could not move along or the carts were moved with greater difficulty. Girdlestone was of the opinion that there would be much greater demand on the part of the Indian traders for rice and hill products of Nepal if the roads in Nepal were better. Further, he added that the exchange of such products would serve to increase the wealth of Nepal.[175]

Again on 7 August 1879, the conversation started between the Prime Minister and the British Resident regarding the construction of roads. The talk was attended by several other Nepalese and British officials.[176] The Nepalese Prime Minister Ranadip Singh argued that Nepal was a poor country, that there was no advantage in making roads, and it was very difficult to keep roads in good condition. He cited an example from the road construction work of the late Nepalese Prime Minister Jang Bahadur Rana. He remarked that the road made by the late Prime Minister from Semrabasa to Bichakoh, and on through Hetauda to Bhimphedi was much damaged every year. He added that recently a road was made from Kathmandu to a place further within the hills where there was a sulphur mine. But it was destroyed by the rain. He himself had once urged Jang Bahadur, the late Prime Minister of Nepal, that there was no use making a road in the middle, i.e. from Hetauda to Bhimphedi, if he did not continue it on both sides. At that time the late Prime Minister had pointed out to him the difficulty of making the roads either in the beds of rivers or on mountains. Upon this the Resident said that he was not speaking of roads in the hills, but of roads in the Tarai from the border to the principal Nepalese marts. The Resident clarified that he did not mean metalled roads but raised roads of earth such as carts might travel along. The roads would be advantageous to both the countries because more of the surplus rice of the country and of forest products such as medicinal herbs, dyes, iron, etc. would go out of the country and broad cloth, cotton, cloth, etc. and cash would be introduced into Nepal. The Resident suggested that to keep existing roads in good condition, it was needed to fill up the routes which he considered would not cost annually more than 20 or 25 rupees per mile. The Prime Minister agreed that such repairs would be done.[177]

Then there was some conversation between the Prime

Minister, the Commander-in-Chief and Mir Subba Balwan Singh as to whether there existed any road from the border to Banke, and as to who had made it. The Resident told the Prime Minister that the road from border to Banki was in a very bad condition. He added that it had probably been made by the British Government before the mutiny of 1857 because Banke was within the British territory. The Prime Minister asked whether the road was raised and not liable to be overflowed by water. He was told that it was well above the level of the surrounding ground. The Resident asked whether the Prime Minister would have any objection if he sent him a list of 8 or 10 main lines of communication which needed repairs. The Prime Minister replied that he would have no objection whatsoever.[178]

Dr. H. Witwell, Officiating Residency Surgeon, prepared a note of the conversation between the Prime Minister and the Resident and he made some comment upon the road policy of the Government of Nepal. He mentioned, "The subject of the inferiorty of road communication in the Nepalese border territory was evidently a very unpalatable subject with the Maharaja; he fenced with it, and showed a singular aptitude in trying to lead the discussion away from the true issues by instituting erroneous parallels regarding the difficulty and expense of first making, and then keeping in order roads in the higher hills in the interior of the country, where the conditions are totally different. And it seemed as if the concesssions made were with a view of pacifying the Resident and closing the discussion, than from a genuine conviction of their necessity and a real determination of having them carried out, the point continually being brought forward with increasing persistence being the poverty of the country to support the strain of these burdens." Further he added that the remainder of the subject under discussion seemed to have been carried on in a much mere earnest and honest manner.[179]

On 12 August, 1879 the Prime Minister of Nepal agreed to make repairs of the road leading to the Banke Bazar. Consequently the Government of India directed Bengal, North Western Provinces and Oudh to send information to the British Reeident in Nepal regarding the main lines of communication between Bengal and

Nepal and latter provinces.

The Government of Bengal sent a list of six important routes leading from Lower Bengal into Nepalese territory, following the Government of India. Similarly, the Government of N. W. Provinces and Oudh sent the list of following routes.[180]

District	**Description of Routes**
Bahraich	Via Sujauli between Golamandi (Nepalese mart) and Motipur. Via Ratgarh between Nepalese mart of Banke and Motipur.
	Via Babaganj between Nepalese mart of Banke and Nanpara.
Basti	Via Morni between Nepal marts of Bahadurganj and Sirsewa and the Basti and Gonda districts.
	Via Uska between the Indian marts and Lotan and Nepal terai.
Gorakhpur	Via Logiabari between Nepal mart of Butwal and Gorakhpur districts.
	Via Bartauli between Gorakhpur district and Nepal Tarai and mart of Butwal.
	Via Thunthibari between Gorakhpur district and Nepal tarai and mart of Butwal.

The Faizabad conference of 1880 also discussed the effect of different means of communication on the trade with Nepal. The conference accepted the view of Charies Girdlestone that the improvement of road communication on Nepal side of the frontier was not possible without strong pressure from the British Government. The conference concluded that the improvement of roads over the mountainous tracts could materially extend the importation of goods required for distribution among the hill tribes, which were chiefly carried by coolies and ponies. It was also pointed out that all the main roads leading to the important marts like Nepalganj required sufficient funds to maintain them, especially at the point of ferry approaches. The conference suggested that the Darbar should be asked to maintain in better order the portion of roads leading to the marts to be traversed by carts on the Nepal side of the frontier.[181] The Government of India decided to influence the Nepalese Government on the question of improvement of Communication as suggested by the Conference. Consequently, the Secretary of State was asked to induce the Nepalese Government to repair and maintain in good order the more important routes leading to the interior of the country. The improvement of routes would assist to develop the trade between these two countries. On the basis of the report supplied by the Government of North Wessern Provinces and Oudh, the Resident Girdlestone informed the secretary of State that the export from Nepal to North Western Provinces and Oudh was 215, 19- maunds in British weight and worth Rs. 1 58,731 when road was bad from 1 April 1875 to 31 March 1880. But from 1 April to 31 March 1880 when the road was good the export from Nepal to North Western Provinces and Oudh was 220,878 maunds and worth Rs. 927,688. Hence, there was an increase in both volume and value when road was good.[182] The Resident mentioned same statistics in his memorandum to the Prime Minister of Nepal.[183]

The Resident had extensive correspondence with the Prime Minister of Nepal regarding the improvement of roads in the Nepalese territory. In his memorandum dated 2 February 1880, he calculated that the more important roads leading from border to the principal tarai marts of Nepal would not be more than 400 miles. The repairs of this distance at Rs 25 a mile would give a total annual outlay of Rs 10,000. He added that considering the taxes levied by the Nepalese Government on trade, it would seem not unreasonable to devote a portion of such revenue to improve the means of communication. Again, he suggested that such improvement would lead to an extension of trade and thereby a direct advantage would accrue to the Durbar as well as to its subjects. Upon the remark of the Nepalese Prime Minister that the people were poor and no aid could be given by them in repairing roads the Resident replied that he did not see any reason to add extra taxes upon the subjects, because a little restriction on the large expenditure of the Darbar would be sufficient for the repair of road.[184]

The Prime Minister replied that his trustworthy Nepalese officials holding the posts of Subba and Captain had informed him that the estimate of Rs 25/– per mile would not be sufficient for the cost of road-repairs in Nepal. He further mentioned that as the rivers at the foot of the hills had no depth, all the roads got damaged in the rainy season. Nevertheless he promised to repair roads leading to the Banke bazar. The Nepal Government expressed its disinclination to meet the British request for the general improvement of roads on the plea of poverty and inability to command the requisite labour.[185] Charles Girdlestone, did not agree to the plea of poverty expressed by the Prime Minister. He argued that many thousand rupees had been spent by the Darbar within the twelve months on a fine approach to one of the temples in the Kathmandu valley. Similarly, hundreds of coolies were employed to carry rice from the tarai to the valley. The rice was collected and stored up as a provision against famine.[186] In his confidential despatch dated September 1880, he mentioned "a yearly expenditure of Rs 10,000 would probably meet all reasonable requirement of Nepal to maintain the road which is equal to interest at 5 per cent on half the sum (i. e. for lakhs of rupees) which the Prime Minister is taking from the State treasury for expenditure on his forthcoming tour in British India."[187] The Darbar complained of serious physical difficulties in the way of making and maintaining roads good for traffic all the year round. This argument appeared reasonable to Girdlestone.[188]

Irritated by the response of the Prime Minister Ranodip Singh, the Resident commented, "His Excellency's character is such that he will agree to a proposal rather than continue a distasteful conversation. But occasionally it happens that he withdraws or modifies his promise, as soon as he has again come under the influence of the bigoted officials by whom he is surrounded. I regret to say that the disinclination then shown to meet the British Government's wishes in regard to the general improvement of roads has been steadily maintained, notwithstanding my efforts to win His Excellency to a more favourable policy."[189]

His predecessor, the Prime Minister Jang Behadur Rana had stated that a very fair road could be constructed through Passage at no great cost but he declined to make the road because he felt that in the near future there would be war between the British and Nepal.[190] In 1851, when Jang Bahadur Rana was pressed to make the road he replied that the prejudices of his contrymen were very strong against it. The people thought that while the roads remained in their present condition no invading army could make its way to the valley. For his own part, he said, since he had been to England and had seen railways, tunnels, etc., he knew the power and skill of the British so well that he was convinced that if he could not make a road over the mountain, he should make a tunnel under it so that no mountain could stop the progress. He added the cat and lion story, "Though the cat cannot fight on even terms with the lion, yet if the lion, drives the cat into a corner the cat will scratch his eyes."[191]

Further efforts were made to coax Jang Bahadur but to no avail. In 1862, the British Resident in Nepal, reported that British attempts to open Tibet for trade were viewed by Jang Bahadur as a threat to Nepal's own commercial interests in the Himalayan trade, which Nepal had for long established in Tibetian trade.[192] The British Government in India had to abandon all hopes of Jang Bahadur's cooperation. But even after his death in 1877, all his successors had followed the same policy of isolation. Ultimately the British Government had to concentrate its attention on Darjeeling and Sikkim routes for trade with Tibet.

The new trade route between Phari in Chumbi Valley and Kalimpong across the Jalep Pass replaced the Kerung and Kuti route via Nepal. By the turn of the nineteenth century, Kalimpong had replaced Kathmandu as the entrepot of trans-Himalayan trade. The construction of the Phari route, besides providing direct contact of Tibet with British India, also helped in making absolute the existing trade route that linked Tibet and South Asia via Nepal. The impact of this changed situation was seen in the behaviour of both the Nepalese and Tibetans. For instance, the Nepalese merchants in Tibet were deprived of the margin of profit, stopped sending wool and yak tails via Nepal to India. The Tibetan Government issued an order which prohibited Nepalese to use route as an artery of commerce. Nepalese traders were compelled to divert the traffic of 3,000 to 4,000 bales of wool on bound towards Darjeeling to Kathmandu.[193] The British attempts to develop Nepal as a highway of Indo-Chinese trade also failed.

Indo-Nepalese trade in general and Nepal's exports earnings in particular were reported to have suffered as a result of the difficult means of transport. The trade was restricted to nearby villages and most of the adjacent valleys. All the Rana Prime Ministers of Nepal had refused to invest money on these developmental works. In his confidential despatch Colonel H. Wylie, the British Resident in Nepal, wrote, "Roads and bridges are being neglected, while funds are squandered on a succession of palaces for himself and his sons. I am informed that these Palaces are considered to be the Ministers' own private property, and he can leave them to whom he pleases, although they are built from State funds."[194] Main lines of roads such as civilization knows were not to be found beyond the British frontier in Nepal. Naturally, it was difficult to have more trade.[195] Mr Braddon, the Superintendent of Excise at Lucknow, complained that absence of made road on the Nepalese side of the border resulted in the restriction to trade.[196] Charles Girdlestone did not accept this view. He argued that the ordinary country carts of northern India did not require good roads. So he advocated that a broad open track should be reserved for traffic. According to the British Resident in Nepal, the main hinderance on the way of transport was the "occurrence of a nullah or water course." He suggested that the banks of the nullah should be connected with rough wooden bridges.[197]

However, the road policy followed by the Government of Nepal did not hinder Indo-Nepalese trade. The increasing volume of trade between these two countries indicates that the routes designed by nature were captured by men. The unchallengable hardship of the roads, could not stand on the way of enterprising traders.

REFERENCES

1. Kanchanmoy, Majumdar, *Anglo—Nepalese Relations in the nineteenth Century*, Calcutta, 1973, pp 78-79.
2. Revenue A. August, 1877, No 22. Girdlestone, Resident in Nepal to T.H. Thornton, Officiating Secretary to the Government of India. Foreign Department, No. 15 p. dated 19 September, 1876. (N.A.I.)
3. *Ibid.*
4. *Ibid.*
5. *Ibid.*
6. *Ibid.*
7. *Ibid.*
8. Jahar Sen, *Indo-Nepal trade in the nineteenth century*, Calcutta, 1977, p. 52.
9. Revenue A. August 1877, No. 22.
10. *Ibid.*
11. H.C. Conybeare, *Gazetteer of N.W. Provinces*, Vol. II, Allahabad, 1881, p. 699.
12. *Ibid.*
13. Krishnakanta Adhikari, "Brief Survey of Nepal's Trade with British India during the latter half of the nineteenth century", *Contribution to Nepalese Studies*, Vol. 2, Vo. 1, February 1975 (Phalgun 2031) (Kathmandu), p. 191.
14. Revenue A. August 1877, Vo. 22.
15. L.S.S. O'Malley, *Bengal District Gazetteer, Champran*, Calcutta, 1907, p. 120.
16. William Wilson Hunter, *The Indian Empire, Its people, History and Products*, London, p. 691.
17. Revenue, A. August, 1877, No. 22.
18. *Ibid.*
19. *Ibid.*
20. *Ibid.*
21. Administration Report of the Patna Division for the year 1872–73, p. 153. (N.A.I.).
22. W.W. Hunter, *Statistical Account of Bengal, Tirhut and Champaran*, Vol. XIII, London, 1877, p. 6.
23. *Ibid.*
24. Revenue, A. August, 1877, N. 22.

King of Nepal Prithvi Bir (c. 1890) who was completely dominated by his Prime Ministers in his policy towards the British India.

Prime Minister Bir Sh

his inauguration in 1885.

Prime Minister Chandra Shamsher,
who diverted trade of Nepal through Sikkim.

25. W.W. Hunter, *op. cit.* p. 177.
26. *Ibid*, p. 178.
27 The General Administration Report of the Bhagalpur Division for the year 1881-82. (N.A.I.).
28. Revenue, A. August, 1877, No. 22.
29. W. W. Hunter, *Statistical Account of Bengal*, *Purnea*, Vol. XV, London, 1877, p. 351.
30. *Ibid*. p. 253.
31. Adhikari, *op. cit.*, p. 192.
32. Revenue A. August, 1877, No. 22.
33. Jahar Sen, *op. cit.* p. 43, Cited from Proceedings of Bengal Govt. Gen. Mis. August, 1876, File No. 120, S. No. 1-2. p. 24 (N.A.I.).
34. *Ibid*, cited from Darjeeling District Records, General Department English Correspondence 1841-1879.
35. *Ibid*, collection XXXXII. File No. 48 of 1885-86, No. 241 G, dated 25 May 1886.
36. *Ibid*. cited from Collection XXX, File No. 55 of 1893-94 dated 9 June 1893.
37. This classification was done by the respective Government of N. W. Provinces and Oudh and Bihar and Bengal.
38. Report on the Foreign Trade of North Western Province and Oudh, during the year 1877-78. N.W.P. and Oudh Gvt. Pvt. Allahabad 1878. p. 4 (N. A. I.).
39. Foreign Department. Political, A. March 1880. No. 303, Rajendra Nath Mitra, Assistant-Secretary to the Government of Bengal to Girdlestone. No. 816 dated, Calcutta, 15 November 1879 (N.A.I.).
40 The Report on the Trade of the N.W. Provinces and Oudh from 1879-1885. (N.A.I.).
41. *Ibid*. p. 55.
42. *Ibid*.
43. *Ibid*.
44. *Ibid*
45. *Ibid*.
46. *Ibid*.
47. Political A. March 1880 No. 305. E. C. Buck, Director of Agriculture and Commerce of N. W. P. Oudh to C. Robertson, Secretary to Govt. of N.W. Province of Oudh, dated 2 December 1979. (N.A.I.).

48. L.S.S. O'Malley, "*Bihar Orissa district Gazetteers*", *Champaran.* Patna, 1938, p. 92.

49. W.W. Hunter, "*A Statistical Account of Bengal*", *Patna and Saran*, Vol. XI, London, 1877, p. 197.

50. L.S.S. O'Malley. *Bengal District Gazetteers. Muzaffarpur, Calcutta*, 1907, p. 157.

51. P. C. Roy Chaudhury, *Bihar District Gazetteers, Darbhanga.* Patna, 1964, p. 304.

52. Imperial Gazetteer of India, 1908, Vol. VIII p. 268, also see Sunil Kumar, *Geography of transport in Eastern India, under the British Raj*, Calcutta, 1980, p. 50.

53. Revenue A. August 1877, No. 22.

54. Orfeur Cavenagh, *Rough Notes on the State of Nepal : Its Government, Army and Resources.* Calcutta, 1851, p. 45.

55. Revenue A. August 1877, No. 22.

56. *Ibid.*

57. *Ibid.* No. 17. The Conservator of Forest of Oudh to the Junior Secretary to the Chief Commissioner of Oudh No. 113 p. dated 28 March 1876. (N.A.I.).

58. *Ibid.* No. 14. The Deputy Commissioner of Kheri to the Commissioner, Sitapur Division No. 681A, dated 6 April 1876 (N.A.I.).

59. Revenue. A. August, 1877, No. 22.

60. *Ibid.*

61. *Ibid.* No. 17.

62. *Ibid.* No. 306-330. The Offg. Deputy Conservator, Oudh Forests, Bahraich Division to Conservator of Forest Oudh No. 196 dated 4 March 1876. (N.A.I.).

63. *Ibid.* No. 22.

64. *Ibid.*

65. Jahar Sen, *op. cit.* p. 48. Cited from Champaran District Records, Serial No. 76 of Register 75. Vol. I. page 23-24, Govt. Circulars, Orders and Letters commencing. . . .

66. It was common practice among the traders to enter into an agreement with the cart owners to carry the commodities. There were leaders among the cartmen who took leases for supply of carts. They were called Chaudhuries. see P. C. Raychaudhury, *Bihar District Gazetteers, Champaran*, Patna, 1960, p. 337.

67. Revenue A. August 1877, No. 22.
68. *Ibid.*
69. P. C. Roy Chaudhury, *Bihar District Gazetteer Darbhanga.* Patna, 1964, p. 304.
70. Revenue A. August 1877, No. 22.
71. *Ibid.*
72. *Ibid.*
73. Arthur Jules Dash, *Bengal District Gazetteers. Darjeeling.* Alipur 1947, p. 169.
74. Jahar Sen, *op. cit.* p. 43.
75. Bhimphedi is at the foot of the first range of hill and Thankot is at the head of the Kathmandu Valley. It is also the main entrance of the capital.
76. External. P. I. June 1902, No. 6. Lieutinant Colonel T. C. Pears, Resident in Nepal to the Secretary to the Government of India, Foreign Department. No. 4 p. dated 8 January 1902. (N.A.I.).
77. Secret, E. September, 1903, No. 95, Lieutenant Colonel C.W. Revenshaw. Resident in Nepal to the Secretary to the Government of Indian. Foreign Department. dated 11 April 1903. (N.A.I.)
78. Perceval London, *Nepal*, Vol. 2, London, 1928. p. 203.
79. The line from Barewa to Kathmandu was introduced in 1875. See Divya Deo Bhatta, "Mass Communication in Nepal". *Nepal, The Himalayan Kingdom.* His Majesty's Government, Ministry of Communication, Kathmandu, 1982, p. 16.
80. However, some Nepalese documents mention that there were postal arrangements in Eastern and Western Nepal. In 1850 there were overwhelming majority of the 4,979 hulaki households who used to provide mail services from Kathmandu to Dhankuta in the east and Doti in the west. Arrangements were made in western hill region to provide each hulaki household with a rice-land allotment of between 40 and 100 muris, depending on the size of the family. On the eve of the Anglo-Nepal War, these arrangements were extended to hulaki porters in the eastern hill region also. This does not mean that each Hulaki household in these regions possessed a rice land allotment. Later on the system was discontinued. Hulaki porters were compensated through exemption from taxes and were given security of tenure without any provision for rice land allotments. On the whole the postal arrangements of Nepal were not well organised as in British India.

Register of Kagate—Hulaki Households in Nepal, 1909 (1852), in Regini Research Collection. Cited in M.C. Regini, *Thatched Huts and Stucco Palaces*. p. 96; "Hulak Regulations for Areas between Dharmathali and the Jamana River" Ashadh Sudi 4, 1866 (June 1809). Cited in *Ibid*, p. 97; Hulak Regulations for Areas Between the Bagmati River and Vijayapur. Baisaku Sudi, 4, 1866 (May 1814); Arrangements regarding Hulaki Households in Dailakh' Bhadra Badi 6, 1886. (August 1839). Cited n Chittaranjan Nepali, op. cit., pp. 328–39. "Register of Kagati-Hulaki Households in Junla" Falgun Sudi 10, 1949 (March 1883), Regmi Research Collection Vol. 22, pp 349–80. Cited in M.C. Regmi, *op. cit*. p. 98.

General B. October, 1881. No. 109. Charles Girdlestone, the Resident in Nepal to the Officiating Secretary to the Government of India in the Foreign Department, Simla. No. 71 p. dated 27 September 1881. (N.A.I.).

81. Foreign Department. Political, A. November 1861. Vo 49. Colonel H.M. Durand C.B., Offg. Secretary to the Government of India Fort William to the Resident in Nepal. No. 114, dated 19 November 1861. (N.A.I).

82. General B. November, 1879. No. 356. Girdlestone, Residence in Nepal to the Secretary of Government of India, Foreign Department, Simla dated 20 Oct 1879. (N.A.I.)

83. General B. October, 1881, No. 109.

84. Abrol Mridula, *British Relations with Frontier States. (1863–1875)*. New Delhi, 1974, p. 41. Cited from the f n. of K.M. Panikkar, Indian States with the Government of India. London, 1932, p. 82-83.

85. Jahar Sen. *op. cit*. p. 77.

86. M.C. Regmi, "The Impact of India's Railway system on Nepal's Economy During the Closing Years of the 19th Century." *Regmi Research Series Year 15, No. 5*, Kathmandu, 1 83, p. 72.

87. Jahar Sen, *op. cit*., p. 71.

88. H. R. Nevill, *The District Gazetteer of the United Provinces, Basti*. Vol. XXXII, Calcutta, 1907. pp. 65–66.

89. Ibid. p. 259.

90. Jahar Sen. *op. cit*. p. 79.

91. M. C. Regmi, *op. cit*. p. 73.

92. *Ibid* p. 72.

93. Jahar Sen, *op. cit*. p. 71.

94. Munsi Sunil Kumar, *op. cit*. pp. 91–92.

95. *Ibid*. p. 92. Cited from Annual Report on the Administration of Bengal Presidency 1880–81, p. 46.

96. Annual General Administration Report of the Patna Division for 1890-91. p. 39.
97. Jahar Sen. *op. cit.* p. 72. cited from Bengal Administration Report for 1880-81. 98. p. 270.
98. *Ibid.*
99. Imperial Gazetteer of India. Provincial Series Bengal, Vol. II. 1909, New Delhi. Reprint 1979. p. 132.
100. *Ibid.*
101. M. C. Regmi. *op. cit.* p. 73.
102. Nepalese railway line ran from Raxaul on the borders of British India to Amlekhganj in Nepal, twenty-four miles in distance but did not reach any of the important towns of the valley.
103. Annual General Report of the Patna Division for 1881-82. pp. 38-39. para 31. (N,A.I.)
104. *Ibid.* for 1884-85, para 31.
105. Imperial Gazetteer of India. *op. cit.* p. 113.
106. Annual General Report of the Patna Division for 1884-85. p. 23. (N.A.I.).
107. Revenue A. August 1877. No. 22.
108. Appendix C. Annual Report of the Foreign Trade of the North-Wesᴛ Province and Oudh for the year ending 31 March 1880 (N.A.I.)
109. Annual Report of the Foreign Trade of the North West Province and Oudh for the year ending 31 March 1880. (N.A.I.)
110. Political. A. July 1880, No. 196. Proceedings of a Conference assembled at Faizabad on 26 January 1880. (N.A.I.)
111. *Ibid.*
112. *Ibid.* Nos. 196-98. K.W. No. 1. (N.A.I.)
113. Revenue. A. December, 1877, No. 2, E. Buck, Director of Agriculture and Commerce. N.W. Provinces and Oudh to C. Robertson, Esq.. Secretary to Government of North Western Provinces and Oudh. NOT-187 C, Allahabad, dated 1 November 1877. (N.A.I.)
114. Jahar Sen. *op. cit.* p. 76.
115. *Ibid.*
116. External B. February, 1893. No. 30. Franklin Prestage, the Chairman of the Darjeeling Himalayan Railway to the Foreign Department Govenment of India Simla No. 103. dated 20 October 1892. (N. A. I.)
117. M.C. Regmi, *op. cit.* p. 72.

118. *Ibid.* p. 73.

119. R.R. Diwakar, *Bihar through the Ages.* Patna, 1959, p. 50.

120. *Imperial Gazetteer of India,* Provincial Series. Bengal Vol. I. 1909. Reprint, New Delhi 1979. p. 98.

121. J.B.S. Burathokey and U.M. Malla, "The Physical Aspects of the Kingdom of Nepal". *Seminar paper on the Ecology of the Tropical Highlands,* Nepal National Commission for UNESCO, 1968. p. 12.

122. Imperial Gazetteer of India. *op. cit.* p. 210.

123. *Ibid.*

124. *Ibid.*

125. *Ibid.* p. 211.

126. J. B. S. Burathokey and U.M. Malla. *op. cit.*

127. Imperial Gazetteer of India. *op. cit.* p. 212.

128. *Ibid.*

129. *Ibid.*

130. *Ibid.*

131. W.W. Hunter, *Statistical Account of Bengal,* Tirhut and Champaran, Vol. XIII, Calcutta, 1877, p. 51.

132. Imperial Gazetteer of India. *op. cit.*

133. J.B.S. Burathokey and U.M. Malla. *op. cit.*

134. Imperial Gazetteer of India. *op. cit.* p. 225.

135. *Ibid.*

136. *Ibid.*

137. J. B. S. Burathokey, *op. cit.*

138. *Ibid.*

139. W.W. Hunter, *Statistical Account of Bengal, Bhagalpur,* Vol. XV, Calcutta. p. 226.

140. *Ibid.* pp. 229–231.

141. *Ibid.*

142. W.W. Hunter, Statistical Account of Bengal, Tirhut Champaran, p. 222.

143. Revenue A. August 1877. No. 22.

144. Jahar Sen. *op. cit.* p. 69.

145. *Ibid.*

146. *Ibid.*

147. *Ibid.* pp. 69–70.

148. *Ibid.* p. 70.
149. Northey W. Brook, *The land of the Gurkhas.* London, 1933, p. 139.
150. Darchula is some three days march above Jhulaghat. The route across the bridge over Kali at Darchula runs to Bajrang and Bajura, the two northerly provinces of Western Nepal. *Ibid.*
151. Revenue A. August 1877. No. 2.
152. H.R. Nevill, *District Gazetteers of the United Provinces of Agra aud Oudh.* Vol. XVII, Allahabad, 1909, p. 78.
153. Secret E. September 1903. No. 95. Lieutinant Colonel C.W. Revenshaw, Resident in Nepal to the Secretary to the Government of India. Foreign Department dated 11 April 1903. (N.A.I.)
154. Orfeur Cavenagh, *op. cit.* p. 95.
155. Jahar Sen, *op. cit.* p. 43. Cited from Darjeeling District Records. General Department English Correspondence. Collection XXXII. File No. 8 of 1885-86. No. 241 G. dated May 1886.
156. Perceval Landon, *Nepal,* Vol. II. London, 1928, p. 200.
157. *Imperial Gazetteer of India*, provincial series Bengal Vol. I 1909. Reprint 1976, New Delhi, p. 100.
158. Revenue. A. August 1877. No. 22.
159. Imperial Gazetteer of India. *op. cit.* p. 111; L.S.S. O'Malley, *Bengal. Bihar, Orissa and Sikkim.* Delhi 1979, p. 47.
160. Jahar Sen, *op. cit.* p. 69.
161. Imperial Gazetteer of India. *op. cit.* p. 114.
162. L. S. S. O'Malley. *Bengal District Gazetteers, Muzaffarpur.* Calcutta, 1907, p. 94.
163. M.C. Regmi, *op. cit.*, p.
164. Register No. 147. Foreign Ministry of Nepal, dated 15 October 1912.
165. "It is estimated that on a good wagon road a single horse power will drag about 3000 lbs at the rate of 3 feet per second, on a railway about 30,000 at the same rate, in water as much as 200,000 lbs." K.T. Shah, *Trade Traffic and Transport in India.* Bombay, 1923, p. 370.
166. *Ibid.*
167. Revenue. A. Aug 1877. No. 14. Conservator of Forest, Oudh to the Junior Secretary to the Commissioner of Oudh. No. 113 dated 28 March 1876. (N.A.I.).
168. P.C. Roy Chaudhury. *Bihar District Gezetteer, Champaran,* op. cit. p. 336.

169. Political, A. December 1880, No. 38. Charles Girchlestone British Resident in Nepal to A.C. Lyall, Esq., C. B. Secretary to the Government of India, Foreign Department. No. 32 p, dated 25 September 1880. (N.A.I.)

170. Political A. February 1875 No. 30. C.E.R. Girdlestone to H. Le Poer Wynne, Officiating Secretary to Government of India, Foreign Department. dated 9 June 1874. N. 18p. (N.A.I.)

171. Niranjan Sharma. *Nepal Foreign trade,* (unpublished Ph. D. Thesis). Delhi School of Economics. University of Delhi, April 1968. p. 29.

172. *Ibid.*

173. Revenue. A. February 1879, No. 2. A.C. Lyall. Esq. C.B., Secretary to the Government of India, Foreign Department to the Resident in Nepal. No. 1R, dated 14 Januaro 1879. (N.A.I.)

174. Political A. October 1879. No. 132. H.L. Harrison, Officiating Secretary to the Government of Bengal to the Secretary to the Government of India, Foreign Department No. 351, dated 7 June 1879.

175. *Ibid.* No. 136. Charles Girdlestone, Resident in Nepal to A.C. Lyall, Esq. Secretary to the Government of India, Foreign Department. No. 37. p., dated 18 July 1879.

176. The Nepalese Officers present in the talk were General Dhira Shumsher Jang Bahadur Rana, Commander-in-Chief, Sirdar Laxmi Bhaga i.e. confidenti l adviser of the Prime Minister, Colonel Ran Singh, Commissioner of Police, Kathmandu, Major Captain Mahabeer Singh, Orderly officer, Mir Subha Balwan Singh, Private Secretary to the Prime Minister. Dr Whitwell, Residency Surgeon and Shew Shankar Singh, Mir Munsi of Nepal Residency were two important British officers. *Ibid.* No. 137. Report by Shaw Shanker Singh, Mir Munshi of the Nepal Residency, of a conversation between the Prime Minister of Nepal and the Resident on the 7 of August 1879.

177. *Ibid.*

178. *Ibid.*

179. *Ibid.* Notes of a conversation held between the Maharaja Prime Minister of Nepal and the Resident on the afternoon of August and prepared by H. Whitewell, Residency Surgeon, on 8 August 1879. (N.A I.)

180. *Ibid.* March 1880. No. 305, E.C. Buck, Director of Agriculture and Commerce of N.W.P. and Oudh to C. Robertson, Secretary to the Government of N.W.P. and Oudh No. 1413C—C.T.V. dated Kanpur, 2 December 1879. (N.A.I.)

181. *Ibid.* July 1880. No. 196. Proceedings of a Conference assembled at Faizabad in North Western Provinces and Oudh on 26 January 1880.

182. General A. January 1882. No. 15. Charles Girdlestone. British Resident in Nepal to Grant, Secretary to the Government of India, Foreign Department No. 69 p. dated 23 September 1881.

183. *Ibid.*

184. Political A. December 1880. No. 44. A Memorandum from the British Resident in Nepal to the Prime Minister and Commander-in-chief of Nepal. dated 2 February 1880.

185. *Ibid.* No. 45. Abstract translation of a memorandum from the Prime Minister and Commander-in-Chief of Nepal, to the Resident in Nepal dated 30 Magh, Samwat 1930 (25 February 1880). (N.A.I.)

186. *Ibid.* No. 38. Charles Girdlestone, Resident in Nepal to A.C. Lyall, Esq. Secretary to the Government of India. Foreign Department No. 32 p. dated 25 September 1880 (N.A.I.)

187. *Ibid.*

188. *Ibid.*

189. *Ibid.*

190. Orfeur Cavenagh, *Reminiscences of an Indian Official.* London, 1884, p. 175–76.

191. William Digby. *A Friend in need 1857 Friendship forgotten.* London, 1890. pp. 25–26.

192. Ravuri Dhanalaxmi. *British attitude to Nepal's relations with Tibet and China 1814–1914.* New Delhi, 1981, p. 86.

193. Prem R. Uprety, *Nepal Tibet Relations* 1850–1930, *Years of Hopes Challenges and Frustrations.* Kathmandu, 1980. pp. 166–67.

194. Secret E. July 1897. No. 76. Colonel H. Wylie, Resident in Nepal to the Secretary to the Government of India Foreign Department No. P 13-3027. dated 16 June 1897. (N.A.I.)

195. A. Husain, *British India's relations with Kingdom of Nepal from* 1857–*to* 1947 (unpublished Ph. D. Thesis). University of MInnesota, U. S. A. 1965 p. 174.

196. Revenue. A, 1877, No. 22.

197. *Ibid.*

Commercial Policy and Monopolies

CHAPTER THREE

The commercial policy of all the Rana Prime Ministers of Nepal was more or less the same during the period under review. Every Nepalese Prime Minister was convinced that if the British were allowed to move freely in their country or their merchants were permitted to carry on trade, it would ultimately lead to the subjugation of Nepal. The Ranas particularly understood that throwing open their country to foreign capital would in no time end their feudal system and would eventually lead to their decline.[1] Although the British Indian Government had assured the Nepalese Government that it had no desire to conquer its country, the Nepalese did not believe it.

The British Indian Government regarded Nepal as a growing captive market for manufactured goods.[2] The secretary of the Society for the encouragement of Arts, Manufacture and Commerce wrote to the Secretary of State for India that it was essential for the Indian Government to use every effort to obtain from Nepal free passage for the British merchants and goods to the Tibetian frontier in return for the full and free access enjoyed by Nepal in the Indian territory.[3] G. Ramsay, the British Resident in Nepal, gave an example of Subha Dharma Narayan, the Nepalese merchant who had several shops in the Indian provinces [4] G. Ramsay tried his best to bring Jang Bahadur back to the term of engagement of 1839. But he was totally unsuccessful. The only remaining alternative for Ramsay was to negotiate a new trade treaty with Nepal. This he saw no hope of achieving, because he simply did not believe that India had anything to offer Nepal as an inducement to enter into a new treaty. He was quite wrong in this regard. The Nepalese Government would have sacrificed considerably, if they could have acquired the right to import arms and ammunition as well as the machinery to make them. The British Government had imposed restriction upon Nepal to import these articles.[5] "This was the real point at issue. The British, on ideological grounds, insisted on the benefits of free trade. They were however not willing to remove their own restrictions on trade. If such a statement makes sense, what they were offering Nepal under the name of free trade—and urging it quite strongly —was a *free* trade in *restricted* items."[6] In fact, it was against the British interest and contrary to British trade policy to sell these items to Nepal. Nepalese were not allowed to import arms and ammunition from any country.

It is interesting to note that a section of the British officials had always considered the Indo-Nepal trade as an unrewarding business. Dr Daniel Write, the British Residency Surgeon remarked, "as regards trade, I am aware that it is generally believed that there is great field for European enterprises in Nepal and through it with Tibet. I suspect, however, that this is an erroneous idea. The people are poor, and have a few wants that are not supplied by their own country. The export trade from Nepal is very small and it is difficult to imagine that it could be much increased, as the country is poor, rugged, mountainous land, just producing enough for the support of its population."[7] But these views were contested by Charles Girdlestone, the British Resident in Nepal. He stated that there was a good trade prospect for European goods in Nepal and Tibet. The Secretary of State for India wrote to the Government of India that considering the natural resources of the country, the trade with Nepal was very small.[8] Since the British Indian Government had disclaimed all the rights to interfere with, even to advise upon, the commercial policy of Nepal, it could do little to press Nepal to give up the protective system generally observed in western part of the country and the policy of isolation throughout the country. In this regard one of the high-ranking British Officials observed, "Nepal in this matter is in her right. She may be (and I believe is) short-sighted but we have no equitable standpoint for protesting."[9] Similarly, Charles Girdlestone remarked, "There is no native state in alliance with us which lays greater stress on the declarations of the British Government than Nepal. In all its communications, the Durbar shows an intense fondness for precedent and an inclination to interpret the clauses of the treaty in the strictest sense····with so deeply rooted a feeling as this on the part of the Durbar, I cannot conceal my fear that if occasion required the words of 1859 would be brought up in judgement against us."[10] As regards the conclusion of a fresh engagement, the Nepalese Government's attitude held little hope to the British. The British Indian Government slowly tried to turn over the commitment of 1859. In 1880 the Foreign Department, Government of India held the view that the declaration of 1859 was not an express agreement. The Government changed the statement stating, "the remark was made in order that the strong remonstrance we were urging against the Darbar's policy might not needlessly arouse Nepalese susceptibilities and so provoke opposition. In other words, the remark was simply a diplomatic phrase to smooth over possible difficulties."[11] The British Indian Government signed a commercial treaty with Sikkim and Bhutan respectively in March 1861 and November 1865. Accordingly, the British Indian Government gained the advantage of "free reciprocal intercourse" and "full liberty of commerce" with Sikkim and "free trade and commerce" with Bhutan.[12] The British Government wanted to conclude a similar treaty with Nepal. It was equally interested to develop free and unrestricted commercial relations with Nepal. But it should be noted that the political status and circumstances of Nepal were different from that of Sikkim and Bhutan.

Charles Girdlestone was quite enthusiastic to develop Indo-Nepal trade. He was the man who took initiative to organise the conference at Faizabad. Besides Girdlestone, the conference was attended by E. Buck, Director, Department of Agriculture and Commerce, North-Western Provinces and Oudh; R. Speeding, Collector, Gorakhpur; R. Demontmorency, Deputy Commissioner, Bahraich; J. Woodburn, Deputy Commissioner, Faizabad; J. Hooper, Assistant Commissioner, Gonda; E. Wood, Conservator, Oudh Forests and D. Pitcher, Assistant Commissioner, Lucknow. The main objective of the conference was to discuss whether any practical suggestions could be made for the development of Indo-Nepal trade. The potentiality of trade between India, Nepal and Tibet and the transportation system were widely discussed in the conference. It was decided that the Resident should be asked to request the Nepal Darbar to remove, the restrictions which forbade the Nepalese traders to cross the Nepal frontier for trade, and forced the Indian traders to use shops in Nepalese marts. But nothing could be done in this respect because, "the restrictive policies practised in Naya Muluk were justified in view of the problem of settlement, and these practices were confined to that area. In other areas along the border normal buying and selling took place."[13]

In the eyes of the British Indian Government the main impediment to the growth of Indo-Nepal trade was the heavy and variable duties levied by Nepal, the artificial means resorted to by the Nepalese authorities to attract the trade to its own towns and the neglect of the trade routes. Charles Girdlestone tried his best to remove all these restrictions, but he completely failed. He ruefully remarked, "Regarding Nepal I do not anticipate that reform will materially increase the trade. There may be less friction, less annoyance and irritation, less uncertainty, a slight reduction of prices and in consequence a slightly larger demand. But with a population of limited extent, and likely to remain so, to whom access is difficult and cannot be otherwise except at inordinate expense, who are compelled by the nature of their country to be self-independent for most of the necessaries of life, whose requirements are simple and habits frugal, who receive through long established sources a considerable supply of such things as they are not able to raise for themselves and who already have the balance of trade in their favour, I cannot see any opening for much greater results than are now attained."[14] The Government of India did not want to make commerce an issue with Nepal, and this remained their settled policy. The Nepalese Government also did not want to damage the bridge of friendship with the British Government. Dr Oldfield, the British Residency Surgeon clarified that Nepalese resistance did not imply hostility towards the British. He added: "Nothing will disabuse them of the belief tha the British are anxious to conquer and annex Nepal. They acknowledge our supremacy in the plains, and they think that the only way to prevent that supremacy from being established in Nepal as well as in Hindustan is to keep us at a distance, and by isolating themselves from all intimate connection with us, avoid giving us the opportunity for gratifying, what they consider the national love of foreign aggrandizement. These considerations form the real and only key to the very exclusive policy which Nepal has systematically adopted."[15] In 1880, Girdlestone saw little prospect for the development of Indo-Tibetan trade through Nepal by the British Governments efforts—a project in which some British Commercial concerns were interested in the later decades of the nineteenth century.[16] Jang Bahadur and all his successors were extremely jealous of British attempts to open up Tibet for trade, fearing damage to Nepalese trade interest in Tibet.

For political reason the British did not press the Darbar for commercial facilities and concessions. In the last quarter of the nineteenth century the British apprehension of France-Russian designs in the Himalayas reached its climax. This highlighted the strategic importance of Nepal for the security of the Gorkha soldiers who were adept in mountain fight. There was yet another underlying consideration in the British mind on the question of inclusion of these soldiers in the Indian army. ' Gorkha Soldiers, whose unflinching loyalty to the superior officers was an established fact, were viewed by the British as an antidote to the rebellious tendency of the Indian sepoys. But the recruitment of the Gorkhas to the Indian army on official understanding with the Nepal Government had been a thorny problem ever since the Anglo-Nepalese war and the two Governments had failed so far to arrive at a satisfactory solution."[17]

Commercial Policy of Jang Bahadur

The visit of Jang Bahadur Rana, the Prime Minister of Nepal, to England in 1850-51 and his help in suppressing the sepoy Mutiny of 1858, made the British Government sure that he would give up his traditional policy of exclusion. They expected that he would introduce certain liberal measures in promoting Indo-Nepal trade.[18] Free trade[19] between India and Nepal got top priority in British India's foreign policy even during the Prime Ministership of Jang Bahadur Rana.[20] But he was not ready to adopt liberal and free trade policy which he had observed in England. Like his predecessors he was aware of the fact that free and unrestricted commercial intercourse might result in economic and political subjugation of Nepal.[21]

Nepal was the only country in South Asia and Indian subcontinent, where Europeans were not allowed to enter in trade.[22] In 1856-57, Jang Bahadur refused permission to Mr Cameron, an English merchant, in whom Lord Clarendon, the British foreign Secretary, was interested and had introduced him to Governor General, to enter and trade in Nepal. "When Colonel Ramsay, the British Resident in Nepal, pressed him to allow Mr Camron to enter into the country, he politely replied, "You say we are independent, The British Government tells us that it has no desire to interfere....with our internal affairs and not even to advise us respecting them. We desire to preserve our independence. We attribute that independence solely to our own peculiar policy (you may call it selfish if you like but we cannot alter it to please you.) We know you are the stronger power, you are like a lion, we are like a cat. The cat will scratch, if it is driven into a corner, but the lion would soon kill the cat. You can force us to change our policy. You can take our country if it pleases you to do so, but we will make no change in that policy, with the strict observance of which, we have preserved our independence as a nation to the present time, unless you compel us to do so. We will not allow Mr Cameron to come into the country, except as a private gentleman and your guest and upon your assurance that he will not attempt to engage in trade or make any enquiries into the resources of the country."[23]

At the time of the annexation of Oudh on February 13, 1856, Jang Bahadur met the British Resident and spoke in the same stream. "What fools the kings of Oudh have always been; If they have only acted as we have done, and had refused to mix themselves up with you in any way, you would not have had any excuse for taking their country." He then said, "I know very well the advantages that would accrue to Nepal for a few years if we were to open the country to British Officers and to British merchants, but even supposing that we were to double our revenue for 10 or 20 years, what good would that do us ? At the end of that time you would probably take the country." He had often pointed to the case of Sikkim. Then the British Resident had reminded him that the Rajah of that country had wantingly seized and had barbarously ill treated Drs Campbell and Hooker upon this, the Prime Minister said, "Well ! but if they had not gone there to gather Rhododendrons, that could not have happened, and the Rajah would not have lost his country. How do I know that some of our officials, through ignorance, or, perhaps, through enmity to myself, might not ill treat some British subject, and then you would take half, if not the whole, of the country. All the other Native states have either fallen entirely under your rule, or you interfere with their management, that would soon happen here."[24]

In 1858-9, Mr William Norris, a timber merchant of North Western Provinces, met Jang Bahadur in Allahabad and asked for permission to carry timber trade with Nepal. Lord Canning, the Viceroy of India, personally wrote to the king of Nepal in his favour. Jang Bahadur quoted such a high price[25] that he decided not to enter into business with Nepal. Similarly, Jang Bahadur also refused to allow Colonel Walker and his party to enter into Nepal for exploration work in 1869 and 1874 though he was pressed by the Governor-General himself.[26] Jang Bahadur had never allowed British Resident to travel in the country according to his wish. On the question of the entry of British and Europeans into Nepalese territory Jang Bahadur tactfully succeeded in keeping them out, and saved his country from their influence.[27]

Lord Canning, the Governor-General of India, informed Jang Bahadur that Calcutta would restore the section of the Tarai taken from Nepal in 1816 and given to Oudh. It was done due to the service rendered by Jang Bahadur in the Mutiny of 1858. Canning thought that Jang Bahadur would be satisfied with the Old Nepal Oudh boundary, but in this he was wrong. Jang Bahadur took a number of steps to express his dissatisfaction. He first requested the recall of Ramsay as Resident. But when Calcutta refused to do it, he later on moved to restrict the activities of British subjects engaged in commerce in Nepal.[28] On 17 July 1858 Jang Bahadur

Prime Minister Chandra Shamsher with his wife (c. 1890).

Prime Minister Chandra Shamshe

Prithvi Bir at his inauguration, 1910.

Chandra Shamsher's son Shankar (right) and his grandson Sridhar.

had asked the Iraqi merchants of Nepal for an undertaking which reads as follows :

"We the undersigned Iraqis do herein write that we will not sell any merchandize on credit from the date of this agreement. We will sell our goods for cash only. If we sell upon credit, we will not come forward to complain against any one, saying that such a one has not paid us. If we do come to complain, do not cause the money to be paid to us. We will make no excuses. We have written this paper willingly and of our on accord in the Suddur Ju: gee Kotwalees Cutcherry at Indra Chowk."[29]

In his report to the Secretary to the Government of India, G. Ramsay, the Resident in Nepal, wrote, "Similar Muchulkas were taken from other merchants, including those from Banares, Bettiah, the Kulwars, Marwarees and from all other classes of British merchants who had establishments in the city, and who had for years past been in the habit of trading with this country upon the same footing as other merchants, subjects of this state."[30]

It seems that the parties who had executed the Muchulka[31] had expressed their consent to see their goods for cash only and to give no credit further. These muchulkas stated that they were signed "Willingly" and ' of their own accord". G. Ramsay, the Resident in Nepal, enquired and asked the reason why they had put their signature. The Principal Iraqi and the other merchants in Nepal, replied that it was the order of the Minister. No one could disobey his order. If they had not signed the paper, they would have been expelled from Kathmandu where they had outstanding debts to a considerable amount, the Iraqi alone owed between two and three lakhs of rupees. These merchants were willing to leave the country provided they recovered their outstanding debts.[32]

The British merchants stated that the Muchulkas were taken from them because many principal Sardars, and Jang Bahadur's relatives were active in business. Their names did not appear but they had privately constituted certain Newar merchants as their agents, to whom they advanced money for the purchase of goods as for employment on loans to other parties and who were allowed a certain small percentage upon their profit. No one could compete with the Sardars, who could take the law into their own hands. All the complaints made by the merchants fell on deaf ears. The Muchulkas greatly handicapped the foreign businessmen so that hence forward they could not do business whereas the Sardars and Jang Bahadur's relatives could do so. According to them, Jang Bahadur wanted the British merchants to abandon their debts and leave the country at once to the great profit of their rivals. When the Resident inquired from Jang Bahadur as to the cause of this undertaking, the Prime Minister answered that the Iraqis were suspicious people and that they could have transmitted false stories and news from Nepal to British India during the Mutiny. Later on Jang Bahadur said that the Iraqis were making numerous claims of outstanding debts in the court, and that some time the individual against whom the case was brought had no means of payment. So he thought that it would be better for them to sell in cash instead of on credit.[33]

G. Ramsay, the British Resident in Nepal, reported that the Prime Minister and his relatives had not the least interest in the country's prosperity, and that the measure that they had taken could ruin the whole trade of Nepal. They had the monopoly of oil, and now they wanted the monopoly of the sale of wood. By monopolizing these articles they could double the price. This would only affect the poorer class. The Resident presented an interesting story about Jang Bahadur's brother, General Krishna Bahadur Rana. The General wanted the Resident to write a letter as the British representative to Indian merchants in Patna and other places to buy opium worth rupees 300,000 at double the price and also to arrange that it should not be checked at the border so that he could earn a handsome profit.[34]

The Governor-General through the British Resident, reminded Jang Bahadur that the policy of exclusion was abandoned even by China and Japan. He expressed his regret over the Muchulkas to the Nepal Darbar. He further added that in European States the restriction which had been placed on British subjects would have been considered as an act of "Undisquired ill will". He also expressed his faith in the friendship of Nepal and stated that Nepal was not influenced by feeling of "unfriendliness". The Governor-General regretfully suggested that if the Darbar wanted to exclude the British subjects from trading in Nepal, it should do it directly instead of indirectly.[35] The polite response of Governor-General of India had a good effect upon the Nepal Darbar. On 22 September 1859 the Prime Minister Jang Bahadur wrote to G. Ramsay "Formerly, on account of the Iraqis having been suspected of taking part in the rebellion in the British Provinces, a muchulka to the following effect was taken from them. As the rebellion is now at an end, I have sent for the Iraqis and have torn up the said muchulka. Moreover I have told them that for the future, they may as was the custom in former days, carry on their trades and dealing in the same manner as Nepalese subjects do and that they will receive the same justice that the Nepalese subjects get."[36]

Jang Bahadur, however, did not make any concession to European businessmen. But in spite of that the trade relations between the Nepalese Government and British Subjects became normal.[37] In the month of December 1862, the British Government pressed the Nepalese Government to reopen negotiations for a less restricted trade. In 1863, G. Ramsay, got an opportunity to press the Nepalese Government to accept the engagement of 1839 but in the absence of original documents, nothing could be done. Jang Bahadur demanded its copies from the Indian Government. On a closer examination it was found that the engagement was quite imperfect. It only included the goods to and from Kathmandu. Leather and hides which were chief commodities of export and imports were not mentioned in the list.[38] Regarding the causes of the absence of original document, G. Ramsay wrote: "I regret to observe that neither the original tariff, nor the engagement itself are in the records of this residency. They were lost many years ago with other papers and records of importance, including three volumes of copies of the Residency yaddast (i.e. to the Darbar) from the year 1816 to 1840 as mentioned in a paper or list dated the 12 of November 1846 bearing the signature of Lieut. Ottley, then officiating Resident. They are supposed to have been taken down into the tarai by the late Sir Henry Lawrence who was encamped near the frontier at the time of the commencement of the first Sikh Campaign in 1845/46, and who upon being suddenly summoned to fill the post of agent to the Governor-General on the North Western frontier in the place of Captain Brodfoot (killed at Ferozeskukur) at once proceeded to join his new appointment, without returning to Kathmandu. Upon my first arrival here, I was informed that efforts had been made to trace these papers but without success. The various enclosures and accompaniments referring to the imports and exports duties and justice to British Subjects residing in Nepal, which appear to have been with them"[39] were also lost. Jang Bahadur expressed total ignorance about it and stated that Nepalese copies of it had been destroyed in a fire.[40] Although the engagement of 1839 was not perfect even then most of the British Residents[41] and representatives mentioned it repeatedly in course of their discussions with the Government concerned.

Nepalese Government had prohibited its subjects from taking their goods from Western Tarai to the British territory with a view to compelling all British Subjects to enter into Nepal Tarai and to purchase Nepalese products and to sell their own. The territory of Naya Muluk, which was restored to Nepal by the British in 1860, flourished under the care of Jang Bahadur. In order to bring the entire Naya Muluk under cultivation and rehabilitation, the Nepalese Government induced and encouraged the British Indian Subjects to settle in the new territory, by giving them many concessions like free grant of lands, lifting of taxation on goods sold for one year.[42] The Nepalese Government issued two orders to attract British Indian traders and other Subjects to settle permanently in the said territory. Jang Bahadur imposed a very light import duty on British goods imported to Nepal and a heavy duty on the articles of export. A cess of one pice per rupee was imposed on all valuable articles, live-stock and other goods, besides a tax called Chungi. In addition, an export or transit duty called Mahsuli Nikasi was levied on goods exported to India.[43] An order issued to the merchants and other people of Jagarkot, Salyan, Dang, Phalabang, Piuthan and Udaypur in Western Nepal, asked them to sell their goods in the Nepalganj market (Naya Muluk) and not to visit Indian territory.[44] It also compelled the British

Indian Subjects to repair to the new Nepalese markets to dispose of their goods. The result of this policy created hardship for the Nepalese traders who used to sell hill products in the Indian markets freely before opening of these markets in Banke district.[45] Similarly, this policy forced the Indian merchants to visit and live in the Nepalese markets to get the hill products which were in great demand in India. Another result of this policy was that the Bazars in British territory, which carried flourishing trade with Nepal before the Mutiny of 1858, were nearly ruined. Some weeks ago Jang Bahadur had informed the British Resident in Nepal. that the Raja of Bahrampur prohibited the merchants residing in his jurisdiction from crossing the border to trade with Nepal. But after the restriction imposed by the Nepalese Government the Raja of Bahrampur had suffered a loss of fifteen to twenty thousand rupees per annum, the amount of duties he formerly took from Nepalese traders. On the basis of the engagement of 1839 when G. Ramsay, protested against the restriction and duties imposed by the Nepalese Government, the Prime Minister of Nepal replied that his Government had every right to do so,[46] because the engagement nowhere mentioned that the rate of the duties could not be revised. Nepal only engaged to forward a statement of authorised duties and assured that unauthorised duties not entered into the list would not be levied upon the Indian traders. Moreover, in 1859 the political Secretary had written on behalf of Lord Canning that the Governor-General "assumes no right to interfere with or even advise upon commercial policy of Nepal."[47]

Jang Bahadur had witnessed the operation of the free trade policy introduced by Sir Robert Peel in England. But he found it useless for him and his country.[48] With regard to unauthorised duties, G. Ramsay told the Prime Minister that the trade in British provinces was quite free and that no duties were subjected to levy by the British Government upon the borders of Nepal. On the contrary the Nepalese Government had imposed such heavy duties in its own bazar at Nepalganj, which greatly exceeded the amount fixed by the engagement of 1839. With reference to this remark, the Prime Minister observed that his .Government was at perfect liberty to make any rules it pleases for the regulation of its own bazaar, and to levy from its own subjects any taxes that it thought proper to impose. Further he added that the duties imposed upon the articles at Nepalganj were not concerned with the British Government because it was not intended to bear upon the subjects of that country.[49] Upon this the British Resident countered that the British subjects were also invited to trade and were the victims of "vexations" charges which were injuring the trade between the two countries.[50] Jang Bahadur promised to send him the names of the merchants who were not allowed to come into Nepal from British territory by the British Indian Government.[51] G.Ramsay, requested Jang Bahadur to alter the trade relations and open the door of the counter for free trade. But the latter refused and explained to the Resident that "the two countries cannot be compared; their Governments are quite different; you have a thousand sources of wealth which we do not have, you are wiser and can understand that, by making apparent present sacrifices, you will be gainers in the end; our people are ignorant and unenlightened; and if I were to make any such change as you desire from time to time, I would lose my Prime Ministership."[52]

It was quite natural for a Prime Minister like Jang Bahadur, whose power rested primarily on the support of the army and the feudal chiefs, to close his country against foreign trade and capital. During the Indian revolt of 1857-58 and afterwards he was vigrorously criticised by a section of the chiefs for surrendering the independence of their country to the British. In fact, in a nation where the people were so sensitive it was too much to expect the Prime Minister to throw open the country.[53] G.Ramsay himself remarked about Jang Bahadur on July 6, 1864, "So weary he is, so suspicious that we are merely biding our times, waiting for an opportunity to insert the point of the wedge, that we may gradually obtain a firm footing in the country, that I think, he would rather counsel the cession to us of a considerable slice of it than consent to a system of free trade and permit English merchants to have transaction in Nepal."[54] G. Ramsay did not believe that Jang Bahadur had any fear from Sardars and the people. He reported that Jang Bahadur was himself the chief obstacle to all free intercourse between Nepal and British Provinces. He was the mainspring, the director of Gorkha's policy. All restrictions emanated from himself not from the Sardars. There was not a sardar who had any voice in the matter. The Prime Minister was absolute, he could do what he pleased. His word was law, his Government was the most perfect autocracy. He could throw open the country tomorrow to English merchants if he so willed it, without a dissenting voice being heard but he did not choose to do so. Further he added that the Resident could not go one yard further from the residency in any direction and it was solely owing to Jang Bahadur's suspicious distrust that these restrictions were then kept up.[55]

In 1862, the Indian goat merchants who used to come over to Kathmandu annually during winter were asked to pay a special tax, "Chumanee" in addition to the annual transit duties levied on the frontier and at other places. The tax was levied at the rate of one anna in each rupee upon the price of their flocks of goats, as valued by the Nepalese authorities in Kathmandu. The goat merchants who refused to pay it were seiged and placed in confinement, and were not allowed to dispose of their goats until they had given security for the eventual payment of the sums demanded. The tax was levied throughout the country. To the objection made by the British Resident against this tax, the Nepalese Prime Minister replied that the tax had been levied for many generations and that it was paid without demur by the Bhotes and all other traders from Tibet and he further added that if the tax were abolished, heavy loss would accrue to his Government.[56]

The Governor-General in Council directed the British Resident in Nepal to forward a copy of an agreement with the Nepal Darbar in 1839, by article six of which the Nepal Government, "engages that an authentic statement of all the duties leviable in Nepal shall be delivered to the Resident, and that hereafter unauthorized imports not entered in this list shall not be levied on the British Subjects." He also asked the resident to be aware of the existence of that agreement "because if it be not abrogated by any subsequent convention it will be incumbent on you to remonstrate against its insuration."[57] The Resident replied that he was well aware of the fact that such a paper had been obtained from the Maharaja of Nepal by the Resident of that time, but that document had been lost. He added, "Those papers would have been, without exception, the most important that have ever passed between this court and the Residency if their terms had, at the time, been strictly acted up to, and British Subjects trading with Nepal would undoubtedly, in such case, have been upon better footing than they now are, but it does not appear that the Durbar has ever been firmly held to them and to the best of my belief they are not once referred to in the despatches of any one of my four predecessors in office."[58] He inferred that the Supreme Government ignored the engagement as a definite commercial one, and that it was not deemed expedient to make any stand upon it. Upon the remonstrance of British Resident, the Nepalese Prime Minister remitted a portion of the tax and this act satisfied the goat merchants from British Indian provinces.[59]

Several efforts were made by the British Indian Government to negotiate a commercial treaty with Nepal, but they failed. The Nepalese Government presumed that the British Indian Government had nothing to give in return for the concession given to them. G. Ramsay, reported, "The Gorkhas have nothing to gain by such an engagement, but, as they fancy, everything to lose, they know that we have abolished the transit duties that were in force when former negotiation failed, and that, since that period, our trade had been entirely thrown open, and that enterprizing Nepalese merchants can trade in British Provinces with the same freedom and upon the same terms as our own merchants do."[60] The Nepalese Government did not see any advantage in concluding any commercial treaty with the British Indian Government. Similarly, the latter was not ready to sanction a retaliative policy. But G. Ramsay was of the opinion that the policy of retaliation would, of course, soon drive the Nepalese Government to solicit a reciprocal treaty. In this regard, the Chief Commissioner of Oudh observed, "the Nepalese authorities would never have adopted the course complained of had they not been well aware that the British Government would not resort to the same illiberal policy."[61]

The commercial interests in England pressed the Government of India to abandon its policy of non-interference in Nepal, because, Nepal offered good prospects for tea gardens, orchards, plantations, woollen mills, saw mills and such other productive industries as could be profitably developed with European enterprise. The Governor General in Council informed the Resident that something might be done to facilitate and encourage trade between the two territories without entering into any such negotiations, especially by inducing the Darbar to improve the communications on the Nepalese side of the border and to remove as far as practicable any inconveniences arising from the Nepalese system of farming revenue. He also suggested to the Resident that in doing so he should carefully avoid anything which might lead the Darbar to suppose that the Government of India desired to interfere with the internal administration of the country. Further, he added that while using his influence with the Nepalese authorities he would make it clearly apparent that his suggestions were limited to the adoption of measures obvionsly as favourable to the Nepalese interest as to those of the British Government.[62]

The desire of the British Indian Government for less restricted trade clearly showed the imperialist designs of the British. An unrestricted Indo-Nepalese trade would have benefited the British. Nepal had, however, her own fear and national interest. For a small and poor country like Nepal to throw herself open to an imperialistic power, which had conquered the whole of India within a century, was a matter of national concern.[63] Jang Bahadur had expressed this sentiment in his several statements. The activities of the British in India showed that behind their demands for immediate justice for their traders there was the policy of imperialism and every Indian State got entangled in that net. Jang Bahadur was not unaware of this fact. His restrictions on free trade were not so much for the protection of Nepalese industries, as to save the independence of his country.[64] Annoyed at the trade policy of Jang Bahadur. G. Ramsay, "I see no hope of establishing a 'free trade' with Nepal during Maharajah Jang Bahadur's tenure of the Ministership. I venture to predict, although I do not think he will consent to enter into any forward engagement with us, that he will in future be more cautious in interfering with trade upon the border, and other mischievous innovations will be averted."[65] The British Residents in Nepal like Hodgson, Lawrence and G. Ramsay might have felt irritated at the restrictions, but they simply could not have realised the feelings of a weak, poor and ignorant country, which had a strong sense of independence and where political power rested in the hands of the feudal elements.[66]

Charles Girdlestone, tried to understand the Nepalese difficulties in developing Indo-Nepal trade. When he was asked to press the Nepalese Government for less restrictive trade, he refused to do so. He was not in favour of political pressure on Jang Bahadur to overcome "self insulating and distrustful policy of the Nepal Government.[67] Unlike his predecessor, he did not find any complaint against the Darbar and the courts of Nepal. He was of the opinion that the Darbar and the courts of Nepal were just and fair in their judgements. In cases which were rather intricate and expensive, the Darbar had ordered special courts composed of some of the highest officers in the country to do justice.[68] On 19 September 1876, Girdlestone reported that the complaints of the traders were amicably settled if reasonably referred to.[69] He did not see any decline in trade and took an optimistic view about it. In the last days of Jang Bahadur's Prime Ministership Girdlestone defended the trade policy of the Nepal Darbar by writing, "We do not appreciate the protective tendencies of American and Australian colonies, but neither do we interfere with them, and I do not see that we have any right to interfere with Nepal which like outselves imposes and maintains duties nor in order to protect a branch of industry but for revenue purposes only.[70]

During the entire period of his premiership Jang Bahadur maintained a protective policy with firm opposition to the entry of Europeans into Nepal for trade. However, two European British Subjects, whose primary occupation was that of tutor in Prime Minister Jang Bahadur's family, were engaged in trade. They were successful only in musk trade. They transmitted the article direct to the agents in England and France. They had large markets for musk trade in Europe. The native merchants could not succeed in musk trade. But in country produce, in Manchester or Birmingham goods, or in woollen fabrics, they could not compete with the native merchants of Nepal. The native merchants purchased European articles of inferior quality at Calcutta at a higher rate. But if they were willing to change the market, they could easily obtain at the same price the first rate articles on Commission from Europe. But they were so jealous of the interposition of Europeans that they preferred to keep the trade on old track. In this situation the Europeans had attempted to introduce European goods into Nepal and the native merchants had combined to undersell these goods in the Nepalese market. They did this wholly of their own accord and were not instigated by the Darbar.[71]

Jang Bahadur never accepted the British proposal for less restricted trade and for negotiating a commercial treaty. Colonel G. Ramsay remarked, "Jang Bahadur is not open to reason upon points connected with the internal policy of his Government, nor will he receive as disinterested, any advice that we may offer him."[72] As a matter of fact, after the abrogation of the Muchulkas he tried to do justice and to avoid any friction with the British Government of trade on the issue. After 1859 he maintained smooth relations with the British Government with the hope that it would not force him to admit European businessmen. He was successful in his policy towards the British.[73] The British Indian Government also did not want to make commerce an issue with Jang Bahadur.[74] It valued his strong and friendly regime which had kept the turbulent tribes of Nepal in lease.[75] It kept its hands off the internal affairs of Nepal. It was during the rule of Prime Minister Jang Bahadur that the foundations of stable relations between the Government of India and Nepal were laid. Jang Bahadur died but his policy survived him. Lord Lytton, the Governor-General, saw in his death "rather an opportunity than an occasion for anxiety."[76]

Commercial Policy of Ranodip Singh

After the death of Jang Bahadur in 1877,[77] Ranodip Singh became the Prime Minister of Nepal according to the Law of succession,[78] which had been made in 1856.[79] He made apparently friendly gestures to prove his honesty to the British but, at the same time, he refused to accept anything which might increase British influence in Nepal.[80] In conformity with Jang Bahadur's style of diplomacy, he informed the British Government in 1885 of Nepal's willingness to offer military assistance "should the rumour prove true that Russians intended to continue their advance through Afghanistan."[81] But the British Government politely declined the offer.

In such a favourable situation, Charles Girdlestone, decided in 1879 to take up the issue of trade with Ranodip Singh and to suggest the ways by which all hinderances to its expansion could be removed. There was a direct talk between Ranodip Singh and Girdlestone, regarding the improvement of Indo-Nepal trade. First of all he wanted to press the Prime Minister to abandon the restriction placed upon the Nepalese traders to cross the Western frontier of Nepal. The Prime Minister clarified that the Nepalese traders were required to sell their articles in five frontier Nepalese "bazars" such as Sirsia, Butwal, Banke, Golamandi and Dhakhanabagh and if they could not sell, they were at liberty to go anywhere they wished. He reminded that it was not compulsory for the British merchants to visit Nepalese markets and settle there. Pucca (brick-built) shops were constructed in these markets by the Government to prevent accidents from fire and rain and theft. The British traders were given privilege to open shops in these buildings. At the same time they could also buy Nepalese products. The Prime Minister added that the restriction was not placed upon the traders in other parts of the country, it was done in Western Nepal in order to make the market popular.[82] After the discussion, Charles Girdlestone believed that the issue raised by the authorities of North Western Provinces near the border of Western frontier of Nepal, "was much exaggeration of actual facts."[83] He remarked that the Prime Minister's explanations were most reasonable and he had no reason to doubt him. He supported the Nepalese contention that the bazaars were established by the Government to develop the trade of of the country and to make the marts larger and popular.[84]

The policy of the Nepalese Government was to encourage its subjects to produce sufficient clothes, food and drinks and to keep them ignorant of the outer world. At the same time the living standards of the people were too low to enable them to purchase foreign goods. They did not depend much on the articles of external manufacture or origin. They, however, obtained foreign products and libitum. They were well-nourished, well-housed and clothed in home spun native clothes. The people exchanged grain for the few commodities from the plains which they could not produce themselves. Hence, it was partly because of the simple habit of the people and partly because of the Government policy that the balance of trade was always in favour of Nepal. Charles Girdlestone, however, wanted to turn the balance of trade in favour of India. He was in favour of material improvements in the export trade from India to Nepal through a radical change in Nepal's national policy and character.[85] On 25 September 1880, Girdlestone reported that the great task for the British Indian Government was to balance trade by getting Nepal ready to take more articles of British origin. Further he suggested that the best chance of increasing the import trade was by placing such things near the border at lower prices than prevalent.[86]

During the rule of Ranodip Singh, the Government of North Western Provinces reported that the policy of the Nepal Darbar was to discourage British goods except silver. The Government feared that after some years Nepalese trade would be one-sided. The transactions were limited to the purchase of Nepalese goods. Except cotton and salt Nepal produced everything to meet the primary needs of the people.[87] There was no scientific machinery to produce goods in Nepal. Girdlestone reported that the hand-looms "from which coarse clothes were woven in the households of the poor for home consumption from imported cotton and wool were of a rude description."[86] He accepted the view of Sir John Macdonald that the main policy of British imperialist was to "accumulate wealth by means of selling in the dearest and buying in cheapest market."[89] Unlike Canada, Nepal's policy of protection was meant for increasing revenue not to stimulate domestic industries.[90]

In his memorandum to the Prime Minister Ranodip Singh, Charles Girdlestone suggested ways and means of improving the trade of Nepal. He advised first, the improvement of road tracks on the Nepalese side so that they would connect the Indian roads with Nepal's business centres. Secondly, he suggested a greater freedom for the merchants of both countries to meet freely, and if possible the abolition of the market system so that Indian merchants could visit the interior of Nepal. Thirdly, he advised that the methods of farming and the collection of revenue from the farmers should be improved and duties and customs levied by the Nepal Government should be made known to the Resident. Lastly, Girdlestone requested for detailed information about the timber trade.[91]

The Prime Minister, Ranodip Singh promised to fulfil some of the demands of the British Resident in Nepal. He agreed to supply the information regarding the rate of customs duties and timber trade.[92] But in spite of pressure from the Resident, the Prime Minister did not do much directly to improve trade facilities between India and Nepal. He did gradually make small concessions which led to some improvement in the volume of trade. During his rule the volume of trade between these two countries increased. It was due to the reform made by the Prime Minister and the suggestion of the British Resident accepted by Ranodip Singh.

Girdlestone was not satisfied with this reform. He suggested coercive measures to secure concessions from the Nepal Darbar.[93] However, the Government of India did not accept his suggestion. The urgent need of Goıkha recruits made the Government of India adopt a policy of mutual concession. On Girdlestone's suggestion, it was decided by the Governor-General to "give arms and ammunition to Nepal as a free gift provided the Darbar would agree to improve facilities for trade. give greater freedom of movement to the Resident and grant full freedom to the British for obtaining recruits for their army."[94] Even this concession was not acceptable to Ranodip Singh. At this critical moment the drama was ended when Ranodip Singh's regime was overthrown by a coup d'etat in 1885 and Bir Shamsher became the Prime Minister of Nepal.

Commercial Policy of Bir Shamsher

The Shamsher family, the second generation[95] of Rana dynesty had had the reputation of being hostile to the British. Dhir Shamsher, the father of Bir Shamsher was anti-British. He had opposed strongly Jang Bahadur's support to the British during the India Mutiny. But the political situation of the country compelled the Prime Minister Bir Shamsher to be on friendly terms with the

British. He had many enemies on the Indian soil. After the coup d' etat of 1885, Jang Bahadur's sons and other relatives who had a claim to the Prime Ministership had fled to India. They left no stone unturned in trying to change the policy of Indian Government in their favour. But they could not get success. The British Government informed Jit Jung, the son of Jang Bahadur, that it had recognised the new regime and warned him that the refugees would not be assisted to overthrow Bir Shamsher.

British relations with Nepal improved during the Prime Ministership of Bir Shamsher. Although he did not give up the traditional policy of isolation and oppositon to free trade, he tried to strengthen the relations between the two countries.

The end of Girdlestone's tenure of office as Resident and the period of service of Major Durand, who succeeded him in 1888, were not a happy time in Indo-Nepalese relations. Just before his retirement from Nepal, Girdlestone reported to the Secretary to the Government of India that Bir Shamsher used "to examine British merchants' letters before despatch."[96] This led to Bir Shamsher's censure by the British Government. Girdlestone was recalled because of his bad relation with the Nepalese Government. Major Durand, like Girdlestone had strong distrust of Nepal. He urged that all measures "short of war should be taken to settle the vexed issue even a war could have only one result : complete defeat of Nepal."[97] Both the Residents were annoyed when they saw that a small nation presumed to limit trade, ban Europeans, restrict the Resident's movements and even complain to the Governor-General of their conduct. The mutual distrust that had developed between these Residents and the Nepalese Prime Minister Bir Shamsher, was not to the advantage of either country.

In 1891, Major Durand was succeeded as Resident by Colonel Wylie who believed in a policy of conciliation and compromise by giving up the previous strong policy which had created so much suspicion and hostility. He regularly submitted a brief report on the progress of Nepal from 1891 to 1899, which gave a clear picture of the country's internal as well as external affairs.[98] He reported that there appeared to be an increasing trade between the two countries.[99] A.C. Lyall, the Secretary to the Government of India, like Colonel H. Wylie, also believed in friendly relations with Nepal. He was opposed to Durand's policy of aggression, which appeared to him imprudent, unwarranted and dangerous, and morally indefensible. Further, he added,"We have no commercial interest in that country, and our native subjects enter it at their own risk; nor does it seem to me humiliating that they should be let in as harmless while we are excluded as formidable visitors."[100] Lyall accepted the truth that Nepal was an independent country and had the right to adopt any policy to safeguard her interests. He disclosed that it was in the British interest to keep Nepal "a half-shut door." European merchants and travellers, if allowed free access to Nepal, might create embarrassing problems for the Nepalese as well as the Indian Government. Lord Ripon, the Viceroy and the successor of Lord Lytton. who was also against any forward policy, "generally agreed" with Lyall.

The British Government had four main objectives in their relations with Nepal. They were (1) increase facilities for obtaining Gorkha recruits, (2) the liberalisation of trade, (3) the removal of the restrictions placed on the movement of the Resident, and (4) abolition of the system of isolation under which the country was closed to European. They wanted to fulfil these objectives in their future negotiations with Nepal. The Government of India wrote to the Secretary of State for India that it did not attach great importance to the last objective, and considered the second and third of "undoubted value". It further mentioned, 'Our merchants are harrassed by uncertain and in some respects heavy duties; and the trade with Nepal, and through Nepal with the countries beyond, might become considerably larger than it is."[101] But later on the liberalization of trade was "regarded by the Government of India as questions of altogether minor importance compared with the free power of obtaining Gorkha recruits."[102] The British objective of Gorkha recruitment was fulfilled during the Prime Ministership of Bir Shamsher. Never before under any previous Prime Minister of Nepal had Gorkha been so freely recruited for the British army.[103] In return for this concession, Bir Shamsher, the Nepalese Prime Minister, got an opportunity to buy arms and ammunition in the open market. The Prime Minister requested Colonel Wylie to supply him with a price list for arms and machinery. He also informed the Resident that the Government of Nepal was ready to spend eighteen lakhs rupees in a year for the purpose[104] Later on, Bir Shamsher submitted a list of large quantities of arms and ammunition to be purchased, together with another list of the machinery needed for manufacturing military equipment in Nepal. The immediate reaction of Wylie to the list submitted to him was, "If the war material mentioned in the list which I refer is purchased, Nepal will be better armed in some important respects than we ourselves are in India."[105]

Bir Shamsher began to exploit the situation in his favour. Contrary to the policy of Jang Bahadur and Ranodip Singh, the late Prime Ministers of Nepal, he started to deposit money in foreign banks. He was acquainted with the wretched financial condition of exiled son and relatives of Jang Bahadur in India. He throught that if there was a similar coup d' etat in the country his sons and relatives might use the money kept in foreign banks for their support.[106] The exploitation of the Nepalese people reached in climax during his rule. He was directly involved in silver and gold trade. On May 1893 (=on Wednesday Jesth Badi 6, 1950) the Prime Minister visited the British Residency in Kathmandu and told the Resident Colonel H. Wylie that the prices of gold had gone up steeply and he possessed gold worth about Rs 750,000, which he had purchased at the rate of Rs 21 or 22 per tola. He added that he would like to send Colonel Mahabir to sell the Gold in Calcutta. The Prime Minister requested the Resident to issue licenses enabling Colonel Mahabir and his party to carry some arms and ammunition with them. Colonel Wylie promised to send the licenses immediately. The Resident remarked, "The Maharaja too is now carrying on trade. I too would have made a big profit had I been in possession of gold worth rupees seven or eight lakhs."[107] This was a sarcastic remark on the conduct of the Prime Minister.[108] Bir Shamsher replied "I am now selling gold which is lying idle. When the price goes down, I shall use the money to buy gold again." After three years, on 17 November 1896 Bir Shamsher sent silver worth rupees twenty lakhs to Calcutta via Sugauli to purchase gold.[109] On 11 August 1897, the British Resident in Nepal informed the Foreign Secretary to the Government of India that the Prime Minister was willing to buy silver worth rupees eighteen lakhs in the Calcutta market because it was very cheap there at that time. He mentioned that the Prime Minister would like to buy silver with the money which he had deposited in the Bank of Bengal. The Prime Minister had a large sum of money in that Bank.[110]

The British Resident reported to the Assistant Secretary to the Foreign Department of the Government of India that the Nepalese Prime Minister had referred to him a news item published in the *Pioneer* of 14 or 16 June 1897 in which it had been mentioned that the British Indian Government had purchased a huge amount of silver duty free for export to Afghanistan and Kashmir and hinted that if this were true he wanted to know whether the same privilege would be extended to Nepal.[111] The Assistant Secretary replied that duty free silver was exported to Kashmir according to the treaty of 1870 with a view to developing trade with Eastern Turkistan. But Afghanistan did not have such privilege. The British Government did not allow Nepal to import silver from India duty free.[112]

The use of luxurious goods was increasing in Nepal during the Prime Ministership of Bir Shamsher. The import of cheap foreign goods had discouraged the native products. The Residential Surgeon and Acting Resident, Lieutenant Colonel G.H.D. Gimlette wrote, "Cotton cloth is also made for use in the country, very stout and durable, but the cheaper, more flimsy Indian and European clothes are rapidly taking the place of the native made article."[113] The trade policy of Bir Shamsher was not favourable to the country. It favoured British Indian merchants who used to export large amounts of European and Indian goods. Muslim and Kashmiri merchants were mostly engaged in this lucrative trade.[114]

The Nepalese officials in the border districts had informed Bir Shamsher that there were many wine shops close to the border of both countries which were the primary cause of confrontation between the people of both sides. On the basis of this report the

Prime Minister requested the Government of India to remove all the wine shops to a distance of two miles from the border because it was the only way whereby to lessen the tension.[115] The Deputy Secretary to the Government of India asked the Bengal and North Western Provinces and Oudh Governments to send their opinion regarding the removal of wine shops. The Chief Secretary to the Government of Bengal replied that all the wine shops in the Darjeeling district adjoining Nepalese border were situated on the main road within two miles from the border. He further added that there would be very considerable loss of revenue to the Government if the wine shops were closed. He did not agree that there was any great dispute between the people of the two countries.[116] The Commissioner of Excise, North Western Provinces and Oudh reported that the reports of disturbances, which had been sent to the Prime Minister of Nepal, were without foundation, and that after full enquiry there appeared no reason to alter existing arrangements.[117] The Secretary to the Government of the North Western Provinces and Oudh wrote to the Deputy Secretary to the Government of India, that there would be no objection on the part of this Government to remove all the liquor shops in both territories to a distance of one or two miles from the border, provided that strict measures were taken to secure the observance of the terms of the agreement by the Nepalese contractors.[118] The main objectives behind this policy were to maintain peace and order in the border and to discourage the production of wine in the country. The people, in the hill and valley, used to prepare wine with rice and other grains. It had created scarcity of grains. Therefore, the Prime Minister had issued an order prohibiting wine production. But he could not check the people. At that time Bhuwan Singh,[119] the reformist and economist of Nepal, submitted an application to the Commander in Chief, Dev Shamsher in which he suggested that since some people of low castes would not give up the habit of drinking wine, they should be encouraged to prepare it with fruits found in abundance in nearby forests. In his opinion it would check rising prices and scarcity of grain.[120] But the autocratic Government had no courage to accept the constructive suggestions of the people.[121] The Government merely imposed restriction on the export of foodgrains to check the rising prices at home.[122]

Like his predecessors Bir Shamsher was also successful in maintaining good relations with the British. But unlike them he exposed the secrecy of his country by showing 'Nakhu Arsenal" of Nepal to the British Resident Colonel H. Wylie. "This mark of confidence enabled the Resident for the first time to make an estimate of the quantity of arms possessed by the Durbar, and how much machinery was available for the manufacture of ammunition."[123] The suspicion and hostility which arose during the Prime Ministership of Ranodip Singh's time were replaced by mutual understanding and cooperation during the time of Bir Shamsher. Colonel H. Wylie also helped him to strengthen the tie of Indo-Nepal friendship. It was at his initiative that Bir Shamsher invited Lord Roberts, the Commander-in-Chief of India to visit Nepal in 1892. A British officer of such a high rank had never before visited Nepal.[124] Hence the rule of Bir Shamsher may be regarded as a landmark in the history of Indo-Nepal relations. Trade and Commerce also increased during his rule.

Chandra Shamsher

After the sudden death of Bir Shamsher, Dev Shamsher succeeded him on 5 March 1901. But he was ousted by Chandra Shamsher within three months in a bloodless coup in June of the same year. Chandra Shamsher ruled the country for the next twenty eight years. The policy of mutual understanding and mutual concession between the British and the Nepalese Governments started during the rule of Bir Shamsher continued to flourish during his rule.[125]

With the turn of the 19th century Indo-Nepal trade Relations took a new turn during the Prime Ministership of Chandra Shamsher, the major cause of which was the British mission of 1903-4. The mission was led by Colonel Francis Younghusband who reached Tibetan Capital on 3 August 1904. Nepal's help to the British contributed to the success of the mission.[126] The Nepalese assistance was both on the physical and diplomatic front. On the physical side the Prime Minister Chandra Shamsher gave 500 yaks[127] immediately and by the end of October 1903 Nepal handed over 3,500 yaks to the British mission.[128] The collection of yaks and furnishing them with saddles and gothalas (drivers) were not an easy task.[129] Nepal also supplied armed troops to assist the mission.

On the diplomatic front, Nepal roughly told Tibet that as the political crisis was Tibet's own creation, Nepal was in no position to come to her aid in the event of a British invasion. In his long eight-paragraph letter to the Tibetan Government, the Nepalese Prime Minister assured Tibet that the British did not have evil designs over their country, for they were not only tolerant in their religious beliefs but also democratic in their diplomatic policies. He warned Tibet not to run into an unnecessary complication with the British Government.[130] Tibet then asked Nepal to follow a strict neutrality in Indo-Tibetan dispute and not to assist the British with troops and transport carriers. Nevertheless, Nepal's diplomatic initiative to solve the Indo-Tibetan dispute continued during the crucial years of 1903 to 1905. With the entry of the British troops in Lhasa, the Nepalese Vakil Jit Bahadur K. C. in Lhasa and the Prime Minister in Kathmandu played an important role in the negotiations between Tibet and the British Government. A convention was finally concluded between Tibet and Great Britain on 7 September, 1904. The object of the convention was to remove the difficulties found in the Anglo-Chinese Convention of 1870 and the Indo-Tibetan trade regulations of 1893. Tibet promised not to station any foreign representatives in Lhasa not to cede, sell or mortgage its land or give concessions for building roads, railways and telegraphs, or in respect of rights to a foreign power. Tibet had to pay a war indemnity of Rs 7,500,000 and also to permit the British to build trade marts in Gyantse, Gartok and Yalung.[131]

The Tibet Government was not satisfied with the articles of the Convention. They particularly resented Article II of the convention, which permitted the British to establish trademarts and station British Officers there. It asked the Nepalese Prime Minister to seek modification of the terms of the Convention with the British Government on behalf of Tibet. The Prime Minister did not appreciate the Tibetan approach. However, in January 1905, with the efforts of Nepalese Prime Minister, the Government of India decided to reduce the Tibetan indenmity from 75 lakhs to 25 lakhs and the period of the occupation of the Chumbi Valley to three years only.[132]

The British Government was quite happy with the timely help of the Nepal Darbar during the dispute and throughout the negotiations.[133] But there was great resentment in Nepal against this help. The general public opinion was sympathetic to the cause of Tibet and against the Nepal Governments bid to force Tibet to accept the British commercial overtures. The confidential dispatch to the Government of India mentioned, "....the people generally are not in favour of the present policy of their Government, the chief reason being that they are averse to the opening of and improvement in trade route between Tibet and India on the ground that this tends to seriously impair the trade between Tibet and Nepal, in which very large numbers of Nepalese are interested."[134] Nepal's interest in Lhasa was of an important nature. Lhasa was the Nepalese Colony where thousands of people were engaged in trade and business operation throughout Tibet under the special privileges and patronage obtained from Tibetan Government. Any move to accommodate the British Indian subjects in the trading community of Lhasa or the attempt to open Tibet through the Darjeeling road was to have serious repercussions on the interest of the Nepalese subjects who were therefore, critical of the conduct of the Nepal Government.[135]

When the Prime Minister of Nepal had put his proposal regarding Nepalese help to the British during the Younghusband Mission before his Council of Nobility many nobles disagreed. They pointed out that such a step would, besides jeopardising Nepal's traditional political and commercial rights in Tibet, would also pave the way for another war with Tibet. But the proposal of the Prime Minister was approved nonetheless. In his letter to the British Resident in Nepal, the Nepalese Prime Minister made disparaging remarks about the nobles who had opposed his plan and called them "Little Nepalanders" as compared to the "Little Englanders" of Britain whose ideas were narrow and limited to the personal affairs of their country.[136]

Chandra Shamsher was blamed for the destruction of trade which Nepal's Kings and Prime Ministers had zealously guarded for 150 years. But he had his own fear and prejudice.[137] By the opening of the present century, Russia was expanding her territory over Manchuria and Western Turkistan. She had annexed Pamirs and was likely to absorb Chinese Turkistan and Mongolia.[138] The Czar believed that a friendly and controlled Tibet was necessary to protect the Russian supremacy over Singkiang and the Pamirs. A secret treaty seemed to have been concluded between Tibet and Russia in which the Czar promised to prevent the English from entering Tibet. This rumour was corroborated by the British Minister in Peking on 2 August 1902.[139] Russian activities in Tibet posed challenge to the British imperialists. They felt that the presence of Russian army in Tibet would complicate matters in South Asia and undermine British prestige in the Orient. The Anglo-Russian rivalry had its impact on Nepal. Her commercial privileges and political influence in Tibet were affected by this rivalry. Although Nepal was not prepared to meet the situation, she had to adjust her policy and remain a strong element in Tibetan affairs. It is true that Nepal was bound by treaty to assist Tibet if she was invaded but the time was not favourable for Nepal to render such assistance. National security were the two significant factors that compelled Prime Minister Chandra Shamsher to assist the British Mission. The Prime Minister felt that the extraterritorial rights of his country in Tibet would be affected by the presence of Russia in Lhasa.[140]

This policy of Chandra Shamsher was however, not favourable to the commercial interests of the country. He sacrificed a profitable position in commerce to achieve a political goal in Tibet. The British Government had nothing to give Chandra Shamsher in reward in proportion to what he had done in order to prevent the growth of Russian influence in Lhasa. From a commercial point of view it was "undoubtedly a foolhardy act." The major loss of Nepal was in the profit on the entrepot trade through Kathmandu and the Nepal Government's Customs profit on it.[141] Hence, with the opening of present century, the foreign trade of Nepal became largely oriented towards India. It was mentioned in a French paper, *Moniteur Official du Commerce*, that Prime Minister Chandra Shamsher created in his royal palace (Thapathali Darbar) an important Bureau of external commerce, at the head of which was his brother. The Bureau had a good deal of correspondence with foreign countries. The Prime Minister had regular business relations with the Hong-Kong and Shanghai Banking Corporation. It also mentioned that Sylvan Levi, Professor of the College de France, had entered into intimate relations with the Nepalese. Since that time the Prime Minister often asked for catalogues and samples of French produce. The paper expressed the hope that the French traders and industrialists would secure profit by the desire of the Nepalese Darbar to enter into trade relations with France. It added that Nepal would be an interesting market for French merchants and goods.[142]

The British were a jealous commercial people. They did not like any country to have good commercial relations with Nepal. They had placed restrictions on Nepal in respect of free commercial intercourse with other European countries. The British themselves were partly responsible for the traditionally exclusive policy of the Nepalese Government. The Nepalese policy of exclusion and non-intercourse with foreigners was from the British point of view an insurance against foreign intrigue in this strategically important country, and so they did not allow Nepal to establish contact with any Western power. In 1862, when Jang Bahadur wished to meet the rulers of France, Austria and Russia as an ambassador of an "independent state", the Government of India warned him that political relations with foreign powers would be prejudicial to Nepal's interest. The British Government's attitude regarding Nepal's contact with foreign powers remained unchanged for quite some time. It discouraged Europeans from visiting Nepal.[143] Thus, when the British heard about the possibilities of French trade with Nepal they made an enquiry about it from the British Resident in Nepal. In reply Colonel C. W. Ravenshaw, the British Resident in Nepal, wrote to the officiating Secretary to the Government of India that there was no such commercial Bureau in Nepal as mentioned in a French paper. There was certainly a foreign goods department attached to the Jinsi Adda, which dealt with Government store in the Public Works Department, and certain of the Prime Minister's domestic requirements. The Department also obtained a few French articles like glasswares, furniture and miscellaneous articles from Paris by way of an experiment. The only French Firm with which the Jinsi Adda Department had any dealing was *Au Bon Marche, Fillot Bicois Lucet and Cie. Paris" and Monsiur Levi's good offices* had been utilised to see that the best things were sent for the price paid. Beyond that Levi did not appear to have taken any action to promote commercial relations between France and Nepal. The British Resident further added, "....the foreign trade in Nepal so far as the import of European manufacture is concerned, may be said to be almost exclusively monopolised by "Messrs D.J. Keymer and Company of No. 1, Whitefairs Street, London."[144]

Chandra Shamsher like his brother Bir Shamsher, took steps to remove country spirit shops from near the border of both the countries. The price of Indian wine was high in comparison with the Nepalese country spirit. Therefore, there was a tendency to smuggle Nepalese wine. By this time, the Government of India was also keen to remove the distillery shops to a distance of two miles from the border of both the territories and to make the borders a "zone free of country spirit."[145] The Nepalese Government informed that the leases of the spirit shops in Nepal had about a year to run before they expired. The Darbar was prepared to remove the shops before the lease terminated, although it would cause a certain amount of hardship to the lessee. It was suggested that the clearance might take place after the rains and the most convenient time would be January or February of 1909. The Nepalase Government also informed that the Prime Minister of Nepal would like to have timely notice of the dates for the removal of the shops so that it might take place simultaneously on both sides of the border and accordingly issued the necessary instructions to the officials.[146] But this proposal was not implemented to the full.

Chandra Shamsher did not care for the development of trade and commerce of the country. Large scale economic development was neither his object nor was it feasible. The construction of the means of communication and transport in an extremely hilly region with numerous rivers and streams was an enormously expensive undertaking for a country with an annual revenue of only fifteen million rupees. Taxation was an unpopular means; it would hit the poorer sections hard because the vested interests of the nobility could not touched. But the greatest impediment to economic development was the Rana economic system itself. Under this system the entire revenue of the country went into the ruling Prime Minister's private treasury. The death of the Prime Minister involved the emptineses of the treasury and the succeeding administration started with no money at all. The progress of the country depended entirely on the whims of the ruling Premier and was determined by the amount of money he had been able to keep.[147]

In spite of all these impediments, Indo-Nepal trade continued to flourish during the Premiership of Chandra Shamsher. Although the export of grain and jute from Nepal decreased[148] and the import of piece goods, twist and yarn and salt increased,[149] the balance of trade was in favour of Nepal.[150] A considerable upward trend in the Nepalese exports which had set in 1905 seemed to have continued till the outbreak of the first World War in 1914, notwithstanding a brief setback during 19๋6-7.[151]

The commodity composition in Nepal export trade was changed during the rule of Chandra Shamsher. The forest products and herbal plants which predominated in the overall exports of the country in the earlier decades had been replaced by food grains. Rice emerged as the major export commodity.[152] Apart from the Younghusband mission of 1904, the First World War was another event which affected Indo-Nepal trade. It remained almost stationary during the first three years of war. The trans-frontier overland statistics recorded the exports from and imports into Nepal at around the stationary level of Rs 3.95 crores and Rs 2.00 crores respectively.[153] The world war also affected Nepal's International trade through India. Indo-Nepal trade started after declining 191?-13 The decline was as much as 20 per cent in case of Nepalese trade with Bihar. "This period is marked by world events of circumscribed area of commerce, restricted trade with neutral countries, trade restrictions, difficulties of foreign exchange and tonnage."[154] The restrictions of the Indian foreign trade were removed only when the war ended. There was a quick restoration of foreign trade due to peace in Europe and its return to political normalcy. Due to heavy dependence of Nepal on Indio, Indo-Nepalese trade had been interlinked with Indo-European trade. It was for this reason that the import of linseed from Nepal decreased by 28 per cent in the year 1912 due to small demand in Europe. Similarly, in the year 1913-14, the import of hides and skin from Nepal into India showed a considerable decline of 63 per cent due to decline in overseas exports from the Calcutta port.[155] India and Nepal had been co-sufferers in matters of foreign trade so far as the international market was concerned.[156]

Government monopoly

The Rana Government also followed the traditional system of monopoly. Tobacco, salt, ghee, raw cotton, copper piece, soap, cigarettes were Government monopoly. The forest products such as timber, ivory, bunkas, wax, honey and lac and the medicinal herbs such as pipal, bay leaves, chireta, musk and dhup wood were also monopolised by the Government.[157] There were two systems of monopoly, viz. direct monopoly and indirect monopoly. The direct monopoly was popularly known as the Amanat system in which Government Officials were appointed to carry out the monopoly. The indirect system involved the contract system or "theeka" which was commonly used as Ijara in which 'theekadar' controlled the monopoly.

This system affected the interests of the Indian merchants, who dealt in articles imported from India.[158] The British Resident Colonel G. Ramsay was naturally irritated at this system. Although the engagement of 1839 had no validity, he claimed that monopolies were directly contradictory to the spirit of the engagement. He sought instruction from the Government of India as to "what steps His Excellency the Viceroy and Governor-General-in-Council may desire me to take in cases in which monopolies already have been, or hearafter may be, established at Kathmandu in articles of imports from Britain Provinces.[159] The Governor-General-in-Council informed him that he did not wish him to move in the matter of monopolies of which he had complained.[160] The British Indian Government had also monopoly in some of the articles such as and salt[161] opium in India.[162]

G. Ramsay reported to the Indian Government that due to lack of opposition in Nepal fresh restrictions were placed upon internal trade and new monopolies were created. He added that Subha Dharma Narayan, the Nepalese merchant had had a great influence upon the Darbar and acquired monopolies. Jang Bahadur established a government monopoly over oil, tobacco, sugar, grain of all kinds, cotton, salt, ghee and other necessaries of life. Nearly all the Sardars were engaged in trade in one way or the other. Many of them had monopoly over timber on behalf of the Darbar, others advanced money to the Newar merchants who dealt in all kinds of miscellaneous goods from British provinces and used to give a portion of their profit to these Sardars.[163] G. Ramsay reported that the Sardars were playing in the hands of each other in monopolysing the trade. He thought that the monopoly was of little advantage to them but was ruinous to the poor classes. This system was seriously and visibly affecting the wellbeing of the people and properity of the country. In the opinion of the Resident the monopoly was like "the killing of the goose for the sake of its golden eggs."[164]

In 1863 Jang Bahadur had tried to control the price of soap in the valley. For that purpose Iraqis were induced to sign muchulkas to sell their soap at the rate of two tolas weight for a piece instead of its former rate of 1½ tolas. They signed the muchulkas because it was only for one year. But again in 1864, Jang Bahadur called them to execute similar muchulkas. When they refused to sign, the Prime Minister issued an order that the soap trade would be controlled by Subha Dharma Narayan and warned that any person who sold it without his licence, or at a higher price than the Darbar might fix for it, would be severely punished. According to him, it was done for the benefit of the people because the Iraqis were making unreasonably large profits by the sale of soap. Later on the Prime Minister cancelled the order and informed the Iraqis that they were free to carry out their trade as they pleased. Now he wanted to reduce the price by encouraging the merchants to sell the soap at a low price. The Resident was happy at this act of Jang Bahadur and remarked that this would promote rather than impede trade.[165]

The monopoly over tobacco was also controlled by Subba Dharma Narayan. No one was allowed to sell tobacco without his license. The British Resident reported that Subba imported tobacco of a very inferior quality which was adulterated by having been mixed with other leaves. He wanted to make it clear that the price was disproportionately high to the quality of tobacco.[166]

The timber trade was the monopoly of the Nepal Government. In 1858 all the timber districts of Nepal were formed to different contractors. The agents of both the vendor and purchaser could arrange and adopt measures for the purchase and sale of timber.[167] From 1868 the Nepal Government employed their own officials under the Amanat system to cut down timber which was afterwards sold by auction at different depots.[168] After 1877, timber was no longer sold to contractors in the forests. It was cut by the Darbar Agency and carried to the depot where it was sold by auction.[169] There were twenty-two forest depots in Nepal where timber was sold by the Government. The Government of Nepal did not allow the merchants from India to fell trees and remove them from the forest for themselves. On 11 November 1880, the Government of Nepal informed the Resident that the mode of transaction in timber in all the depots could not remain always the same.[170]

In 1861, Nabgopal Mukherjee, a sub-Overseer in the Public Works Department, wanted to obtain 6,000 saul wood for Government purpose. Major Pearse, Commissioner at Sugauli, requested the British Resident in Nepal, to interfere in this matter. The Resident refused to interfere and explained, "The Durbar will not enter into any direct dealings with, or order the delivery of a single log of wood to, any parties, be they private traders or contractors on the part of our Government." The Resident suggested that the sub-Overseer should make his own arrangements with various agents on the border who had the right to sell timber.[171] The Government of Nepal appointed agents from east to west of the Nepal frontier to make necessary arrangements for timber trade.

Firewood was also monopolised by the Government of Nepal. The system of monopoly instantly doubled the price of firewood. The poor wood cutters suffered heavily on this account. They had to spend four or five days in a week away from the family to sell firewood. There was a hue and cry against the rising price of firewood. Ultimately, after about a month the arrangement was changed, and firewood then nearly resumed its ordinary price.[172]

General Bhat Jang, the Cousin of Jang Bahadur, had obtained monopoly over the forest from Kalia Peak (lying in the north of the British Residency) to Bagdawar upon the mountain of Sheopuri, for which he engaged to pay annually a sum of Rs 18,000. He was also permitted to make necessary arrangements with the help of woodcutters. The woodcutters were not allowed to cut a single piece of stick without his license, which was difficult to acquire because of its high cost which he had imposed. The woodcutters, who formerly used to sell wood in the market, were thus exploited, finding it difficult to support their family.[173]

There was similar exploitation of the people living in and around the Kathmandu valley by the system of monopoly. The inhabitants of Bulu area of Lalitpur district in the Kathmandu Valley were under the obligation to supply charcoal to the Government by rotation. Each household required to cut wood and manufacture charcoal for fourteen days in a year. The inhabitants of other villages, including Sunaguthi and Thecho, were under the obligation to transport charcoal to prescribed destinations. These arrangements had been reconfirmed in the course of the revenue settlements of 1854 and 1868. There was no other obligation imposed on them. But in 1871, levies totalling Rs 4 or 4½ were imposed on each household instead of the obligation to supply charcoal. The arrangement continued for sixteen years from 1871 to 1887. The economic condition of the people belonging to these areas, was wretched. They did not have a single piece of rice land, while their Pakho land (barren land) did not yield adequate food to meet their needs for the whole year. Even on these lands they could grow food only after maintaining a watch day and night to protect them from bear, monkeys, birds and rats. If they were unable to continue the watch even for a single moment, their maize and other crops would be eaten up by wild birds and animals. Even if they succeeded in harvesting the crops, the quantity would barely suffice to meet their need for six months in a year. They gathered wild fruits and roots to feed their families. It was under such conditions that they had discharging their obligation to the government. In addition to this, after 1887 the villagers were brought under obligation to pay Rs. 4-4½ as well as to supply firewood as usual. Thus the people had to fulfil a double obligation. The villagers submitted a petition to the Government against extra obligation. Ultimately, the Prime Minister abolished the previous obligation of cutting and supplying firewood and remitted some of the amounts of taxation.[174]

Wax and papers[175] were also monopolised by the Government of Nepal. On May 1862, a public notice was issued to the village headmen and producer of wax and paper in which the monopolists were under the obligation to supply wax of pure quality (Galawal) everyday in the stipulated quantity and also to supply additional quantities when required at the rate of Rs 2½ per dharni. Similarly monopolists were also under the obligation to supply writing paper to the palace at the rate of one anna per dhep (20 sheets) in the required quantities. The notification also mentioned that the Government had received reports that Jagirdars and Birta owners did not let the monopolists procure wax and paper produced in the areas under their jurisdiction and made their own arrangements for the sale of both the commodities. It warned them not to do so.[176]

In June 1879, Sahu Ram Das, the monopolist of paper and wax, complained that the wax and paper were being sold elsewhere in contravention of the monopoly regulations. The Government Officials also procured papers from other sources. He asked how he could operate these monopalies and pay the stipulated amounts to the Government if the practice continued to exist. He, therfore, requested that an order be issued prescribing a fine amounting to double the profit that would have accrued to the monopolist, and confiscation of the commodities, if wax and paper were sold by anyone to persons other than the monopolist. The Petition Office (Hukum Nikasai Jhagada Patti Ek Lambur Adda) recommended that such an order be issued according to section 25 of the Law on Revenue Contracts (Rairakamko) mentioned in Civil code (Muluki Ain) and the terms and conditions stipulated with the monopolist. The Council (Bharabari) accepted the recommendation and directed the Court of Customs to issue a notification accordingly.[177]

The Government of Nepal exercised monopoly on copper also. In June 1900, the Amanat system for the management of copper, iron, and lead mines in the Eastern hills of Nepal was abolished. But in other parts the Amanat system continued. The monopoly was given to Dittha Bhaktadhwaj Chhetri on jhara basis for a three-year period. Accordingly, the jharadar was under the obligation to pay Rs 10,301 to the Government every year, and to supply copper and lead in the required quantities to the Sadar Jinsikhana in Kathmandu at the rate of Rs 3-12 dharni for copper and Rs 1-12 for lead. the ijardar was allowed to use inferior copper for the manufacture of utensils. However, he was denied authority to mint coins.[178]

The copper monopoly in the Eastern hills of Nepal led to a scarcity of the metal for the maunfacture of utensils. The use of even scrap copper for this purpose required a permit from the monopolist. The coppersmiths had to go on journey for eight or nine days to acquire copper. The local coppersmiths, therefore, prayed that they be allowed to import copper from India on payment of import duties. The Government, however, rejected the demand and reconfirmed the ban to import copper.[179]

The Government monopoly for export of goat and sheep skins was given to Jamaluddin Ranke, one of the Iraqi merchants, in the Kathmadu valley. He had obtained a contract for monopoly procurement and export of hides and skins (Charra rakam) in Eastern Nepal north of the Churia hills. Another person was given the monopoly in the South of Churia hills. The Iraqi merchant was informed that his jurisdiction did not extend to areas in the south.[180]

Rakam Bandobasta Adda (Revenue Contracts Office) received offers from different Muslim and Iraqi merchants, for monopoly

Dev Shamsher with his wife Sharada
and his son Mussorie in India after his deposition (c.1910).

Prime Minister Dev Shamshe

wed the monopolicy of trade.

Prime Minister Dev Shamsher with
the King of Nepal Prithvi Bir, 1901.

procurement and export of goat skins from Mahottari, Sarlahi and Rauthat districts of Nepalese Tarai. Finally in November 1904 the monopoly was given to Mahmud Raki, who was staying at Indra Chok in Kathmandu.. He promised to pay Rs. 5,751 for the period of 2 years, 7 months and 8 days. It was the highest amount offered for contract. Mahmud Raki made the offer on behalf of Makhu Miya, a resident of Gorakhpur in India. The monopolist was permitted to procure skins of goats and sheep slaughtered for meat, or dying natural death, at prescribed prices. He had no right to demand skins consumed by the owner, or used by him for domestic and agricultural purposes. The monopolist was permitted to procure[181] only such skins as were actually offered for sale. He was empowered to seize skins being smuggled to India and hand over the smuggler to the Birgunj Revenue Office for appropriate action. He was also required to pay export duty at the prescribed rate on skins exported to India.[182]

Kharidar Krishna Prasad and Bhairav Prasad, residents of Bhotahiti in Kathmandu, had been granted monopoly in cigarette trade. The total payment stipulated by them under the monopoly amounted to Rs. 100/a year for two districts of Lamjung and Kaski. On November 19, 1904, the Prime Minister Chandra Shamsher ordered that the monopoly be granted to Principal Babu Batukkrishna Maitra without inviting bids. Under the monopoly, the Principal was required to pay Rs 258.30 yearly, or Rs. 774/80 during the three years for which the monopoly was valid. The regulations were promulgated in the name of the monopolist, which provided that if any other person was found trading in cigarettes in the area under his jurisdiction, he shou ld be taken to the Rakam Bandobast Adda (Revenue Administration Office) for necessary action. He would be punished with confiscation of his goods for the first offence. If he repeated the offence his goods would be confiscated, and a fine of an equal amount would be imposed. It was also mentioned that no duty would be collected on cigarettes brought for the use of His Majesty, the Prime Minister. The above mentioned action was to be taken if cigarettes were smuggled in by Nepali or British Indian post or otherwise. Customs offices were ordered not to collect any duty on cigarettes imported by the monopolist. However, consignments were to be opened for customs inspection. The amount stipulated by the monopolist was payable in four instalments during the three years yeriod. No remissions was to be allowed in any circumstances.

Meanwhile, the monopoly trade in cigarettes in other parts of the Kingdom had been given to Subba Kalidas Upadhyaya, Bhairav Prasad Upadhyaya and Krishna Prasad Upadhyaya. The former got monopoly in the Kathmandu valley on payment of Rs. 7000/- yearly (Nepalese currency). The remaining two persons got the monopoly in the hill except Kaski and Lamjung districts and in Tarai districts respectively. The monopolists were to pay Rs 720/for hilly region and Rs 2,530 (Indian currency) yearly for Tarai area. On the expiry of their terms, fresh bids were to be invited. The highest bids were offered by Principal Babu Batukrishna Maitra. The Principal offered Rs 22,551.83 N.C. for the Kathmandu Valley, Rs 1,135.28 for the hill region except Kaski and Lamjung and Rs 3,584.10 (annas) for the Tarai region. On 17 December 1904, Prime Minister Chandra Shamsher ordered that the monopolies be granted to the Principal. The monopolies were valid for a three-year term. Regulations laid down for Kaski-Lamjung monopoly were made applicable to these monopolies also. The amounts stipulated by the monopolist were payable in four instalments every year.[183] It is interesting to note that the Principal[184] of a Nepalese College in the Capital was involved in the monopoly. This might have been because the Rana autocratic regime wanted to control intellectuals by providing monopolies to the College Principal.

The Government monopoly of cardamom was governed by the Law of revenue collection (Rairakam Ko), contained in the Muluki Ain (Legal Code) promulgated in 1854. It provided, "In case it is proved that cardamom and other commodities which must be sold only in galas and other Government establishments are sold elsewhere, these shall be confiscated, and the seller and the purchaser shall each be punished with a fine amounting to half the value thereof."[185] In November 1861 Chandrabir Bista Chhetri was appointed Captain with seven golas and Udayapur Gadhi under his jurisdiction to carry on business in cardamom.

His duties included state trading in cardamom and other commodities. The Rana Government had established a cardamom Depot (Alainchi-Kothi) at Patna in Bihar and started exporting cardamom through it. The regulations were issued in the name of Chandrabir Bista Chhetri, Section 8 of these regulations mentioned "Purchase on behalf of the golas such commodities arriving there from the hill region as can be traded with profit at prices current according to the season. Commodities purchased in this manner, including cardamom, cardamom seeds, wax, fish (sidra), soap nut (rittha), pindalu, long pepper (pipla), other medicinal herbs and drugs (piplamul, bikh, bikhma, jatamasi, silajit, kutki), lac, musk, yak-tails, ganja, Charas, and borax, shall be despatched to Patna after making arrangements for payment of wages to porters and boatmen."[186]

Sometimes the Nepalese Government had to suffer loss of revenue on account of the system of monopoly. The monopoly of the cardamom trade entailed such a loss. In January 1901, the stock of this commodity in the possession of the Nepalgunj Bazar Adda amounted to 824 1/4 maunds. The cost price was calculated at Rs 29 per maund. The firm of Mahabir Ramphal in Nepalgunj offered to lift the entire stock of cardamom in the possession of the Nepalgunj Bazaar Adda within eight months if the rate was fixed at Rs 23-0 per maund (4 *sers*, or 92 *tolas*). Sardar Dhundi Raj Shahi of the Naya Muluk Goswara Adda ordered the Nepalgunj Bazaar Adda to invite tenders on the basis of the offer made by Mahabir Ramphal. However, no other tender was received. The total amount offered by Mahabir Ramphal was only Rs 19, 421-10½ at rate of Rs 23-9 per maund. The Nepalgunj Bazaar Adda thus suffered a loss of Rs 4, 481-13.[187]

Sometime it was found that the Central Government sent some officials to collect Cardamom in eastern and western Nepal. Otherwise, the State trading operation had the right to export it. The state trading authority at Brahmadeo Mandi in far western Nepal had monopoly to export cardamom.[188]

The export of hides from Dailekh, Surkhet and Butwal was monopolised by the Government. In Butwal monopoly included horns also. The monopolists were under the obligation to pay the amount fixed by the Government in addition to export duty. In March 1886, Bidulal, the resident of Chilli in Dang district, was given monopoly on the payment of Rs 500 every year for a three-year period in addition to export duty. His area of monopoly was confined to Dang district. He promised to purchase hides at fair prices. Bidulal was bound to purchase hides sold by the people of Dang district willingly.[189]

The import of Tibetan salt was also a monopoly of the Government.[190] Nepal imported Indian salt only when there was friction between Nepal and Tibet. People mainly in the Northern part of the country preferred to use Tibetan salt. They explained to the British Resident that they were unable to import salt from as far away as India. The British Resident remarked "I believe they will be delighted at any arrangement by which they can obtain Tibetan salt again, dirty though it be."[191] He futher added, "It will be seen that the exports largely increased when the Nepalese fell out with the Tibetans. If they make up their differences we must expect the trade to fell up."[192]

Dr Daniel wright, the British residency Surgeon, mentioned that broad cloth was the monopoly of the Government. But Girdlestone, the British Resident in Nepal, did not agree with his view. He stated that the broadcloth for the army was only monopolised. The clothing of the army was procured readymade from Calcutta on contract from the tailoring firm of Rankeen & Co. A report from Gorakhpur mentioned elephant as the subject of monopoly. But, practically no valuable elephant was called to leave Nepal.[193]

The commercial policy of all the Rana Prime Ministers was guided by their desire to monopolise the lucrative Indo-Nepal trade. All the senior civil and military officials of the country were engaged in monopolistic trade. Monopoly rights were sold to favourite merchants, who remitted a share of their huge profit to the Prime Minister. When the monopolists created artificial scarcity of goods, the Nepalese Government asked the British Government's help for the supply of those goods from India at reasonable prices. But the British Government usually refused to help on such occasions,[194] for two reasons. The first reason was that such help meant playing into the hands of monopolists and secondly it would have been against the commercial interest of the British Indian merchants in Nepal. The British Resident regarded the system of monopoly "as one of the crying abuses in the administration of Nepal."[195] F. Fenvey, the Officiating British Resident in Nepal reported that the Banking firm of Dhurba Narain and Co., who were closely connected in pecuniary matters with the late Sir Jung Bahadur, enjoyed a contract for the exclusive sale of tobacco for chewing and smoking, and for dried fish. The result was that tobacco was both bad and dear, and the cost of one of the most common articles of food was greatly increased. This monopoly had been abolished by Sir Ranodip Singh, who had also taken off for one year the toll of one pice on every person entering the valley. The loss to the state involved in these concessions was about Rs 13,000 per annum.[196]

The Rana Government of Nepal followed the system of monopoly vigorously. According to the law on Revenue Collection (Rakam Tahasil Ko), "No person shall sell elsewhere any commodity which has been placed under a monopoly by the Government, and must be sold at the prescribed place, or which can be sold only on payment of a duty. In case he does so, the value of the commodity shall be realized from him, and he shall be punished with a fine of an equal amount, or with an amount ranging between rupees 20 and rupees 500 or with imprisonment for a term ranging between four months and nine years, according to the gravity of the offence, at the discretion of the Prime Minister."[197]

The system of monopoly was adopted because it was the only way to divert the attention of the Sardars, Officers and intellectuals from politics to commerce. The Rana Government wanted to make them satisfied with the monopoly of lucrative trade. These people used to raise their voices whenever their commercial interests were ignored by the Government.[198] In 1901 the country gained a profit of Rs 59,075 from the system of monopoly in different articles.[199]

REFERENCES

1. Ramakant, *Indo-Nepal Relations 1916–1917.* Delhi, 1968, p. 356.
2. Piers Blaikie, John Cameron, David Seddon, *Nepal in Crisis, Growth and Stagnation at the Periphery.* Delhi, 1980, p. 31.
3. Foreign Department. Political A. October 1873. No. 134. Secretary of the Society for the Encouragement of Arts, Manufacturers and Commerce to the Secretary of State for India, Indian Office, London. dated 4 June 1873, No. 10. (N.A.I.)
4. Foreign Department, Political A. August 1864, No. 51. Colonel G. Ramsay, British Resident in Nepal to Colonel H. M. Durand, C.B. Secretary to the Government of India in the Foreign Department, with the Governor General, Simla, No. 1, dated 6 July 1864. (N.A.I.)
5. Ludwig F. Stiller, S J., "A note on Himalayan trade". *Journal of the Tribhuvan University. Kirtipur*, Nepal, Vol. 4, No. 1. November 1972. Kathmandu, p. 25.
6. *Ibid.* pp. 25–26.
7. Daniel Wright. *Nepal, History of the Country and People*, Delhi, 1983, p. 69.
8. Foreign Department. Revenue. A. June 1879. No. 1–2. Secretary of State for India. London Office to Government of India. dated 13 February 1879. (N.A.I.)
9. *Ibid.* July 1880. Nos 194–95. A note of the revenue Secretary to the Government of India, Foreign Department. (N.A.I.)
10. Foreign Department, Revenue A. August 1877, No. 22.
11. Foreign Department. Political A. July 1880 Nos 194–9.
12. Jahar Sen, *Indo–Nepal Trade in the nineteenth century.* Calcutta, 1977, p. 139.
13. Foreign Department. Political A. July 1880, No. 196.
14. Revenue A. August 1877. No. 22.
15. Henry Ambrose Oldfield, *Sketches from Nepal.* London. 1880, Vol. I, No. 2., p. 201.
16. Kanchanmoy Majumdar. *British Impact on Nepal. Bengal Past and Present.* January–June, 1971, p. 5.
17. S. K. Jha, "British India's policy towards Nepal". *Journal of Bihar Research Society.* Vol. LX. Pts 1–4, p. 214.
18. Ramakant, op. cit. p. 316–17.

19. "Free trade does not mean that there shall be no taxes but that taxes shall be levied solely with a view to revenues, and not partly for revenue and partly for protection." C.J. Hamilton, *The Trade Relations between England and India (1600–1896)*. 1919, Reprint, Delhi 1975, p. 237.
20. Rishikesh Shah, *Essays in the Practice of Government of Nepal,* Delhi 1982, p. 87.
21. *Ibid.*
22. M.H. Ansari. *Nepal in World Affairs.* (unpublished Ph. D. Thesis), Vikram University, Ujjain, 1974, p. 13.
23. Political A. August, 1864, No. 51. Colonel G. Ramsay, Resident in Nepal to Colonel H.M. Durand, C.B. Secretary to Government of India, in the Foreign Department, with the Governor General, Simla. No. 1, dated 6 July 1864.
24. *Il id.*
25. Jang Bahadur supplied the following statement showing the length, breadth, the thickness and price of timber.

No. of timber	Length of timber in feet	Breadth of timber in inches	Thickness of timber in inches	Price Rs
200 (Beams)	32 to 33	15	12	40 each
400 (")	27	12	9	30 "
800 (")	22	11	8	15 "
5000 (")	12	8	5	5 "
15,000 (Poles)	20 to 40	8	2 to 3 1/2 in dimension	6 "

Foreign consultation 31 December 1858. No. 1717. F.B. Norris to L. Bouring, Private Secretary to the Governor General. 8 April 1858; Ibid No. 17–25. Khareeta from Jang Bahadur to Lord Canning, Viceroy of India dated (4 Jesth 1915) 31 May 1858 (N.A.I.)

26. Abrol Mridula, *British Relations with Frontier States (1863–1873)*. New Delhi, 1974, pp. 46–47.
27. Ansari, *op. cit.*
28. Leo E. Rose, *Nepal Strategy for Survival.* Bombay, 1971. p. 132.
29. Foreign Department, Foreign Consultation. 26 August 1859. No. 212. Translation of Muchulka written by the Principal Iraqi merchants who have Firms in Indra Chowk in Nepal. dated (Asarh Sudi 6, Saturday, Sambat 1915) 17 July 1858.

30. Ibid. No. 211–14. Colonel G. Ramsay, the British Resident in Nepal to Cegil Beadon, Secretary to the Government of India in the Foreign Department, Fort William. No. 100 dated 6 August 1858. (N.A.I.)

31. The Assistant Resident in Nepal reported that the Muchulka did not include Kashmiri and Newar merchants, the former as well as the latter being subjects of Nepal. Foreign Consultation. 20 May 1859. No. 260–262. Captain C. H. Byers, Assistant British Resident in Nepal to G. F. Edmonstomed. Foreign Department, Allahabad dated 24 August 1858 (N.A.I.)

32. *Ibid.*

33. *Ibid.*

34. *Ibid.*

35. Ibid. 26 August 1859. No. 213. Cegil Beadon, Secretary to the Government of India in the Foreign Department. Fort William to Colonel G. Ramsay, the Resident in Nepal. No. 5280, dated 26 August 1859. (N.A.I.)

36. Foreign Department, External A. 77. 14 October 1859, No. 170. Abstract translation of a yaddast from Maharaja Jang Bahadur to the address of Ramsay, the British Resident in Nepal. dated the 10th of Guruwar Thursday Sambat 1916 Corresponding with 22nd of September 1859. (N.A.I.).

37. A. Husain, *British India's Relations with the Kingdom of Nepal from 1857 to 1947* (unpublished Ph. D. Thesis). University of Minnesota, U.S.A., 1965, p. 174.

38. Foreign Department, Political A. August 1864, No. 51.

39. Foreign Department, Political A. December, 1862. No. 398. Lieutenant Colonel G. Ramsay, the Resident in Nepal to Under Secretary to the Government of India. Foreign Department. Fort William dated 18 February 1862. (N.A.I.)

40. Ramakant, *op. cit.* p. 321.

41. B. H. Hodgson, G. Ramsay and Charles Girdleston were the prominent among them.

42. Adhikari, *op. cit.* p. 190. Cited from the Register kept in Kausi Tosa Khana, Nepal, dated (Bikram Sambat 1920) 1863–64. An Order from Jang Bahadur to Lieutenant Buddhinath Upadhyaya regarding the opening of market in the Kanchanpur district.

43. *Ibid.*

44. *Ibid.*

45. *Ibid*, Cited from the Register kept in Kauri Tosa Khana, Nepal, dated (Bikram Sambat 1920) 1863-64. An order issued by Prime Minister Jang Bahadur to the people of Jagarkol, Salyan, Dang, Phalabang, Piuthan and Udayapur.
46. *Ibid.*
47. Political A. August, 1864, No. 51.
48. Foreign Consultation, 26 August 1859. No. 213.
49. Political A. August 1864, No. 51.
50. *Ibid.*
51. Jang Bahadur made it clear that similar restrictions were placed on the British subjects by their Government see *Ibid*.
52. *Ibid.*
53. Ramakant, *op. cit*, p. 321.
54. Politicai A. August 1964, No. 51.
55. *Ibid.*
56. Foreign Department, Political A, November 1862, No. 103-104. Colonel G. Ramsay, the British Resident in Nepal to Colonel H.M. Durand, Secretary to the Government of India in the Foreign Department. Fort William dated 16 October 1862. No. 24. (N.A I.)
57. Ibid. Secretary to the Government of India, Fort William, Foreign Department to the British Resident in Nepal, dated 19 November 1862. No. 1079. (N A.I.)
58. Revenue A. August 1877. Nos 1-4. K.W. Vol. Office notes. (N.A.I.)
59. *Ibid.*
60. Political A. August 1864, No. 51.
61. *Ibid*.
62. Revenue A, February 1879 No. 1. Department of Revenue, Agriculture and Commerce No. 328. dated 11 September 1978, K.W. No. 2. (N.A.I.)
63. Ramakant, *op. cit*. p. 320-21.
64. *Ibid.*
65. Political A, August 1864. No. 51.
66. Ramakant, *op. cit*. pp. 321-22.
67. Shushila Tyagi, *Indo-Nepalese Relations*. (1858-1914) Delhi, 1972. p. 103.
68. Revenue A. August 1877, No. 22.
69. *Ibid.*
70. Extra Supplement of Gazettee of India, August 14th 1875, p. 2. Cited in Husain, p. 128.

71. Political A, February 1875. No. 30.
72. Foreign Department. Revenne A. August 1877. Nos 1–4. K.W. No. 1. Office note.
73. Husain, *op. cit.* p. 123.
74. Kanchanmoy Majumdar. *op. cit.* p. 240.
75. *Ibid.*
76. *Ibid. Anglo–Nepalese Relations in the nineteenth century.* Calcutta, 1973, p. 8.
77. S. K. Jha, *op. cit.*, p. 215.
78. According to the law of succession the ruling Prime Minister would be succeeded first by all his brothers (or cousin) successively in order of seniority of age and then in the same manner by all his sons (or nephews). Cited from Satis Kumar, *Rana Poliiy in Nepvl, Origin and Grnwth.* Delhi 1967. p. 64.
79. *Ibid.*
80. S. K. Jha, *op. cit.*
81. Perceval Landon, *Nepal*, Vol. II, London, 1928, p. 64.
82. Foreign Department, Political A. 1879. No. 134. Charles Girdlestone, the British Resident in Nepal to A.C. Lyall, the Secretary to the Govern ment of India. dated 30 June 1879. No. 22. (N.A.I.)
83. *Ibid.*
84. *Ibid.*
85. *Ibid.*
86. *Ibid.* December 1880. No. 38. C. E. R. Girdlestone, Resident in Nepal to A. C. Lyall, Secretary to the Govt. of India. dated 25 September 1880. No. 32 p. (N.A.I.)
87. North Western province Report for 1878–79 para 3. Cited in margin. *Ibid.*
88. *Ibid.*
89. The Times Weekly Edition, August 13, 1880, cited in *Ibid.*
90. *Ibid.*
91. *Ibid.* Memorandum of Verbal Representation, put in writing at the request of the Prime Minister of Nepal. Nepal Residency. dated 18 July 1879. No. 136. (N.A.I.)
    Ibid. Translation a memorandum from Prime Minister of Nepal. dated 12
92. *Ibid.* Translation of a memorandum from Prime Minister of Nepal. dated 12 August 1879. No. 139.
93. *Ibid.*

94. *Ibid.*
95. The second generation of the Ranas was called Shamsher, the first being Jang Bahadur and his six brothers who staged the coup d'eat in 1846.
96. Husain. *op. cit.* pp. 131–33.
97. Kanchanmoy Majumbar. *Political Relations between India and Nepal 1877-1923.* Delhi, 1973, pp. 32–33.
98. Husain, *op. cit.* p. 135.
99. Foreign Department, Secret E. June 1893. No. 389. Lieutenant Colonel H. Wylie, C.S.I. Officiating Resident in Nepal to the Secretary to the Secretary to the Government of India. dated 27 may 1893. No. 35 p. (N.A.I.).
100. *Ibid.* June 1884. No. 460. Government of India, Foreign Department Secret to the Right Honorable, the Earl of Kimberly,
101. *Ibid.*
102. Secret F. November 1884. No. 234 K.W. 3. Cited in Jahar Sen *op. cit.* p. 140.
103. A. Husain. *British Relations with Nepal 1857–1947.* London, 1971, p. 138.
104. *Ibid.*
105. *Ibid.*
106. Ghyana Mani Nepal. "Nepal Ko Dhan Vidashi Bankma" (Nepali) (Nepal's wealth in Foreign Bank). *Arthik Nepal* Kathmandu. November 1982, p. 18–19.
107. *Ibid.* p. 21–22.
108. Ghyan Mani Nepal. *op. cit.* p. 20.
109. *Ibid.* p. 22.
110. *Ibid.*
111. External. B. October 1897. No. 156. H. Wylie, The British Resident in Nepal to John Lang, Assistant Secretary to Foreign Department dated 11 August 1897. (N.A.I.)
112. *Ibid* John Lang, Assistant Secretary to Foreign Department, Government of India to H. Wylie, the British Resident in Nepal dated 22 September 1897. (N.A.I.)
113. Col. G.H.D. Gimlette, *Nepal and the Nepalese* London. (n.d.). p. 81.
114. Bhuwan Singh, "*Maharg Niwaran.*" (Nepali) (Priee Control Measure)–edited by Devi Chandra Shrestha. Kathmandu (2030 Kartik) 1973. p. 29.
115. External A. November 1897. No. 153. Colonel H. Wylie, Resident in Nepal to Captain H. Doly, Deputy Secretary to the Foreign Department Government of India. dated 17 May 1897. (N.A.I.)

116 *Ibid.* No. 156 (Demi Official) C.W. Balton, the Chief Secretary, Gevernment of Bengal Darjeeling to Captain H. Daly, Deputy Secretary to the Government of India. Foreign Department. dated 17 July 1897. (N.A.I.)

117. *Ibid.* No. 157. Report of North Western Provinces and Oudh, W. G. Jackson, Commissioner of Excise North Western Province to the Deputy Secretary to the Government of India. Foreign Department, dated 21 September, 1897. (N.A.I.)

118. *Ibid.* No. 156. (Demi-Official) Secretary to the Government of the North Western Provinces and Oudh to Captain H. Daly. Deputy Secretary to the Government of India. Foreign Department dated October 1897. (N.A.I)

119. Hc was imprisoned at that time. Bhuwan Singh. *op. cit.* p. 23.

120. *Ibid.* p. 19.

121. *Ibid.*

122. Political A, July 1881. No. 372–76.

123. Husain, *op. cit.* p. 139.

124. *Ibid.*

125. Husain. *op. cit.* p. 149.

126. Prem Uprety, *Nepal Tibet Relations 1850-1930 Years of Hopes, Challeange and Frustration*, Kathmandu 1980, p. 123.

127. Foreign Department, Secret E., Proceedings No. 197 of 1903.

128. "Nepal-Tibet Negotiations" Under Secretary, Government of India. Foreign Affairs, to the Military Department. September 26, 1903. p. 25. Cited in Uprety *op. cit.*

129. Foreign Ministry Nepal, Cha P ka No. 104 Maharaja Chandra to Colonel Harka Jung Thapa, Bada Hakim. Cited in *Ibid.*

130. Foreign Ministry of Nepal, Cha Poka No. 104. A conversatian between Col. Harka Jang Thapa and Col Younghusband at Ghoom Undated; Major Tek Bahadur Khatri to Maharaja Chandra, Kartik 4, 1961 (October 1904) cited in *Ibid.*

131. *Ibid.* Foreign Department, Secret E. Proceeding No. 147. of 1903 "Tibet Negotiations". Maharaj Chandra to the Four Kazis of Kasyal. Cited in ibid. p. 124.

132. *Ibid.* p. 125.

133. *Ibid.* p. 125-26.

134. Foreign Department, Secret E, Proceeding No. 999 of February 1905. Assistant Secretary. Government of India, Foreign Department to Lt Colonel C. W .Ravenshaw, October 20,1904. p. 35. cited in *Ibid.* p. 125.

135. Foreign Department, Secret E. February 1903. Nos 93–107, Cited in Niranjan Sharma, *op. cit.* p. 67.
136. Foreign Department, Secret External B, pro. No. 188 of February 1904, Maharaja Chandra to C. W. Ravenshaw, January 25, 1905. Cited in Prem R. Upreti. *op. cit.* np. 151.
137. Ludwig Z. Stiller, *op. cit.* p. 29.
138. Prem R. Upreti, *op. cit.* p. 121.
139. *Ibid.* p. 120.
140. *Ibid*, p. 122.
141. Ludwig F. Stiller, S. J. *op. cit.* p. 30.
142. Foreign Department. External B. March 1905. N. 1. Enclose 2. Translation of an extract from "Moniteur Official du Commerce" article for M. Raoul Bloch, page 17. (N.A.I.)
143. Kanchanmoy Majumdar, "British Impact on Nepal". pp. 19–20.
144. Foreign Department. External B. March 1905. No. 3. encloser 1652–1.2.5. Lieutenant Colonel C. W. Ravenshaw, the British Resident in Nepal to S.M. Fraser, Esquire, C. I. E. Officiating Secretary to the Govern ment of India, Foreign Department, Calcutta. dated 30 January 1905. No. 19. (N.A.I.)
145. Foreign Department, External A. October, 1908. No. 18–21. J.M. Holms, Chief Secretary to the Government of United Provinces to the Secretary to the Government of India, Finance Department. dated 28 February 1908. No. 104 (N.A.I.)
146. Foreign Department. External A. October 1908. Pro. No. 20. Lieutinant Colonel F.W.P. Macdonald, officiating Resident in Nepal to the Secretary to the Government of India in the Foreign Department. 24 August 1908 No. 109. (N.A.I.)
147. Kanchanmoy Majumdar, *op. cit.* p. 8.
148. Foreign Department, Secret E, December 1207, Nos 121–123. Annual General Report on Nepal for the year 1906–7. (N.A.I.)
149. Foreign Department. Secret E. August 1912. Pro. No. 23. Lieutenant Colonel H. L. Showers, Officiating Resident in Nepal to the Secretary to Government of India Foreign Department (Confidential) dated 11 July 1912. No. 88 (N.A.I.)
150. Foreign Department. Secret E. December, 1907. Nos 121–123.
151. Niranjan Sharma, *Nepal Foreign Trade* (unpublished Ph. D. Thesis) University of Delhi, 1968. p. 46.
152. *Ibid.* p. 45.

153. *Ibid.* p. 52.

154. P. C. Rawat, *Indo-Nepal Economic Relations.* Delhi. 1974. p. 58.

155. Imperial Gazetteer of India, 1908. Vol. xxi, p. 2.

156. *Ibid.*

157. Foreign Department. Revenue A. August 1877. No. 22.

158. Foreign Department, Political A. October 1864, Nos 63 Colonel Ramsay, Resident in Nepal to Colonel H. M. Durand (C.B., Secretary to Government of India, Foreign Department, dated 21 July 1864, No. 63. (N.A.I.)

159. *Ibid.*

160. Political A. October 1864. No. 64. Under-Secretary to the Government of India, Foreign Department with the Governor General to the Resident in Nepal. dated 13 September 1864. No. 483. (N.A.I.)

161. *Ibid.*

162. Revenue A. August 1877. No. 22.

163. *Ibid.* Political A. August 1864. No. 51.

164. *Ibld.* Foreign Consultant. 26. August 1859. No. 211.

165. *Ibid.* Political A. June 1864. No. 203. Colonel G. Ramsay, British Resident in Nepal to Colonel H.M. Durand, C.B. Secretary to the Government of India. dated 24 June 1864, No. 19.

166. Foreign Department. Political A. October 1864. No. 63.

167. Nepal Residency Records Register No. 10. pp. 41–42. Cited in Jahar Sen. "The Tune of Timber in Indo-Nepal Relations". *The Galcutta Historical Journal.* Vol. VII. No. 1. July-December 1982. p. 57.

168. *Ibid.* Register No. 13, Lawrence to Aitchison. dated 18 July 1870, pp. 77–78. Cited in *Ibid.*

169. The Gazetteer of the Provinces of Oudh 1877. Vol. I. p. 137.

170. *Ibid.*

171. Indian Embassy, Nepal Pre 1872 Records. Register No. 11, p. 94. Ramsay to Major Pearre. No. 30. dated 16 May 1861. Cited in Jahar Sen, *op. cit.* p. 58.

172. Foreign Department, Foreign Consultion, 26 August 1859, No. 211.

173. *Ibid.*

174. Mahesha Chandra Regmi, "Supply of firewood from Bulu" *Regmi Research Series.* Year 13, No. 3, 1 March 1981. pp. 44–45.

175. The paper manufacture of Nepal was incomparably than that of India. It was strong and dnrable as leather and quite smooth to write on. See

Brain H Hodgson "On the Native me}hod of Making the paper, denominated in Hindustan, Nepalese" *Journal of the Royal Asiatic Society of Bengal*. Vol. 1, No. 1 January 1832. p. 11.

176. Mahesha Chandra Regmi, "The Wax and Paper Monopolies" *Regmi Research Series*. Kathmandu. year 13, No. 11, November 1, 1981, p. 162.

177. *Ibid.*

178. *Ibid.* "The copper monopoly. A.D. 1900". *Regmi Research Series*. Kathmandu Year 14. No. 1–2. January Zebruary, 1982, p. 20.

179. *Ibid.*

180. *Ibid.* "Monoply for Export of Goat and sheep skins". *Regmi Research Series*. Kathmandu, year 13, No. 7, 1 July 1981, p. 101.

181. The procurement prices were fixed as follows :

Size	Price
Less than 30 inches in length	8 annas each
Damaged skins	—do—
More than 30 inches in length	12 annas

Cited in Ibid. p. 102.

182. *Ibid.*

183. *Ibid.* "Monoply trade in Cigarettes" *Regmi Research Series*. Kathmandu, Year 12, No. 11, 1 November 1980. p. 162–63.

184. Triratna Manandbar, "Rana Kalin Pancba Estihar", *Voice of History*. Journal of History Instruction Committee, Kathmandu, Vol. III 1976, p. 71.

185. M. C. Regmi, "Cardamom Farming in Nepal." *Regmi Research Series*, Year 15, No. 4, April 1983, p. 54.

186. *Ibid.* p. 55.

187. *Ibid.* "Sale of Cardamom in Nepalgunj". *Regmi Research Series*. p. 140

188. *Ibid.* "Stare Trading at Brahmadeo Mandi". *Regmi Research Series*. Kathmandu, year 13, No. 10. 1 October 1981, p. 145–46.

189. *Ibid.* "Export of Hides from Dang District" *Regmi Rcsearch Series*, Kathmandu, year 12, No. 10; 10 October, 1980, pp. 154–55.

190. Revenue A, August 1877, No. 22.

191. Foreign Department. External B. September 1895, No. 125. British Resident in Nepal to Mr Hayes Sadler, Assistant Foreign Secretary to the Government of India. dated 15 July 1895, No. 119. (N.A.I.)

192. *Ibid.*

193. Revenue A. August 1877. No. 22.

194. Shushila Tyagi, *op. cit.* p. 100.

195. Foreign Department, Political A. May 1877, No. 55. Z. Henrey, Officiation British Resident in Nepal to T.H. Thornton, Officiating Secretary to the Government of India. dated 26 March 1877. No. 12, A.P. (N.A.I.)

196. *Ibid*.

197. M. C. Regmi, "Smuggling of Cardamom". *Regmi Research Series.* Year 13, No. 5, May 1981, p. 76.

198. The Sardars were dead against the Nepalese Prime Minister Chandra Shamsher when their commercial interests in Tibet were ignored by him in 1903–4.

199. Revenue from miscellaneous monopolies in 1901 was as follows :

1.	Liquor monopoly in the rcgion between the Koshi and Trisuli rivers and Hetauda-Indrayani	Rs.	33,543
2.	Chaudhari levies	Rs.	13,475
3.	Wax monopoly	Rs.	3,908
4.	Paper monopoly in Marsyandi-Dudhkoshi Region (except Khinchet)	Rs.	3,771
5.	Monopoly in Charas	Rs.	3,711
6.	Monopoly in buffalo horn in the Kathmadu Valley	Rs.	667
	Total	Rs.	59 075

See, M.C. Regmi, "Notes on the Revenue System of Nepal during the 19th century." *Regmi Research Ssries.* year 11, No. 5, 1 May 1979. p. 68.

Volume and Exchange of Commodities

CHAPTER FOUR

4.1. Volume of commodities transacted

Compared with all the northern countries [1]India's trade with Nepal was quite significant.[2] In the period under review, the volume of articles exported from and imported into Nepal was higher than that of all these countries. The trade with Nepal constituted about 92 per cent of the whole trade carried across the frontier of Bengal.

In the year 1877-78, Nepal exported articles worth Rs 1,054,00/- and imported articles valued at Rs 633,000/-. The total registered trade of Nepal with British India was Rs 1,687,000/- of which more than two-third was conducted through Bengal.[3] This volume of trade tremendously increased in 1878-79. The registered international trade of Nepal with British India was valued at Rs 22,322,457 in that year. Nepal's export to India was valued at Rs 13,968,953/- and import from India worth Rs 8,355,504/- in 1878-79. Out of the total amount of export from and import into Nepal, the articles worth Rs 9,862,800/- were exported and Rs 6,437,479/- were imported through Bengal and the rest through North Western Provinces and Oudh.

The volume of Indo-Nepal trade decreased in the year 1879-80. The total value of trade was Rs 14,059,492/-. It was less by Rs 8,262,965/- than the previous year. However, both exports and imports into Nepal through North Western Provinces and Oudh increased to Rs 1,699,330/- as compared with the previous year. But the exports from Nepal through Bengal decreased that year by Rs 2,049,648/- as compared with N.W.P. and Oudh. The total registered trade with Bengal was also less by Rs 1,383,524/- as compared with the North-Western Provinces and Oudh. In that year Nepal exported articles worth Rs 7,834,770/- and imported articles worth Rs 6.224,722/-. In all the cases export from Nepal exceeded import, as will be clear from Table 1.

The British Resident in Nepal believed that the downward trend in the Indo-Nepal trade in 1879-80 was due to the trade policy pursued by the Nepalese Government.[4] However, a comparative study of the trends in India's foreign trade in those days reveals that the effect of India's overall trade performance in a particular year was transmitted to Indo-Nepalese trade the next year. For example over-trading and reckless speculation that prevailed in India during 1877-78 and the slump in India's overall trade during 1878-79[5] were followed by the visible fall in Indo-Nepalese trade in 1879-80.

Table 1[7]

Comparison between the value of commodities exported and imported into Nepal through Bengal and North Western Provinces during 1878–79 and 1879–80

	1878–79		1879–80	
	Exports from Nepal	Imports to Nepal	Exports from Nepal	Imports to Nepal
	Rs	Rs	Rs	Rs
Bengal	9,862,800	6,437,479	2,892,566	3,445,418
N.W.P. and Oudh	4,106,153	1,916,025	4,942,204	2,779,304
	13,968,953	8,353,504	7,834,770	6,224,722

	1878–79	1879–80
	Rs	Rs
Total registered trade with Bengal	16,300,279	6,337,984
Total registered trade with N.W.P. and Oudh	6,022,178	7,721,508
	22,322,457	14,059,492

Indo-Nepal trade increased in the year 1880-81. The total value of trade amounted to Rs 24,878,629/- in that year. Nepal exported articles valued Rs 16,040,560/- and imported articles worth Rs 8,838,069/-. Out of the total trade larger amount of commodities were transacted through Bengal.[6]

Table 2
Value of Indo-Nepalese Trade
1880-81 to 1889-90

Years	Exports to British India from Nepal Rs	Imports into Nepal from British India Rs	Total Rs
1880-81	16,040,560	8,838,069	24,878,629
1881-82	13,457,436	8,133,468	21,590,904
1882-83	13,326,704	8,124,349	21,451,053
1883-84	14,694,763	9,386,416	24,081,179
1884-85	14,055,191	9,573,645	23,628,836
1885-86	16,633,552	8,391,077	25,024,629
1886-87	17,993,354	8,533,715	26,527,069
1887-88	17,872,111	11,110,714	28,982,825
1888-89	15,097,010	10,652,568	26,049,578
1889-90	15,406,349	11,530,656	26,937,005

Sources : Report on the External Trade of Bengal with Nepal, Sikkim, Bhutan and Tibet 1880-81 to 1889-90. Note on the Trade of the North Western Provinces and Oudh for the year ending 31 March 1879; Annual Report of the Foreign Trade of North Western Provinces and Oudh for the year 1880-90.

The intense trade conflict between Nepal and Tibet that started since the late 1880's[8] gave an impetus to the growth of Indo-Nepalese trade. Nepal diverted her trade from Tibet towards India.

The total trade of Nepal with India was valued at Rs 21,590, 904 in 1881-82. Nepal exported articles worth Rs 13,457,436 and imported articles worth Rs 8,133,468. As compared with the year 1880-81, Indo-Nepal trade declined by Rs 3,287,725 during 1881-82. This decline continued till 1882-83. There was a considerable falling off in Indo-Nepal trade during these years. The reason given by the Collector of Champaran was that owing to the shortness of the aghani harvest and disturbance with Tibet, the export of grain from Nepal was stopped for some time. A Chainpatia mahajan, who cultivated land in Nepal complained to the sub-divisional Officers of Bettiah that he was not allowed to export his grain.[9]

During 1883-84, Indo-Nepal trade increased[10] as compared with the previous two years. It increased by Rs 2,630,126 against Rs 215,904 in 1881-82 and Rs 2,490,275 against Rs 21,451,053 in 1882-83. The imports into Nepal were also highest that year as compared with all the previous years.

The value of commodities again decreased by Rs 352,343 in 1884-85 against Rs 24,081,179 in 1883-84. But after 1885-86 until 1887-88 the volume of Indo-Nepal trade gradually increased. During 1885-86 the total value of the trade increased by Rs 1,395,793 as compared with Rs 3,628,836 in 1884-85.[11]

The total value of commodities increased by Rs 1,402,440 in 1886-87 as compared with Rs 25,024,629 in 1885-86. However, it decreased by Rs 2,933,247 in 188 -89 as compared with Rs 28,982, 825 in 1887-88. As compared with the entire period of one decade from 1880-81 to 1889-90, the volume of Indo Nepal trade reached at its peak during 1887-88. Similarly, Nepal imported the largest quantity of commodities during 1889-90. It was the highest amount of imports of the decade. The imports were worth Rs 11,530,656 against the total exports of Rs 15,406,349.[12]

Since 1887-88, the imports into Nepal from British India registered a rapid expansion as compared with the relative increase in Nepal's exports to India. It resulted partly from the decline in the export of Nepalese forest products and partly from the growing demand for imported goods from the newly established ruling class in Nepal. Nepal's trade conflict with Tibet also stimulated the imports from India of goods which were till then imported from Tibet.

During 1890-91 Nepal transacted articles worth Rs 22,179,431 through Bengal. After that it continuously decreased till 1893-94.

As compared with 1890-91 it decreased by Rs 2,324,804 in 1891-92, Rs 4,678,641 in 1892-93 and Rs 2,608,775 in 1893-94. The reason for this decrease was the decline in timber export from Nepal. However, the exports again increased by Rs 2,394,649 in 1894-95 against Rs 19,570,656 in 1893-94.[13]

Table 3 indicates that the total value of commodities transacted was highest during 1897-98 as compared with previous five years. The imports into Nepal was also highest. But the exports from Nepal were less in comparison with previous years. It was because the Nepalese Government prohibited the export of certain articles into British territory and due to shortage of the crops in Nepal.

Table 3
Value of Indo Nepal trade
1895–96 to 1899–1900

Years	Export to British India from Nepal Rs	Imports into Nepal from British India Rs	Total Rs
1895–96	18,478,417	13,250,397	31,728,814
1896-97	18,930,554	15,367,519	34,298,073
1897–98	20,565,292	18,038,103	38,603,395
1898–99	21,409,805	16,063,496	37,473,301
1899–1900	20,934,021	13,374,745	34,678,766
Grand Total	100,318,089	76,464,260	176,782,349

Sources : Report on the External Trade of Bengal with Nepal, Sikkim, Bhutan and Tibet for 1895–96 to 1899–90; Annual Report on the Foreign Trade of N.W.P. and Oudh for 1895–96 to 1899–1900.

With the turn of the present century till the First World War Indo-Nepal trade rapidly increased. The balance of trade remained in favour of Nepal as in the earlier years. Table 4 demonstrates that there was remarkable increase in the imports from British India during 1900. It was probably due to the imports of huge amount of construction materials for palatial buildings. On 11 September 1901 J.E.O' Coner, the Director General of Statistics of Bengal reported. "There was an exceptional increase in the exports of treasure, caused by a demand for gold in connection with the construction of a temple by the Nepalese Darbar."[15]

From 1900-01 to 1904-05 there was no significant change in the exports of commodities from Nepal. It was due to the good harvest in India during these five years.[16] Indo-Nepal trade suffered some setback during 1906-07. Both the exports and imports decreased and as a result of the total value of trade declined by 48%. Regarding the fall, Annual General report mentions, "This is the result of a partial failure of the autumn crops in the tarai. As regards exports from Nepal, the most remarkable decline appears in grain and jute. The principal imports affected were cotton piece goods, twist and yarn, and salt. The fall in the value of the first-two named articles imported is thought to be due partly to the fact that prices ruled high during the year which tended to reduce importation, and partly to depression of trade owing to bad harvest. The decrease in the value of the salt imported is partly accounted for by the reduction in the duties charged and the consequent reduction in price."[17] Moreover it was also as a result of the slump in India's exports and imports during this period.[18] Nepalese exports recovered during 1907–08, but there was stagnation in Nepalese exports during 1907–08 and 1908–09. It was also due to the bad harvests and high price for the food-grains in Nepal which reduced exports. Even then, Nepal's trade balance in these years continued to be surplus and amounted to one third of the total Indo-Nepalese trade.[19]

The export and balance of trade in favour of Nepal increased fantastically during 1911–12 and 1912–13. The imports into Nepal were also highest except in the year 1900–01. The imports into Nepal increased by one third of the total trade and amounted to Rs 2.26 crores in 1911–12. The export increased by 21% and amounted to Rs 4.54 crores. But this amount exceeded in 1912–13. Out of total trade of Rs 6.87 crores commodities worth Rs 4.65 crores were exported. However, imports into Nepal decreased. It amounted to Rs 2.22 crores against Rs 2.26 crores in 1911–12. The surplus trade balance of Nepal increased to a record figure of Rs 2.43 crores in 1912–13.

Table 4
Value of Indo-Nepal Trade
1900–04 to 1913–14

(in million rupees)

Year	Exports from Nepal to British India	Imports into Nepal from British India	Trade balance
1900–01	24.4	22.7	+ 1.7
1901–02	27.4	16.5	+10.9
1902–03	26.2	14.3	+11.9
1903–04	26.7	13.7	+13.0
1904–05	26.4	15.0	+11.4
1905–06	35.3	16.1	+19.1
1906–07	22.4	12.0	+10.4
1907–08	35.5	15.7	+19.8
1908–09	35.5	17.3	+18.2
1909–10	32.9	16.1	+16.8
1910–11	37.3	17.2	+20.1
1911–12	45.4	22.6	+22.8
1912–13	46.5	22.2	+24.3
1913–14	38.3	19.2	+19.1

Source : The annual confidential despatch of the British Resident in Nepal to the British India. British Residency Record (N.A.I.)

The growth of Indo-Nepal trade did not continue till 1913–14. It declined by nearly 20%. The exports from and imports into Nepal amounted to Rs 3.83 crores and Rs 1.92 crores respectively. In comparison with the previous year exports declined by 21% and imports by 13%. During the First World War Indo-Nepal trade remained almost stationary.

Export and Import of Commodities

Nepal exported a large variety of indigenous goods and among which foodgrains, timber, hide, wax, ghee and metal wares wers the principal items. The forest products and herbal plants which predominated in the overall exports of the country in the earlier decades of the 19th century were replaced by foodgrains at the end of the century.[20] This change was probably because "in the early stages of economic growth the production of goods for exports was determined largely by natural resources.[21] Therefore with the dawn of the present century rice smerged as the major export commodity. Approximately half of Nepal's exports consisted of food grains including rice and other foodgrains.[22] The most voluminous item of import from Nepal was rice of which more than 200,000 maunds entered the district (Gorakhpur) in a single year.[23] During 1877-78 Nepal exported 661,986 maunds of foodgrains valued at Rs 1,225,584 to North Western Provinces and Oudh out of which 501,340 maunds consisted of rice (husked and unhusked) only.[24] The other foodgrains exported were 20,494 maunds of wheat, 71,070 of gram and pulse and other miscellaneous items.[25]

The amount of rice exported from Nepal through Bengal was also high in comparison with other foodgrains. Out of 1,997,114 maunds of foodgrains exported rice constituted 1,607.882 maunds during 1878-79. This pattern was followed in the entire period under discussion. But the exports of rice gradually decreased after 1878-79 "due to the absence of demand on account of the excellent harvest and low price throughout the country (India)."[26]

During 1887-88, the exports of rice again increased by 9,126 maunds as compared with 990,644 maunds in 1878-79. But it decreased in 1888-89 to 1898-99. The exports of rice greatly increased during 1899-19C0.[27]

Table 5 clearly indicates that the exports of rice exceeded the amounts of all the foodgrains exported from Nepal. The quantity of rice exported was higher than paddy (unhusked rice) until 18 2-83, but it was reversed after 1883-84 onward i.e. the amount of paddy exceeded that of rice. The highest rice exporting year was 1899-1900 and the lowest amount of rice was exported during 1883-84 because in 1884,Nepal imposed restrictions on the export of rice, "owing to the scanty produce of grain in Terai, and on account of the necessity of collecting russud for the Tibet expedition, no hope is entertained of the usual export of grain from Nepal to British districts."[28] The Nepalese Prime Minister informed the British Resident that the Nepalese Officers in Tarai were instructed to

Prime Minister Bhim Shamsher (c. 1910).

Prime Minister Bhim Shamshe

anese ambassador and his wife (c. 1930).

King Tribhuvan's twenty-fourth birthday, 1930.

Table 5

Food-Grains Exported from Nepal to India Through Bengal 1878-79 to 1889-90

(in Mds)

Years	Description of food-grains						Total
	Wheat	Gram & pulse	Other spring crops	Rice (husked)	Rice (unhusked)	Other Rain crops	
1	2	3	4	5	6	7	8
1878-79	9,467	31,415	25,730	990,644	617,238	322,620	1,997,114
1879-80	7,606	54,089	23,019	811,105	665,457	244,039	1,805,315
1880-81	13,556	78,209	74,530	791,191	495,772	187,020	1,640,278
1881-82	8,360	64,762	43,162	747,268	640,690	173,415	1,677,657
1882-83	12,890	58,258	58,164	832,516	758,458	228,069	1,948,355
1883-84	16,455	63,842	37,526	508,288	644,137	275,142	1,545,390
1884-85	7,432	43,300	27,920	361,560	541,118	213,995	1,195,325
1885-86	9,375	30,937	33,157	613,117	649,504	293,849	1,629,939
1886-87	39,618	95,790	53,626	786,411	811,946	201,778	1,989,169
1887-88	69,979	113,501	50,546	999,770	1,184,152	333,926	2,751,874
1888-89	22,903	40,127	38,460	376,922	632,623	152,745	1,263,780

1	2	3	4	5	6	7	8
1889-90	7,272	23,496	14,179	704,401	977,587	276,019	2,002,954
1890-91	29,112	122,955	43,301	879,926	1,296,506	235,754	2,607,554
1891-92	43,813	81,247	45,113	441,520	700,887	142,508	1,455,088
1892-93	6,878	70,705	11,605	460,539	857,579	309,066	1,716,372
1893-94	7,558	84,298	20,107	582,219	909,282	162,132	1,765,596
1894-95	28,199	143,671	86,905	659,651	1,009,555	886,595	2,814,576
1895-96	56,293	179,414	131,100	761,696	991,522	279,951	2,399,982
1896-97	44,111	158,919	113,184	690,970	709,656	570,946	1,987,786
1897-98	17,083	160,298	59,739	737,316	893,881	361,831	2,230,148
1898-99	31,471	145,267	95,137	634,598	1,032,352	287,977	2,226,802
1899-1900	34,808	162,477	89,575	1,136,688	1,520,563	498,779	3,442,890

Sources : Report on the External Trade of Bengal with Nepal, Sikkim and Bhutan—!878-79 to 1899-1900.

direct the zamindar and tenants to store up the grain for their whole year consumption "before selling any part of it."[29]

Nepal exported wheat in the smallest quantity as compared with other foodgrains, because she did not produce much wheat as "it did not form a favourite article of food." It was used only for "manufacturing coarse beer and spirit."[30]

Timber

After foodgrain, Timber was the next important article exported from Nepal.[31] Larger amount of timber was exported through North Western Provinces and Oudh than through Bengal. For inst ance out of 569,409 maunds of timber 48,373 maunds were exported through Bengal and the rest through North Western Provinces and Oudh during 1878-79.[32] But the opposite was the position in respect of rice. More rice was exported through Bengal than

Table 6
Export of Timber from Nepal to India
1878-79 to 1889-90

Years	Quantity Mds	Value Rs
1878–79	569,409	845,110
1879–80	679.235	1,489,994
1880–81	1,492,721	3,110,042
1981–82	1,290,623	1,891,194
1982–83	1,763,097	2,635,669
1983–84	1,850,276	2,536,662
1984–85	2,517,341	3,634,130
1985–86	2,110,105	2,930,375
1986–87	2,222,383	3,024,613
1987–88	2,430,756	2,350,040
1988–89	1,423,007	2,054,123
1989–90	451,001	699,206

Sources : Report on the External Trade of Bengal with Nepal Sikkim and Bhutan 1878-79 to 1889-90. Annual Reports of the Foreign Trade of North Western Provinces and Oudh 1878-79 to 1889-90.

through the latter. This was largely due to geographical factors. During the nineteenth century, Western Nepal adjoining North Western Provinces and Oudh, was a "vast tract of forest lands, whereas cultivated tracts were few and dispersed."[33] Eastern Tarai adjoining Bengal and Bihar produced more foodgrains and was ideally suited for the cultivation of rice.[34]

Table 6 indicates that during 1979-80, the total exports of timber increased by 109,826 maunds as compared with 1878-79 but the export through North Western Provinces and Oudh decreased by 74,874 maunds as compared with 521,036 maunds during 1878-79. On the contrary, the export of timber through Bengal increased by 184,700 maunds as compared with 48,373 maunds during 1878-79. However, the exports of timber through Bengal was less by 213,089 maunds as compared with 446,162 maunds through North Western Provinces and Oudh. The export of timber through North Western Provinces and Oudh was always high on account of the heavy construction of railway line in that part of India.[35]

As compared with 1879-80, the export of timber from Nepal increased by more than double during 1880-81. It was 1,492,721 maunds against 679,235 maunds in 1879-80. The value of timber exported in that year was Rs. 3,110,042. It was the second highest timber exporting year between 1878-79 and 1889-90.

Nepal exported the highest amount of timber during 1884-85. She exported 3517,341 maunds of timber worth Rs. 3,634,130. Thirty-eight per cent of the total value of timber was imported by North Western Provinces and Oudh. The exports was above average this year because heavy rains washed down a large amount of timber.[36]

The greatest fall in the export of timber occurred during 1889-90. Nepal exporten 451,001 maunds of timber worth Rs. 699,206. It was less by 118,408 maunds valued Rs. 145,904 as compared with the minimum exported during 1878-79. The Nepalese government prohibited its sale owing to some misunderstanding and friction between Indian merchants and Nepalese officials[37] and also because it found extensive fraud committeed by the Officials (agents).[38] Another reason for the decrease was the internal disturbance in Nepal during these years.[39]

Hides

Hides were also exported in larger quantities. During 1877-78, 2,047 maunds of hides valued at Rs. 32,723 were exported through North Western Provinces and Oudh.[40] On 6 April 1876 the Deputy Commissioner of Kheri reported that three hundred and ninet-yfour pieces[41] of hides worth Rs. 314 were exported only through Singhai.[42] During 1878-79, Nepal exported hides worth Rs. 39,527 through Bengal. But it greatly increased during 1879-80. In comparison with the entire period of one decade from 1878-79 to 1889-90, it was the highest amount of hide exported that year. Nepal exported 70,706 pieces of hide worth Rs. 167,927, during 879-80. But as regards the value of hide exported, the year 1882-83, broke the record of 1879-80 because during that period Nepal exported 64,969 pieces of hide worth Rs. 178,665 as against 70,706 pieces worth Rs. 167,927 during 1879-80. Nepal exported larger amount of hide through Muzaffarpur than through other districts. Out of the total 70,706 pieces of hide, 31,879 pieces were exported through Muzaffarpur.[43]

Ghee

Ghee was the most important commodity exported from Nepal. On 6 April 1876 the Deputy Commissioner of Kheri reported that 111 maunds 32 seers of ghee worth 2,898 rupees 3 anna and 9 paisa were exported only through Singhai and Ram Nagar post.[44] On 1 November 1877 the Director of Agriculture and Commerce of North Western Provinces and Oudh informed that Nepal exported ghee worth Rs. 126,350 which was 4.5 per cent of the total amount of exports.[45]

During 1877-78 the total amount of ghee exported through North-Western Provinces and Oudh was 11,933 maunds worth Rs. 260,055. It was exclusive of some ghee exported from Dang and Deokhuri of Nepal by the Dara pass, which was not registered on its entry, "though possibly some may have been caught at

Table 7

Exports of Ghee from Nepal to India through Bengal 1880–81 to 1889–90

Years	Quantity Mds	Value Rs.
1880-81	4,284	138,088
1881-82	5,881	188,192
1882-83	10,352	300,208
1883-84	7,239	209,931
1884-85	7,244	211,558
1885-86	5,640	168,810
1886-87	3,460	111,975
1887-88	5,127	171,397
1888-89	9,075	289,021
1889-90	11,295	349,636

Matariaghat; 3,037 maunds (from Butwal) were registered at Lotan, and 5,875 from Banke at Babaganj."[46] Butwal was the main centre of ghee export. Large amounts of ghee were collected in that market. It was reported that some years ago, 5,000 maunds of ghee was destroyed there by a fire that broke out in the market.[47] During 1878-79, the export of Nepalese ghee through Bengal was 7,378 maunds valued at Rs. 236,096. After that the export of ghee started decreasing till 1882-83. The exports of ghee decreased by 2,589 maunds in 1879-80 as compared with the previous year.

Table 7 shows that the exports of ghee gradually increased after 1880-81 except in 1886-87. The export touched its peak during 1889-90. Nepal's export of ghee was 11,295 maunds worth Rs. 349,636. The export increased by 3,220 and 6,168 maunds as compared with the year 1888-89 and 1887-88 respectively. As compared with the point of entry, largest amount was recorded through

Bairagania in Muzaffarpur. Out of 11,295 maunds, 2,843 maunds worth Rs. 87,982 were recorded through that post. Darjeeling was the second highest ghee importing district after Muzaffarpur. Out of the total export of ghee, 2,672 maunds worth Rs. 82,706 was exported through Sukiapokhari and Goompahar in Darjeeling district.[48]

Import of Commodities

The principal imports of Nepal were cotton, salt, sugar and tobacco. Luxurious goods were also imported for nobles and rulers.

Cotton

Large amount of raw cotton, yarn and European as well as Indian piece-goods were imported into Nepal from British India. On May 1876, the Officiating Personal Assistant to the Chief Commissioner of Oudh wrote that the export to Nepal consisted entirely of cotton goods, the value of which was estimated at Rs. 248,045 in 1873 and Rs. 285,398 in 1874.[49] A report by a Special Committee on Statistics (1874) mentions that the trade of Oudh with Nepal was not great, only a small quantity of cotton "about two lakhs of rupees"[50] was exported to Nepal. However, another paragraph (250) mentions that the figures of the external trade of Oudh were not accurate.[51] This cannot be accepted because the table given below (Table 8)[52] indicates the accurate figures of the different types of articles imported into Nepal from North Western Provinces and Oudh.

The above table clearly indicates that seventy-eight per cent of the total value of imports from North Western Provinces and Oudh were cotton and cotton manufactures. The import of raw cotton was less than that of cotton goods. In this regard the report of the North Western Provinces and Oudh 1877-78 mentions "Cotton is but little imported in the raw state, its transport being probably too expensive for the trade to be remunerative. Only 458 maunds were exported during the whole year. It is said that cotton cultivation is to some extent being introduced in the Nepal Tarai near

Table 8

Imports of Commodities from North Western Provinces and Oudh Into Nepal 1877

Name of articles	Total value imported Rs.	Percentage of (the total value of each article to) the total value of imports
Raw cotton	14,820	1.4
Yarn and piece goods (European)	219,160	21.5
Yarn and piece goods (Indian)	437,534	42.90
Salt	97,178	7.8
Sugar	44,205	4.4
Others	224,130	22.0
Total	1,019,027	100.0

Banki, and that weaving industry on a small scale has sprung up there. The Tarai, however, is too damp ever to be a cotton-growing country, and so long as the Nepalese use cotton they must rely on trade for a supply of it. The cotton manufactures sent to Nepal are by far the most important feature in the export trade."[53]

During 1877-78 Nepal imported 23,406 maunds of cotton goods from North Western Provinces and Oudh. Out of it 363 maunds worth Rs. 12,407 were Indian spun twist, 4,643 maunds valued at Rs. 427,987 were European piece-goods and the rest 18,400 maunds valued at Rs. 772,266 were Indian piece goods (cloth). The total value of cotton goods imported amounted to Rs. 1,212,660. Of the European piece-goods, 1,132 maunds were registered at Thunthibari and 789 maunds at Babaganj. Of the Indian cloth 1,164 maunds were imported through Nautanwa; 4,157 maunds through Marni and 4,579 maunds through Babaganj.[54]

Table 9
Imports of Cotton and Cotton Goods from Bengal into Nepal 1878–79 to 1887–88

Years	Raw Mds	Cotton Rs	Piece goods (European) Value Rs	Piece goods (India) Value Rs	Total Value Rs
1878–79	6,511	104,176	1,887,996	295,842	2,252,014
1879–80	7,011	119,187	1,724,118	297,426	2,140,731
1880–81	5,721	96,306	2,174,290	184,979	2.455,575
1881-82	5,623	95,591	1,834,818	232,693	2,162,102
1882–83	8,154	138,618	1,819,592	178,058	2,136,268
1883–84	8,069	132,750	2,135,246	247,540	2,515,536
1884–85	5,849	88,264	1,864,682	336,557	2,289,503
1885–86	7,198	99,123	1,557,508	162,654	1,819,285
1886-87	5,454	86,072	1,646,4 7	173.627	1,906,136
1887–88	5.836	87,768	1,927,111	307,190	2,322.060

Sources : Report on the External Trade of Bengal with Nepal, Sikkim and Bhutan. 1878–79 to 1887–88. (N.A.I.)

The table No. 9 indicates that Nepal imported more piece-goods than raw cotton. The highest amount of raw cotton imported during 1882-83 through Bengal were 8,154 maunds worth Rs. 138,618. After that the import of raw cotton started falling. The lowest quantity of cotton was imported into Nepal during 1886-87. The import of cotton started falling because Nepalese government also took initiative to start cultivation in the country. In 1897, cotton plantation was started in Nuwakot district in Nepal under the auspices of the government. Lt. Colonel, Devi Bahadur Sijapati was deputed to administer the project. The plantation started with 34 labourers and employees on pay roll on 13 April 1897.[55]

There was greater demand of European piece-goods than Indian goods in Nepal. In most cases the import of European piece goods was nine times greater than Indian piece goods. During 1878-79 Nepal imprted European piece goods valued at Rs. 1,887,996 as against Indian piece goods worth Rs. 259,892 in the same year. But during 1879-80 the import of Indian piece goods increased by Rs. 37,584 as compared with Rs. 259,842 in 1878-79 whereas the import of European piece-goods decreased by Rs. 163,878 same year as compared with the previous year. After that import of Indian piece goods started falling till 1884-85. The imports of Indian piece goods reached its peak during 1884-85. After that year the import drastically fell off. It decreased by Rs. 173,903, Rs. 1 2,930 and Rs. 29,367 during 1885-86, 1886-87 and 1887-88 respecively.[56]

The European piece goods highest in number, were imported in 1880-81, and the lowest in 1885-86. During 1885-86, the import of Indian piece goods as well as the total value of cotton goods also decreased. It was partly owing to the internal disturbance in Nepal[57] and partly because the prices ruled high during the year which tended to reduce imporation, partly due to depression of trade from the bad harvest.[58]

The cotton cloth made in Nepal was stout and durable but the cheaper, more flimsy Indian and European cotton cloth was rapidly taking the place of native cloth.[59]

Salt

Salt was the most important of imports into Nepal for which the inhabitants of eastern Nepal almost entirely depended on British territory.[60] But the people in the hill and the valley preferred Tibetan salt. In his report for the year 1867-68, the Commissioner of Customs in North Western Provinces and Oudh, quoted a letter from British Resident in Nepal who wrote to him, "Nepal, proper, or the hills of which the country is composed and the valley of Kathmandu, is supplied entirely with salt from Tibet. The taxed salt from British territory is not imported here at all, and is looked upon with disfavour. The importations from Tibet are more than sufficient for the want of the people, and the price at which it sells in the bazaars here (Kathmandu) is 6½ seers per rupee."[61] But the cost of Indian salt (Sambhar and Lahori rock salt) was 3 seers per rupee.[62] The Tibetan salt was cheaper than Indian because, "the salt of Tibet costs little on the bank of lakes where it is collected, and is carried on sheep and goats, which graze their way and realize something as butcher's meat at the end."[63] But the salt of the Sambhar lake sold at 10 annas per maund on the spot with the addition of customs duty @ Rs. 3/– per manud in Nepal. Indian salt was consumed in Tarai. In the hill Lahori salt was used only in times of mourning when Tibetan salt was forbidden.[64]

Of all the commodities imported into Nepal from North Western Provinces and Oudh, in 1877, salt constituted 7.8 per cent worth Rs. 97,178.[65] During 1877-78, altogether 29,191 maunds of salt was imported against 14,509 maunds in the previous year.[66] The imports of Indian salt through Bengal reached the peak during 1879-80. It was 87,510 maunds worth Rs. 393,777 against 80,708 maunds worth Rs. 363,186 in 1878-79.[67] After that the value of salt imported into Nepal decreased gradually but the volume increased after 1883-84 because India reduced its customs duty at a uniform[86] rate of Rs. a maund all over India in 1882. The inland customs line was also abolished. Salt was then far cheaper in India as "a whole than it was 50 years ago, or at any earlier stage of Indian history."[69] Not only the rate of duty was lowest but the cheapest facilities of transport provided by the extension of railway also helped to reduce the price of salt.[70] As a result the price of Indian salt was also reduced in comparison with Tibetan salt.

Regarding the increased volume of salt imports into Nepal the British Resident in Nepal wrote to the Secretary to the Government of India that owing to disagreements between Nepal and Tibet, concerning the price and quality of salt supplied by the latter country to the former much larger imports of this commodity was made from India than ever before.[71]

Sugar

Sugar and tobacco were also imported into Nepal in large quantities. Refined and unrefined sugar in the form of shira or molasses was imported. In 1877 sugar worth Rs. 44,205 or 4.4 per cent of the total value of imports was imported.[72] In 1876 the Deputy Commissioner of Kheri reported that 19 maunds 7 seers of sugar worth Rs. 118 annas 8 and 334 maunds 27 seers of molasses valued at Rs. 1746 were imported into Nepal only through Singhai and Ramnagar Chowki.[73] The amount of shira imported through that route was 430 maunds worth Rs. 784.[74] During 1877-78, Nepal imported 791 maunds of refined sugar and 25,347 maunds valued at Rs. 82,986 of unrefined sugar including shira or molasses. None of the registering posts in North Western Provinces and Oudh recorded more than 3,000 maunds of import.[75]

During 1878-79, Nepal imported 10,662 maunds valued at Rs. 170,592 of refined sugar and 20,847 maunds worth Rs. 145,929 from Bengal. The imports of refined sugar gradually decreased till 1887[76] but the import of unrefined sugar was stationary except a fall in 1879-80 and little fluctuation in other period. There was a great demand of unrefined sugar especially molasses.

Molasses was the Government monopoly in the 19th century. The agent of the government was instructed to purchase molasses at reasonable prices, and collect fines from any person who sold the commodity to others. At the same time, he was warned not to harass traders by purchasing molasses from them at unduly low price.[77]

The import of refined as well as unrefined sugar was high in 1887-88 as compared with all the previous years. Nepal imported 12,486 maunds valued at Rs. 134 545 of refined sugar and 46,854 valued at 215,450[78] of unrefined sugar. The import of unrefined sugar increased by more than double as compared with all the previous years. Its import into Nepal was larger than that of sugar in all the cases.

Tobacco

Tobacco was imported into Nepal "as a luxurious item."[79] The British Resident in Nepal was irritated at the monopoly and tax imposed upon this article. Its cultivation was lately started in Nepal.[80] Land under tobacco was the most heavily taxed.[81]

During 1877-78 Nepal imported 4,735 maunds of tobacco worth Rs. 34,288 from North Western Provinces and Oudh. Out of it 2,294 maunds were imported through the Babaganj post.[82] The imports of tobacco from Bengal were 12,642 maunds valued at Rs. 75,852 in 1878-79.[83] The volume and value of the imports of tobacco gradually increased with the passage of time. For instance the import increased by 78,480 maunds worth Rs. 286,551 in 1887-88 as against 12,642 maunds (valued at Rs. 75,852) in 1878-79 and 19,276 maunds (valued Rs. 125,314) in 1879-80.[84] The Eastern Tarai region of Nepal adjoining Bengal imported larger amount of tobacco because the tobacco grown in that part was "uncommonly good".[85]

There were fluctuations in imports into and exports from Nepal in all the commodities mentioned above. The reason given by the Collector of Darbhanga was that the fluctuations were governed by the variations in the incidence of taxation along the different routes. He added that the traders naturally used to choose such routes as best suited their convenience, costs of carriage, taxation, price charged or given for commodities. But Faulder, the sub-divisional Officer of Madhubani did not believe that the traders followed their route according to the dues levied, finding them higher in one place than another. Rather they followed from year to year the particular road to which they heard their fathers had been accustomed for years and they knew nothing of the other routes. The Collector of Bhagalpur concluded that the difference in the rates of duty had very little to do with the fluctuations in the amount of traffic at different places. The amount of traffic was dependent more on the demand for different articles in different places.[86]

4.3. Smuggling

Smuggling was a common practice on the Indo-Nepal border. Large amounts of commodities such as opium[87], cardamoms[88] and timber[89] were smuggled from Nepal into India. Arms and ammunition[90] from India were smuggled into Nepal and salt from Tibet. The people of both the countries were equally involved in this illegal trade.[91] Opium was smuggled because its imports was prohibited by the Indian Government.[92] Timber and cardamoms were smuggled to escape registration and customs duty. Tibetan salt was smuggled during the Nepal-Tibet conflicts.[93] Smuggling if detected was fined with double duty and confiscation of goods.

4.4. Slave Trade

Human traffic was legal in Nepal but sale of free-born person was prohibited.[94] The child of a slave woman by her free-born master was not a slave. Before the rule of Jang Bahadur, private sale of children was a common practice among parents belonging to the lower castes of the Newars and other hill tribes.[95] But Jang Bahadur imposed some restrictions on this practice. The persons selling free-born human beings were to be fined Rs. 360 and in default of payment of the fine, were to be imprisoned for a period of three years and four months or until the whole amount was accounted for, by the deduction of Rs. 9/- every month that the prisoner remained in jail.[96] Jang Bahadur also passed a law to the effect that no person from whose hands water could be taken according to the laws of caste, should be reduced to slavery. But he could not abolish the custom altogether. Because some forces were pulling him from behind. Some aristocrats and the owners of the slave were dead against it. He was bound to permit "even those members of higher castes who were already slaves as well as their children to remain in slavery."[97]

The Indian Act V of 1843 made slavery illegal in India, and the Indian Penal Code of 1860 rendered keeping or trafficking in slaves a penal offence.[98] Therefore the British Officials were keen to check the flow of this traffic on the Indo-Nepal border. However, it remained unchecked. They blamed Nepalese officials who were deputed near the border for this.[99] But they should not be blamed because it was more an economic than social or political problem. The Nepalese aristocrats inherited slaves as ancestral property, agriculturists maintained slave for work in the field, traders purchased slaves for the sake of their business and others reared slaves like cattle and sold them for profit.[100]

The slaves were purchased from among the poverty stricken people of Bihar and the North Western Provinces. The purchases were made in India at Rs. 4 or 5 and sold in Nepal for Rs. 30 or 40 each.[101] The price was much more higher in Kathmandu and in other towns. On 1 December 1836 the price for full grown-up male slave was Rs. 80 each and for full grown female slave as Rs. 100 each. Boy slaves cost Rs. 40 each and girl Rs. 50 each.[102] In 1877 the price for female slaves ranged from Rs. 150 to 200 and for male slaves from Rs. 100 to 150.[103] At that time there were twenty to thirty thousand slaves in Nepal It was a quite profitable business. Many slaves were sold by their parents or other relatives. Some were stolen and brought into Nepal. There was a great rise in the traffic of slaves during eighteen months in 1866 67 as a result of famine in Champaran and other districts. The people of these places came in search of food and took shelter with well-to-do persons. Jang Bahadur himself admitted that the reason for the large influx of slaves from India into Nepal was more economic than anything else. During the famine of 1866-67 several people from Bihar entered into the Nepalese territory to obtain food which was then distributed as charity in Nepal. They began to sell their children when they failed to get sufficient food.[104] In this regard the view expressed by the Officiating Commissioner of Patna Division was also similar. He reported that during periods of scarcity parents sold their children to the Nepalese in large numbers. They wanted home and other necessities for their children.[105]

Some of the people in far Western Nepal used to sell their children to Muslims[106] and other people who used to come from the Tarai and Tibet. They also kidnapped and sold the children of others. To check this practice, the Nepalese Government issued a proclamation to the effect that "any person who sells or purchases (human beings) in this manner will be punished with his life and property. The goods of the people who come from the Madhesh (India) and Tibet to purchase (human beings) shall be confiscated."[107] The prices of slaves in the hill and mountains were quite low. For example, a slave could be bought for Rs. 20 and entire family consisting of parents and two children for Rs. 80 in Jumla. The prices were determined by the low capitalized value of human labour as well as by demand and supply. A poor and mountainous region like Jumla where the supply of slaves was possibly higher and the demand lower than in the capital town of Kathmandu, the prices of the slaves would be naturally low.[108]

Slaves were also kept in bondage. They remained in bondage as long as they failed to repay the loan. In 1865 a blacksmith in a village in Doti district complained to the concerned authority in Kathmandu that some local people had unlawfully claimed his mother to be slave and kept her in detention. The woman had been bounded by his father several years previously for a loan of Rs 6. The loan remained unpaid for at least two decades. [109]

There was no such case as kidnaping of children for the purpose of despatch as slaves to Nepal in North Western provinces and Oudh. Mac Mullin, the district Superintendent of Police in Basti reported that such practice did not exist in his district although Rajputs of the district sold their girls to the Nepalese Rajputs ostensibly as wives, who might subsequently be subjected to slavery; also that in time of scarcity children might be sold or bartered by their parents to Nepalese, but he was not aware of any children being kidnapped for the prurpose.[110] The Deputy Commissioner of Bahraich quoted the report of D.S.P. that he did not find any case except a few kidnappings during the tenure of four years in office. He calculated that in four cases out of thirty-three the defendants were apprehended on their way to Nepal. But according to the D.S.P. it was not too excessive to draw the conclusion that there was anything like a system of kidnapping for slavery in Nepal.[111] The District Superintendent of Police in Gorakhpur also failed to trace any case of kidnapping except a woman involved in such case in a different manner. He mentioned that a woman had an intrigue with a man in Nepal by whom she had a child that died, the man turned her out, and the woman subsequently kidnapped a child from Gorakhpur district intending to pass it off as the man's second child to gain his favour.[112] In most cases except these minor incidents, parents willingly sold their children as slaves to gain some money. J. Beams, the Magistrate of Champaran wrote, "In times of famine especially, but more or less at all times, native British subjects voluntarily sell their children to any one who will take care of them often asking no questions as to what will be done with them."[113]

In some cases the purchasers used to keep the slaves in India with them and were not taken into Nepal until they were of a marriageable and a saleable age. "The original sale took place when they were very young, so that children lost all memory of their real parents and did not even know their names; they believed themselves to be the children of their purchasers; or perhaps they neither knew, nor cared to know who their parents were."[114] In such a case no clue would be obtained as to their origin if these slaves were arrested on crossing the Indo-Nepal border. J. Beams suggested that it was better to live as slave than to die in starvation. In his own word, "it would be a very mistaken kindness to take them away from their rich protectors, who kept them in comfort, and restore them to poverty-stricken parents with whom they would starve, and on whose resources they would be a heavy burden. The result of such a measure with females would be that they would be sold for purposes of prostitution in British territories and I submit that of the two fates that wait them; that of being the slave concubine of a Nepalese official, is less revolting to morality and less prejudicial to the individual than that of a public prostitute."[115]

It was not easy for the British Government to check this traffic in such a frontier which was wide open on all sides except north. And also because the slaves were usually taken to Nepal one by one and not in batches. It would be blunder on the part of Indian officials to arrest persons walking into Nepal with children who went willing and who might seem to be their own. Hence, the slave traffic could not be stopped.[116] In such a situation Jang Bahadur sent an order to his officials that, "although they were not to encourage the sellers, they were not to prohibit any one from purchasing children."[117] He ordered liberation of several slaves who had been purchased during the year 1866-67. Altogether 450 emancipated slaves were taken to the British Residency at Kathmandu for return to India. Jang Bahadur asked them that they would be sent to their homes, if they so desired of, if they preferred, they could stay in Kathmandu and take service with any one. Some women slaves complained that many of their companions were kept back secretly at some places.[118] However, some of the female slaves who were brought to the Indian side of the frontier requested to go back again to Nepal as they were reluctant to part with the links they had formed there. Slaves were assisted to go back to Nepal when they were found really sorry.[119] A Nepal law provided that a fugitive slave who had settled in Naya Muluk, and district of Morang in the Tarai, could not be enslaved again.[120]

According to British Officials if the slavery were treated as criminal in Nepal it would die out.[121] But at the same time they agreed that as long as the demand of the slave was great in Nepal and India had the problem of growing population of poor people, the system of slavery would continue.[122] The British Resident in Nepal suggested that the persons who came to the Tarai for this traffic should be sent to the Indian police post with the statement of their offence. But the Nepalese Prime Minister flatly refused on the ground that the method would be the violation of the Treaty with British India by which British subjects apprehended within the Nepalese territory should be punished by Nepalese Court on the basis of Nepalese Law. He requested that this practice should be allowed to continue.[123]

Neither British nor Nepalese officials could check this nefarious trade. Ultimately on 28 November 1924 Chandra Shamsher made an appeal to abolish slavery. A new law was passed to make slavery a penal offence. Out of a total of 59,875 slaves, the Government paid compensation for 51,782 slaves, 4,651 slaves were liberated by their masters without compensation, 1984 died, 1342 fled, and 114 paid for their own release.[124]

4.5. Entrepot Trade

Nepal's export trade to India constituted the mainstay of the nation's economy whereas exports of primary products and handicrafts to Tibet were mostly concentrated along the border. Entrepot trade with Tibet was not so profitable as a whole because it enriched only some persons involved in this trade.[125] The vast bulk of Nepal-Tibet trade was entrepot trade.[126]

The Newars of the Kathmandu valley and Kashmiri and Gosain traders from India were getting the maximum profit. They generally specialized in articles of great value and small bulk. The Newar monopoly in the Tibetan trade did not last long. With the coming of the foreign traders the commercial activity of Newars was limited. The foreign merchants had agents and large establishments at different centres in India, Nepal and Tibet But the Newar merchants had no such commercial link in India for the supply of goods. Therefore, their role in Nepal-Tibet trade was confined to the export of commodities brought by Indian traders to Kathmandu and retail trade in Tibet. Some of the so-called imports of Indian and foreign goods into Nepal were for the sake of re-export to Tibet.[127]

Tibetan trade was much more profitable for the merchants than the Nepalese trade, because foreign goods were sold in Tibet at double the price than the rate in Nepal. For instance, silk cotton piece-goods and cotton staples brought 25% profit when sold in Nepal and 60% in Tibet; Kuff of diamonds and indigo 25% in Nepal and 100% in Tibet. Similarly if broad cloth was sold in Nepal net profit would be 25% and if in Tibet it would go up to 60%; ornaments made of conch shells would bring a profit of 25% in Nepal and 100% in Tibet and coral would bring a profit of 37% in Nepal and up to 75% in Tibet.[128] However, the difficulties on the path going to Tibet and cost of transportation could not be ignored.

Out of 18 passes, the Kerung and Kuti routes were the shortest and most convenient between northern India and Tibet. The towns of the Kathmandu Valley and of Patna in Bihar were the main links in the trade that was conducted along those routes. From Kathmandu, Kerung[129] lies at a distance of 141 kilometres which then was usually covered in eight days. The route to Kuti was shorter by ten kilometres but was more hazardous and arduous and so required one day more. After travelling 19 days from Kerung, and 16 days from Kuti, traders reached the town of Digarcha, from where Lhasa lies at a distance of 273 kilometres, which could be covered in 11 days more. A journey from Kathmandu to Lhasa thus required about 38 days through Kerung and about 36 days through Kuti. The routes leading from the Kathmandu Valley to the south were less hazardous. Hetauda was the main centre for the movement of goods between the Kathmandu Valley and India. Goods imported into the Kathmandu Valley from India were transported through porters. They were packed in loads of 32 dharnis each. Each such load was called *bakku*. In Kathmandu, the goods were repacked in bakku load of 16 dharnis each for onward transit to Tibet owing to the extreme difficulties of the road, which would not permit a man to carry more than that weight upon his back.[130] The cost of conveyance would be naturally high in such a difficult path.

Nepal was the principal channel through which English commodities and products of Bengal were carried to Tibet.[131] Broad cloth was in great demand in Tibet. All colour except yellow were liked by the people. About Rs. 300,000 worth of broad cloth was sold every year. Coral was also in great demand among the army and Sardars of China and in parts of Tibet.[132] The Tibetans exchanged Pashmina or shawl wool, salt, borax, musk, quicksilver and gold dust for Nepalese metal wares, European peace goods, Indian cotton goods and spices.[133] The Nepalese traders on the Tibetan frontier used to get salt in barter for rice and other grain.[134] Salt was packed in bags forming loads of about 15 lb each, which were brought across the snows fastened to the backs of sheep.[135] Thak village in the north western frontiers of Nepal was the centre and depot for the great quantities of Tibetan salt.[136]

A large portion of the trade profits went to foreigners.[137] However, the state revenue derived from different taxes levied on the commodities exported from and imported into Nepal from Tibet was also high. Customs duties were levied on goods imported into the Kathmandu Valley from that country, but no information is available about their rate.[138] In 1861 such duties yielded a revenue of Rs. 5,489. The transit duties known as jagat were also collected at various points on such goods. Other duties known as Nirkhi and Kirana were also levied on goods exported to Tibet. In 1860 Nirkhi duty on goods exported to Tibet amount to Rs. 4,456 while Kirana duty yielded Rs. 6,028. Both these duties were levied on goods of Nepalese origin. The rate of Nirkhi duty was 1½ ad valorem and Kirana at 2 per cent. The total value of

Nepali goods exported to Tibet may be estimated at approximately Rs. 300,000 in that year.[139] Apart from this, monopoly trade in specified goods imported from Tibet constituted a supplementary source of revenue. These monopolies included silver, gold and borax.[140] The last commodity was imported from Tibet mainly for reexport to India.[141] The trade was highly lucrative for a large volume of Tibetan gold passed through Nepal the value of which, in Kathmandu was 50 per cent less than when brought to Patna.[142] Much more trade between India and Tibet went through Nepal than by any other route but figures are lacking. The trade of Bengal with Nepal was between 20 and 25 times as great as that with Tibet.[143]

Since 1856 the Nepalese Government had enjoyed a privileged position in Lhasa, with extra territorial rights.[144] The Nepalese traders were under the jurisdiction of the Nepalese Government, rather than Tibetan Government. The latter had no authority to collect any taxes from them. On the other hand, the Government of Nepal used to collect customary fee and payments from traders, merchants and retail shopkeepers living in Tibet through the chief of the community there. That functionary kept one sixth of the proceeds for himself and transmitted the balance to Kathmandu. The Nepalese Government also appointed judges to adjudicate in disputes among the trading community in Lhasa. The fines and penalties collected by that official while dispensing justice constituted yet another source of revenue. A special tax was collected from Newar traders on their return home from Tibet at Rs 3 each. [145]

Since the opening of trade route between Tibet at Kalimpong in North East Bengal, Indo-Tibetan trade through Nepal dwindled to a negligible quantity. [146] Another reason for this fall in entrepot trade was the young-husband mission of 1904-05. This trade was again greatly affected by the political change that occurred in Tibet in 1959. Nepali and Tibetan traders were no longer allowed to engage in border trade. This had a great impact on the life of the people living in the border area of northern Nepal. [147]

REFERENCES

1. These countries include Afghanistan, Central Asia, Persia, Tibet, Sikkim, Bhutan, Shan States and Western China. For example, in the year 1913-14 Afghanistan exported articles worth Rs. 12 884/-; Central Asia Rs. 1,333/-; Persia Rs. 267/ ; Tibet Rs. 3.323/ ; Sikkim Rs. 3,089/-; Bhulan Rs. 2,086/-: Shan States Rs. 20,166/ ; Western China Rs. 2,892/-; Nepal Rs. 43, 275/-; to India. Similarly Nepal imported from India articles worth Rs. 20,480/-; Afghanistan Rs. 15,233/-; Central Asia Rs. 1818/-; Persia Rs. 2,163/-; Tibet 1,962/-; Sikkim Rs. 1,601/-; Bhutan 1,766/-; Shan States 18,270/ ; Western China 5,615/-. See, K.T. Shah, *Trade Traffic and Transport in India*, Bombay, 1923, p. 101.
2. These data differ from the data available in other documents. However, it should be noted that the volume of commodities exported from and imported into Nepal was always high in all the documents. It was difficult to determine the actual value and volume of the articles exported from and imported into Nepal during the period under review mainly for three reasons. First there is paucity of records of the trade transacted through North Western Provinces and Oudh before 1877. Secondly, owing to the multiplicity of traffic routes and smuggling, the figures for the external trade can not be considered accurate. Thirdly, for geographical reasons, an article of Nepalese origin was transferred to some other parts of Nepal by an easier way through India. Likewise, some unsold articles returned from Nepal were also listed in export and import items. However, on the basis of the trade registered on the Indo-Nepal border and the volume of articles mentioned in the report of the British Resident in Nepal it can easily be admitted that the balance of trade was always in favour of Nepal. See Revenue A. August 1877. No. 2. K.W. (N.A.I.) ; also see Report on the External Trade of Bengal with Nepal Tibet, Sikkim and Bhutan for the year 1896-97.
3. W.W. Hunter, *The Indian Empire, Its people and products.* London, 1892, p. 691.
4. *Ibid.*
5. Parimal Roy. *India' s Foreign Trade since 1870.* London, 1934, p. 52.
6. Report on the External Trade of Bengal with Nepal, Sikkim and Bhutan, and Tibet 1880-81. (N.A.I.)
7. This chart was supplied by British Resident in Nepal to the British Indian Government for the year 1878-79 to 1879-80. Political A, December 1880, No. 38. (N.A.I.)
8. Niranjan Sharma, *Nepal Foreign Trade.* (Unpublished Ph.D. Thesis) University of Delhi, 1968, p. 39).

9. Report on the External Trade of Bengal with Nepal, Sikkim, Bhutan, Tibet 1882-83. (N.A.I.)
10. In 1883 Nepal-Tibet conflict reached its climax, when Nepalese shops at Lhasa were looted by Tibetan monks., see, Kanchanmoy Majumdar. *Anglo-Nepalese Relations in the nineteenth century.* p. 118.
11. Report on the External Trade of Bengal with Nepal, Sikkim, Bhutan, Tibet 1883-84 to 1885-86.
12. *Ibid.* for 1886-87 to 1889-90.
13. *Ibid.* for 1890-91 to 1893-94.
14. The trade of Bengal with Nepal, Tibet, etc. for the year ending March 31, 1901, Calcutta. September 11, 1901. (N.A.I.)
15. *Ibid.*
16. Foreign Department, Secret E. December 1907, Nos 121. Annual General Report on Nepal for the year 1906-07 (N.A.I.)
17. Parimal Roy. *op. cit.*
18. Badri Prasad Shrestha, *An Introduction to Nepalese Economy*, Kathmandu, 1966, p. 158.
19. *Ibid.*
20. "As development proceeds, increased availability of capital and skilled labour broadens the product-range over which a country can effectively compete in the international market." See Vijaya Katti, "Commodity and geographic concentration in Indo-Nepalese Trade". *Foreign Trade Review* (18) (3). October December, 1983, p. 322.
21. M.C. Regmi, *The State and Economic Surplus, Production, Trade and Resource Mobilization in early 19th century Nepal.* Varanasi 1984, p. 224.
22. District Gazetteers of U.P. , Gorakhpur District Vol. xxxi. pp. 78-79.
23. Report on the Foreign Trade of North Western Provinces and Oudh during the year 1877-78. (N.A.I.)
24. *Ibid.*
25. Report on the External Trade of Bengal with Nepal, Sikkim and Bhutan 1880-81. (N.A.I.)
26. *Ibid*, for 1899-1900.
27. A General E. March 1884. No. 3. Extract from the Nepal Dairy for the week ending the 1884. (N.A.I.)
28. *Ibid.*
29. *Imperial Gazetteer of India, Afghanistan and Nepal.* Calcutta 1908, p. 115.

30. Regmi, *op. cit.* The exports of salwood was one of the principal sources of income to the Nepalese Government ; also see Eden Vansittart 'The Goorkhas.' Reprint of ed 1890, New Delhi, 1980. p. 6.
31. Report on the Foreign Trade of North Western Provinces and Oudh 1877-78. (N.A.I.)
32. Mahesh C. Regmi *Thatched Huts and Stucco Palaces, Peasants and Landlords in 19th century Nepal.* New Delhi, 1978, pp 5-6.
33. *Ibid.* p. 5.
34. External B. September 1906. No. 50. Annual Report on the Foreign Trade of the United Province with Nepal. (N.A.I.)
35. Jahar Sen, "*The Tune of timber in Indo-Nepal Relation*". *Calcutta Historical Journal.* Vol. VII, No. 7, July December 1982, p. 64.
36. Report on the Administration of the North Western Provices and Oudh for the year ending 31 March 1899. Allahabad, 1900. (Rattan Tata Library, Delhi University)
37. Jahar Sen, *op. cit.*
38. *Ibid.*
39. Report on the Foreign Trade of North Western Provinces and Oudh. 1877-78. (N.A.I.)
40. Report of N.W.P. and Oudh recorded exports of hide in maund whereas all other documents mention it in number.
41. Revenue A. August 1877, No. 14.
42. Report on the External Trade of Bengal with Nepal, Sikkim and Bhutan. 1879-1900.
43. Revenue A. August 1877. No. 14.
44. *Ibid.* December 1877. No. 2.
45. Report on Foreign Trade of North Western Provinces and Oudh 1877-78. (N.A.I.)
46. *Ibid.*
47. Report on the External Trade of Bengal with Nepal, Sikkim, and Bhutan 1872-1900. (N.A.I.)
48. Revenue A. August 1877, No. 13. Captain A. Murray, Officiating Personal Assistant to the Chief Commissioner of Oudh to T.H. Thornton, Officiating Secretary to the Government of India. dated 31 May 1876. No. 2489. (N.A.I.)
49. Ibid, No. 3. Extract paragraph 6 from a report by a Special Committee on Statistic relating to India. dated 10 December 1874, No. 73. (N.A.I.)

50. *Ibid.*
51. *Ibid.* No. 2.
52. Report on the Foreign Trade of North Western Provinces and Oudh. 1877-78. (N.A.I.)
53. *Ibid.*
54. M.C. Regmi, "Cotton Cultivation in Nuwakot." *Regmi Research Series*, Year 12, No. 2. February 1980, p. 23
55. Report on the External Trade of Bengal with Nepal, Sikkim and Bhutan. 1878-88.
56. Yagya Acharya, *Nepal Ko Itihas*. Kathmandu, (2039 v.s.) pp 214-15.
57. Foreign Department, Secret E. December 1907 No. 121-123. Annual General Report on Nepal for the year 1906-7. (N.A.I.)
58. G.H.D. Gimlette. *Nepal and the Nepalese*. London, (n.d.) p. 81
59. Revenue A. August 1877, No. 22.
60. Report on the Foreign Trade of North Western Provinces and Oudh. 1877-78. (N.A.I.)
61. *Ibid.*
62. *Ibid.*
63. *Ibid.*
64. Revenue A. August 1877. No. 2.
65. Report on the Foreign Trade of North Western Provinces and Oudh 1877-78. (N.A.I.)
66. Report on the External Trade of Bengal with Nepal, Sikkim and Bhutan 1877-78. (N.A.I.)
67. *Ibid.* for 1878-79.
68. Before 1882 customs duty was not uniform in India. From times immemorial a tax on salt was a source of revenue in India. In 1858 the salt tax was Rs 2½ a maund (about 82 lbs) in Bengal, Rel a paund (including cost of manufacture) in Madras, 12 annas in Bombay, and Rs 2 a maund in North India. In 1859 the rates were raised to Rs 3, Re 1, and Rs 2½ respectively and in 1861 they were again raised to Rs 3¼ in Bengal, Rs 3 in Madras and in North India. In 1878 the salt duty was raised in Madras and Bombay and reduced over the rest of India and ultimately in 1882 it was fixed and made uniform all over India. See, *Memorandum on Some of the Results of Indian Administration. During the Past Fifth Years of British Rule in India.* Calcutta, 1911, pp. 2–3.
69. *Ibid.*

70. Foreign Department. Secret E, June 1892. No. 136. Lieutenant Colonel H. Wylie, Officiating British Resident in Nepal to the Secretary to the Government of India dated 24 May 1892. No. 36p. (N.A. I.)
71. Revenue A. August 1877. No. 2.
72. *Ibid.* No. 14.
73. *Ibid.*
74. Report on the Foreign Trade of North Western Provinces and Oudh. 1877-78. (N.A.I.)
75. Report on the External Trade of Bengal with Nepal, Sikkim and Bhutan. 1878-79—1886-87.
76. M.C. Regmi, "Monopoly Trade in Gur". *Regmi Research Series.* Year 14 No. 9. September 1982, p. 138.
77. Report on the External Trade of Bengal with Nepal, Sikkim and Bhutan. 1887-88. (N.A.I.)
78. Revenue A. August 1877. No. 14.
79. Tobacco had been introduced in India by the Portugese during the early seventeenth century and later on its cultivation started in the eastern Tarai region of Nepal. See M.C. Regmi, *The State & Economic Surplus.* p. 46.
80. *Ibid.*
81. Report on the Foreign Trade of North Western Provinces and Oudh 1877-78. (N.A.I.)
82. Report on the External Trade of Bengal with Nepal, Sikkim and Bhutan. 1878-79.
83. *Ibid.*, for 1887-88.
84. Francis Hamilton, *An Account of the Kingdom of Nepal.* Reprint of 1819 ed. New Delhi 1971. p. 62.
85. Report on the External Trade of Bengal with Nepal, Sikkim and Bhutan. 1882-83. (N.A.I.)
86. Finance B. February 1882. No. 40 C.E.R. Girdlestone, the British Resident in Nepal to the Officiating Lieutenant to the Government of India in the Foreign Department, Calcutta dated 27 January 1882. No. 4 p. (N.A.I.)
87. M C. Regmi, "Smuggling of cardamom" *Regmi Research Series.* 1 May 1981. p. 75.
88. External A. November 1889. No. 51. Major E.L. Durand, the British Resident in Nepal to the Secretary to the Government of India. Foreign Department dated 12 October 1889. No. 92 p (N.A.I.)

89. The British Government blamed the Nepalese Government for the smuggling of arms and ammunition. See Secret E. June 1884. No. 438. Departmental Note by the Secretary to the Government of India dated 20 February 1884. (N.A.I.)

90. Ibid., 1890. No. 529. Note in the Foreign Department dated 3 May 1890. (N.A.I.)

91. The opium was the monoply of both the Governments. Therefore the British Indian Government wanted to restrict the exports of Nepalese opium to India or other countries. The Nepalese sought permission to export opium to overseas countries through Bombay on payment of pass duty Rs. 700 per chest. But the request was rejected on the pretext that the Government of India had no desire to encourage the cultivation of opium in Nepal. Nepal opium being inferior if exported through Bombay would naturally discredit the Malva opium. General B. July 1881, No. 104. Foreign Department of the Government to the British Resident in Nepal dated 13 May 1881.

92. Salt was smuggled from Tibet during the Nepal-Tibet Conflict which led to the shortage of this commodity in Kathmandu and elsewhere. The traders who smuggled salt from Tibet without paying customs duties were punished with a fine amounting to half the value of the smuggled salt.

    M.C. Regmi, *Regmi Research Series*. "The Sa t Trade during the Nepal-Tibet War." p. 18.

93. Political A. November 1867. No. 84 Abstract translation of a yaddasht from Jang Bahadur Rana to the British Resident in Nepal dated 28 October 1867. (N .A.I)

94. British Residential Record, Confidential P.N. 32 of 1877. File No. 890-G of 1877. (N.A.I.)

95. Political A. November 1867. No. 84. Abstract translation of yaddasht from Jang Bahadur Rana to the British Resident in Nepal dated 28 October 1867. (N.A.I.)

96. Political A. October 1877. No. 376. F. Heuvey, Officiating Resident in Nepal to T.H. Thornton, Officiating Secretary to the Government of India, Foreign Department No. 32 p. dated 29 June 1877. (N.A.I.)

97. The French, the Portuguese and the English companies carried on traffic in slaves and there was a slave market in Calcutta in the eighteenth century. On the basis of humanitarian ground during the first half of the 19th century slavery was abolished and the Indian act of 1843 removed legal recognition of slavery. See S.N. Srivastava, *Harijans in India*. Lucknow, 1980. p. 245. Also see Jahar Sen, "Slave Trade on the Indo-Nepal Border

in the Nineteenth Century". *Kailash.* Kathmandu, January-February 1973. p. 160.

98. Political A. November 1867. No. 83. An English version of yaddasht from Colonel G. Ramsay British Resident in Nepal to Jang Bahadur Rana, Prime Minister of Nepal dated 3 October 1867. (N.A.I.)

99. K. Majumdar, "British Impact on Nepal." *Bengal Past and Present.* January-June, 1971, p. 140.

100. Jahar Sen. *op. cit*, p. 161.

101. A. Campbell, *Notes on the Agriculture and Rural Economy of the Valley of Nepal.* Kathmandu, 1836, p. 32.

102. Daniel Wright. *Nepal : History of the Country and the People*, 1877, Reprint, New Delhi, 1983, p. 45.

103. Political A. November 1867. No. 82. Colonel G. Ramsay, British Resident in Nepal to the Secretary to the Government of India. Foreign Department. Viceregal Camp at Lucknow dated 8 November 1867. No. 35. (N.A.I.)

104. Proceedings of the Government in the Political Department for August 1867. No. 27. Jekins, the Officiating Commissioner of Patna division to the Secretary to the Government of Bengal. No. 28 dated 29 July 1867. (N A.I.)

105. The number of Musalmans were increasing in Nepal. They were zealous in purchasing girls, and in propagating their sect. Similarly Musalmans and Syyed women were taken by the Rajput and were turned into slave girls in India. They were taught the art of dancing also. Brahman and Rajput were also enslaved forcefully in the region between the Bheri and Mahakali river in Western Nepal. Therefore, the Government of Nepal proclaimed, 'no Brahman or Rajput shall be enslaved except with their consent in presence of the respectable person of the village, not through the use of force.' See, Hamilton, *op. cit.* p. 88; Srivastava, *op. cit.* p. 241. M. C. Regmi, "Documents on Slavery". *Regmi Research Series.* Year 1 No. 2. December 1, 1969. p. 44.

106. *Ibid.*

107. Regmi. *Thatched Huts and Stucco Palaces. Peasants and Land Lords in 19th Century Nepal.* New Delhi, 1978, pp. 127–28.

108. *Ibid.*

109. Political A. March 1878. No. 2. E. Tyrwhit, Inspector General of Police. North Western Provinces and Oudh to C. Robertso, Secretary to the Government of N.W.P. and Oudh dated 3 January 1878. No. 7. (N.A.I.)

110. *Ibid.*

111. *Ibid.*

112. Proceedings of the Bengal Government in the Political Department for August 1867. No. 30. J. Beams, Magistrate of Champaran, to the Commissioner of Patna Division No. 76. dated 11 July 1867.

113. Jahar Sen, *op. cit.* p. 164.

114. Proceedings of Bengal Government in the Political Department for August 1867. No. 30. (N A. I.)

115. *Ibid.*

116. Political A. November 1867. No. 84.

117. Political A. October 1867. No. 225. G. Ramsay, the British Resident in Nepal to J.W.S. Wyllie, Under-Secretary to the Government of India in foreign Department No. 29. dated 23 September 1867. (N.A.I.)

118. Bengal Administrative Report during 1867–68. p. 245.

119. K. Majumdar, *op. cit.* p. 14.

120. Proceedings of the Bengal Government in the Political Department for August 1867. No. 32. H.A. Cockerel Officiating Magistrate at Tirhut to the Commissioner of the Division. No. 120 dated 24 July 1867. (N.A.I.)

121. *Ibid.*

122. Political A. November 1867 No. 84.

123. Mc Leish Alexander, *The Frontier People of India.* London. 1931. pp. 124–125.

124. The re-shipment of imported goods, i.e. entrepot is not as much profitable as brisk indigenous trade. Almost the whole prices of the object sold comes back to enrich the exporting country in case of latter but a few persons get profit from the former. See Ludwig F. Stiller S.J. "A Note on Himalayan Trade". *Journal of Tribhuvan University.* Kirtipur, Nepal, Vol. VII, No 1, November 1972. p. 1.

125. M.C. Regmi, "The Kathmandu Valley Entrepot Trade". *Regmi Research Series.* Year 12, No. 1, 1 January 1980, p. 185.

126. *Ibid. A Study in Nepali Economic History.* New Delhi, 1971. p. 24.

127. K.C Chaudhury, *Anglo-Nepalese Relations from the Earliest Times of British Rule in India Till the Gorkha War.* Calcutta, 1960, p. 91.

128. Kerung and Kuti were two important trade centres in Tibet.

129. Regmi Research Series. *op. cit.* pp. 187-88.

130. Camman Schuyler, *Trade Through the Himalaya the Early British Attempt to Open Tibet.* Princeton, 1951, p. 162.

131. K.C. Chaudhury, *op. cit.*

132. William Digby. *Nepal and India, A Friend in Need : Friendship Forgotten*. London, 1980, pp. 20-21.
133. Report on the Foreign Trade of North Western Provinces and Oudh. 1877-78. (N.A.I.)
134. Eden Vansittart, *op. cit*. p. 6.
135. Ikbal Ali Shah, *Nepal, the Home of the Gods*. London n. d. p. 235.
136. M.C. Regmi, *A Study in Nepali Economic History*. p. 25.
137. Regmi Research Series. *op. cit.* 191.
138. *Ibid.* p. 190.
139. *Ibid.*
140. *Ibid.*
141. Parshotam Mahra, *The Younghusband Expedition*. Bombay, 1968, f. n. p. 46.
142. Alastair Lamb, *Britain and Chinese Central Asia : The Road to Lhasa 1767 to 1905*. London, 1960, p. 346.
143. *Ibid.*
144. *Regmi Research Series*. op. cit.
145. W. Brook Northey and C.J. Morris. *The Gurkhas, Their Manners, Customs and Country*. 1928 reprint, Delhi 1974. p. 84.
146. Harihar Acharya, "Uttare Sima Vyapar" *Gorkhapatra* 5 May 1980.

Commercial Taxes and Trade Registration Centre

CHAPTER FIVE

5.1 Commercial taxes levied on the border

Different kinds of taxes were levied by the Nepalese Government on the Indo-Nepal border and in the Nepalese markets. These taxes included customs and transit duties, license fees, house-rent, market taxes, etc. These taxes were also called Sair.[1] The customs and transit duties were levied by the Government on both exports and imports. The whole frontier of Nepal was divided into a certain number of sections, known as Sair Mahal which were farmed-out for a term of certain years to contractors called Thekedars. The customs duties varied according to the region and routes by which the goods were imported or exported. On the Western frontier of Nepal, the Government imposed high export duties on Nepalese traders and very light import duties on Indian traders. It was done to compel the Nepalese traders to sell their goods in Nepalese markets and to attract the Indian traders to inhabit and promote trade in the new region which was under-developed and sparsely populated. Besides export duty, a cess of six pice per rupee was imposed on all valuable articles, live-stock and other goods. In addition, an export and transit duty called Mahsuli Nikasi[2] was levied on goods exported to India. On the one hand this policy created difficulties for the Nepalese traders who used to sell hill products in the Indian markets freely before the opening of these markets in Banke district, and on the other forced the Indian merchants to visit and live in the Nepalese markets to get the hill products. Consequently, the Indian traders had to live permanently in Nepalese markets, deserting their former shops in the British territory. On 13 December 1875, the Deputy

Commissioner of Bahraich estimated that the Nepalese Government earned an average income of Rs. 55,000 in Banke district through various dues as indicated below.[3]

1. Cesses from hillmen bringing their goods in the market	4,000
2. Mahsuli Nikasi (export duty) paid chiefly by British traders	41,000
3. Import duty paid chiefly by British traders	8,000
4. Baithaki Mahsul (licenses to seel)	500
5. Rent for shops paid by British traders located there	1,500
Total	55,000

The British traders had to pay rent for the shops built by the Nepalese Government. If no shops were available at time, they had to pay a Baithaki Mahsul or permit due to admit them as traders at the rate of rupees 1-8 per annum for each trader.

The rate of Customs and Transit duties varied from place to place in the western part of Nepal adjoining British districts of of Kumaun, Gonda, Basti and Gorakhpur. The table below clearly indicates the diversities in the taxation system.[4]

Table 10

Taxes Levied on the Commodities Exported from British Provinces to Nepal

Commodity	Rate of taxation per maund on the frontier of											
	Kumaun			Gonda			Basti			Gorakhpur		
	Rs	a	p	Rs	a	p	Rs	a	p	Rs	a	p
Salt	0	2	0	0	6	0	0	4	0	0	6	0
Sugar	0	2	0	0	6	0	0	4	0	0	6	0
Potatoes	0	1	6	0	4	3	0	10	0	0	6	0
Tobacco	0	2	0	0	2	0	0	4	0	0	6	0

It was a general belief that the rate of duty in Nepalese district adjoining Kumaun was ten per cent ad valorem for export and import. But the duty was levied in lump sum on the com-

Table 11

Taxes Levied on the Commodities Imported into British Provinces from Nepal

Commodity	Rate of taxation per maund on the frontier of				
	Kumaun	Gonda		Basti	Gorakhpur
		For Resident	For non-Resident		
	Rs a p	Rs a p	Rs a p	Rs a p	Rs a p
Iron Ploughshares	Not known	1 5 0	1 12 0	Not known	0 6 0
Ginger	1 9 6	1 3 0	1 7 9	,,	0 3 0
Honey	1 9 6	1 3 0	1 12 0	,,	0 6 0
Cardamom	2 4 0	1 4 0	3 0 0	5 0 0	0 3 0
Turmeric	1 7 0	Not known	Not known	1 12 0	0 3 0

modities exported and imported from Bareilly. On payment of the duty a pass was issued which protected the goods from any further charges. The duty on export from Nepal was estimated to be from 10 to 12 per cent. It was levied per weight and per load of article not ad valorem in Bareilly. Metal and grain were taxed by weight, cloth by load and timber by measurement. The Assistant Collector of Pilibhit stated that it was impossible to estimate the duties levied on imports into Nepal as the trade was in the hands of the Nepalese.[5]

According to one British trader, who used to trade at Golamandi, Rajapur and other places in Naya Muluk, the import charge taken by the Government on European cloth was 3 per cent ad valorem. The duty on country or Indian cloth per piece was between Rs. 1 and Rs. 3.24. The export duties on goods like red-pepper and catachu were between Re 1 and 6 per Nepali maund.[6] Charles Girdlestone, the British Resident in Nepal, reported that the duty on export and import was both on weight and ad valorem. He pointed out that the large dealers could often make arrangements with the contractors by which they get the reduction of 25 per cent. Import duties were levied at only one time. The tarriff seldom varied and the rate of the customs was known to all concerned. Certain persons of high rank or position had the privilege of purchasing free of duty.[7]

The rate of customs duty was heavier at Brahmadeo Mandi than at Jhulaghat, Asgad, Auluang and Darchula. As a result the producers and traders preferred to export their commodities through these four places, rather than through the former. It caused a loss of revenue to the Government and smuggling increased. Therefore, it was suggested by Colonel Siddhiman Singh Rajbhandari that revenue might go up and smuggling checked, if customs tariffs at these four places were collected at the same rates as at Brahmadeo-Mandi. The Prime Minister Jang Bahadur Rana accepted the suggestion and ordered that the consolidated accounts of customs tariffs should be submitted to the 'Dafadar-khana Kumari Chok' (Government treasury).[8]

There were differences between commercial taxes paid by the residents and nonresidents or itinerant traders. The traders residing in the Nepal bazars were taxed at lighter rates than non-residents. The itinerant traders had to pay 25 per cent more taxes than the residents. The report of the North Western Provinces critically mentioned, "The resident traders though nominally allowed to export at the lower rates, are not really allowed to do so as long as there are itinerant traders to pay the higher rates and compete with them. The so-called residents are all British subjects who go to the Nepalese bazars at the beginning of the cold season and return before the rains set in. The advantages residence is supposed to give them in the lower rates at which they are taxed often appear to be disallowed when they conflict with the interests of the Nepal exchequer, and if we may believe report the residence of the richer traders is rather enforced by official pressure than tempted by benefits to compensate for the trouble and expenses.[9] Although the mode of taxation appeared to be irregular. it would be difficult to make generalization from the report mentioned above.

In addition to customs dues and Rawana or pass fee, there were other taxes levied on residents and non-resident traders at Nepalgunj, Golamandi and Dhakhnabagh.

The resident traders at Nepalgunj had to pay Octroi (chungi) at the rate of $1\frac{1}{4}$ seer per maund and non-resident had to pay this tax ad valorem at the rate of $4\frac{1}{2}$ pies per rupee of price. In both the cases, they recovered the tax from Nepalese traders who brought the goods to sell. The resident traders had to pay Arhat or Commission at the rate of $1\frac{1}{2}$ pies per maund whereas non-resident traders paid at the rate of $1\frac{1}{2}$ annas per maund for all goods except cardamom. Cardamom was levied at the rate of $2\frac{1}{4}$ annas.[10] The traders had also to pay taxes called *hath* and *gatthi*. The hath was a market cess usually levied at the rate of 12 annas per one hundred pieces of cloth whether coarse or fine, and gathi was an import duty also levied on cloth, usually at the rate of $7\frac{1}{2}$ annas per score for fine, and $2\frac{1}{2}$ annas per score for coarse texture.[11] Dastur adhani at the rate of 6 pies per maund was paid by both the resident and non-resident traders. It was an all-round tax. As its name implies it was a half anna fee. All these taxes except adhani, were levied on the resident and non-resident traders at Golamandi and Dhakhnabagh. The non-resident traders at Dhakhnabagh had to pay chungi ad valorem at the rate of $\frac{1}{2}$ anna per rupee of price while the goods were in their hands. There were differences in taxation at Dhakhnabagh in respect of goods in their custody and goods in course of export. In the latter case there was a rawana or pass fee at the rate of 1 anna on the unit on which the tax was levied. The imposts (Mahsul) except in cloth, were the same in Golamandi as in Dhakhnabagh. But, at Nepalgunj, in addition to the Mahsul there was another tax called Roshan Chungi. This tax was levied at an allround rate of 2 annas per maund in case of the resident traders and 3 pies in case of non-resident traders. *Roshan Chungi* was literally a fee towards defraying the expenses of lighting the bazar,[12] but in fact the proceeds went into the pocket of the Rana Prime Minister.

There was no customs duty on food grain on the border of Western Nepal. But a tax was imposed on its production, and cultivators had to pay a cess called "Sayer Galla".[13]

There were thirteen passes over Dundwa range in Western Nepal adjoining Indian territory of Gonda district. At the top of each there was a customs post. At twelve of these posts customs dues were levied only on the products of the Dundwa range.The products were chiefly, dhup, bankas grass and rough wood. No other commodities were allowed to cross through these passes except by the Dara Pass. On the Dundwa range there were two separate taxing establishments, one for hill products which was stationed at the top of the passes and another for the trade near the border. Mr Happer, Assistant Commissioner of Gonda, found the Customs on hill products to be very irregularly levied. On bankas grass the duty was levied both in kind and in cash. It was levied five plaits (or atis) and five Nepalese pice per headload.Dhup was taxed one anna per headload, but no tax was levied on this article when carried by women. Rough wood was taxed Rs 0-1-6 per cartload. Timber, cut and roughly shaped in the hills, was taxed as follows (Table 12).

Table 12
Taxes on Exports of Timber

		Rs	A	P
Sugar–Mill Pestles each	duty	0	10	0
	Katai	0	8	0
	Hakk Thekadari	0		0
	Total	1	4	0
Cart Sheels (per pair)	duty	2	8	0
	Katai	2	0	0
	Total	4	8	0
Axles, each	duty	0	2	0
	Katai	0	1	0
	Total	0	3	0

Some receipts for the tax paid which Mr Happer obtained from traders, contained no amount of duty paid but merely describing the article on which duty was levied. There was some export and import of commodities between the Nepalese district of Dang and Deokhuri. These commodities were not taxed at the hill post, but at the post called Kakrahwa near Deokhuri. If the trader was taxed on the load (man or animal) and returned with his goods unsold, he could claim a refund at the same rate, and occasionally, if he were well-known, the duty was not levied till his return. The cloth imported from India was nearly all of native manufacture and was chiefly confined to 'dhotis' known as 'garha'. On this the duty was levied at 3 piece (Gorakhpuri) per than on European cloth the duty was levied per piece 2 annas for markin (American drill) and one anna for 'nainsukh'. The demand for these fabrics was so great in Deokhuri that the duty was almost nominal to encourage import.[14] The following[15] were the rates of duties levied on the goods crossing Dandwa range by the Dara Pass opposite Gonda district.

Table 13 (a)

Rate of Duty on the Goods Exported from Nepal to India through Gonda District

Name of article	Rate of duty Rs	a	p	How levied	Percentage on average value Rs	a	p
Oil seeds, Lahi	0	3	0	per horse or bullock load	4	2	8
Linseed	0	3	0	,,	4	2	8
Rice (husked)	0	2	6	,,	3	14	6
Other grains	0	2	0	,,	5	9	0
Ghee	2	0	0	,,	6	4	0

Table 13 (b)

Rate of Duty on the Goods Imported into Nepal from India through Gonda District

Name of article	Rate of duty Rs	a	p	How levied	Percentage on average value Rs	a	p
Salt	0	6	0	per horse or bullock load	2	5	6
Coarse sugar (Gur)	0	6	0	,,	4	2	8
Molasses (Shira)	0	4	0	,,	6	4	0
Tobacco	0	2	0	,,	0	8	9
Potatoes	3 or 4 annas			,,	Not known		
Onions	0	2	0	,,	Not known		
Cloth country	0	0	3	,,	1	14	0
Cloth European							
Markin	0	2	0	,,	1	14	9
Nainsukh	0	1	0	,,	1	12	7

One trader, who used to take salt to the Dang Valley and bring back Lahi (rope) seed said that goods coming from and going to Dang were taxed lighter than those from or to Deakhuri. He used to pay 4 annas for salt and 2 annas for Lahi (rope) seed per bullock load instead of 6 annas and 3 annas respectively.

The customs dues in the Western part of Nepal were levied on all the valuable articles of import and export from the Nepalese bazar. It was done with a view to collecting the taxes easily and to promote the prosperity of the towns or the market. The dues on the goods imported from Gonda district were calculated on the load (carried either by men or animals or in carts), on the weight, on the number, or on the value. Bamboo paper was taxed by the headload, the coarse blankets (known as Bhangras) by the score, salt and sugar ad valorem, and cloth on the score of 20 Nepalese thans. Besides customs dues, there were two other taxes, one was called "Khunt" and the other was known as Chungi or Octroi. The tax "Khunt" was taken from non-resident traders on their entry into the town or in the market. The tax was one of the means of inducing traders to take up their residence in the bazars. It was levied at the rate of 2 annas per bullock load, 1 anna per pony load, 1 pice per head load. The Octroi was calculated in kind, but levied in cash. It was calculated at the rate of one bisola (or $1\frac{1}{4}$ Nepalese seer) per Nepalese maund. In the case of the larger traders the Octroi was not levied at the time of purchase, but in a lump sum at the end of the season, according to the attested entries in customs official's book.[16]

The duties were collected under the jurisdiction of only one contractor in the Nepalese tarai, north of Gorakhpur district. The tax was levied according to the cart load if brought by cart and according to weight for the rest of the articles. The weight was determined by guess. The Deputy Collector of Gorakhpur was of the opinion that the import into Nepal and export from that country were taxed twice. He remarked, ". . . if the articles which cross the frontier into Lukauli, are declared to be for sale within the Lukauli jurisdiction then double rates than those entered above (those in the schedule) are at once levied at the Gorakhpur frontier posts, while, if the goods after paying a single rate as above cross the Bootwal jurisdiction, three-fourths of the original rate are again levied there . . . . Further there are exceptional increase to these additional inland charges, for instance, the frontier charge on a male buffalo is 1 anna 6 pie, but on reaching the Bootwal Ilaka 4 annas 3 pies additional are levied".[17] The import duty was levied on several articles at different places. The tax was levied for the first time for crossing the frontier and other taxes for crossing for other parts under others' jurisdiction. The taxes were levied until the articles reached their destination. This complicated system was not prevailing in other parts of the kingdom. The Deputy Collector estimated that the initial duty at the border was $1\frac{1}{4}$ per cent ad valorem for exports from, and $2\frac{1}{2}$ per cent ad valorem on imports into Nepal. He thought that the aggregate of all the charges on imports were equivalent to 5 per cent ad valorem, or even more. In the ad valorem case, the valuation entirely depended on the market prices both at the place of purchase and the place of sale. The valuation of commodities charged according to the changing prices of the market. The system of taxation in the Nepalese territory adjoining Champaran, Muzaffarpur, Darbhanga, Bhagalpur and Purnea was not complicated.

The duty was levied only one time for the commodities exported from Champaran into Nepalese territory. Except Chokidari dues nothing was paid en route till the traffic reached Kathmandu from Sugauli. The trader, who had paid taxes in Kathmandu for export had nothing to pay at other places on the way. But he had to get pass as the proof of having once paid. The rate of customs duties were levied according to the engagement of 1839. The Deputy Collector of Purnea remarked that the wealthy merchants, who conducted the trade used to make their own terms with the tax collector. There were several customs houses en route from Kathmandu to Indian territory. These existed at Chapkaiya, Kowahli, Katchorwa Semrabasa. Semraungadh, Hetauda, Bhimphedi, Sisagadhi and Kathmandu. Duties were levied at fixed rate in these customs houses. Some of these customs houses were nothing but checking offices.

The customs duties were levied on goods imported into and exported from Nepalese districts adjoining Muzaffarpur district on the basis of entry point. The Collector of Muzaffarpur stated the following rates of duties at the different points of entrances.[18]

Bairgania : 1 anna a cart, ½ anna a pack animal

Majorgunj : 2 per cent (? ad valorem) up to the border, and 4 pice a cart intending to cross the border.

Sonbarsa : 2 per cent (? ad valorem) on tarai articles and 8 per cent in articles from Kathmandu.

Sursand : 6 annas a cart, 2 annas a pack animal, 4 pice a coolie.

Madhawa-pur : 1 pie per rupee for common things, and 2 per cent for valuable things.

No duties were levied at the ghats during 1892 to 1895 on imports into and exports from Nepal but the undermentioned tolls were levied by Thekedars (contractors) at the ghats near Sonbarsa and Bela on the following articles exported from Nepal.[19]

Table 14
Tolls Levied by Thekedar

Articles	Loaded cart			Pack bullock			Coolies		
	Rs	a	p	Rs	a	p	Rs	a	p
Sabey	0	10	0	0	1	0	0	0	3
Khar	0	6	0	0	1	6	0	0	3
Bamboos	0	10	0	0	1	0	0	0	3
Leaves of Malhan	0	8	0	0	1	0	0	0	3
Foodgrain	0	0	6	0	0	1	0	0	½

There was one customs house at Jaleshowar in Nepal on the opposite side of Sursand.[20]

The duty was generally levied by the cart or bullock load, irrespective of the weight or value of the goods in the Nepalese territory on the other side of the Darbhanga district. There was no import duty on food grain or tobacco. There were customs houses at Jalipur, Malangwa, Bishanpur, and Sarsar. The traders were allowed to pay customs duty at the Court (Kachahari) in the village where they carried on their trade.[21]

General Gahendra Shamsher with his wife(c.1920)

Prime Minister Chandra Shamsher

family at Singh Durbar (c. 1920).

King Prithvi Bir with high-ranking Ranas and family members.

None of the goods were allowed to pass into Nepalese territory from the Bhagalpur district without paying customs duty in Nepal. The taxes were levied partly by load, and on animal per head. A shopkeeper had also to pay one pie in one rupee on his sale. The Sub-divisional Officer believed that the rate of taxes were arbitrarily not fixed. The right to levy duty was in the hands of one contractor (farmer) who collected it through subordinates. They collected dues on exports according to the rates in the schedule and on sale of imports. Taxes were levied by zamindar at the fairs. The Collector of the Bhagalpur district remarked that the Nepalese customs officials were strict and rigorously levied duties without favour.[22]

The duties were levied on all goods exported from and imported into Nepalese district on the other side of Purnea district. The taxes were collected by the contractor with the help of subordinates along the frontier. They collected duties in cash not in kind. Although the Nepalese Government fixed the rate nominally, it varied according to locality and the sublessees, the latter being under no real control. Mustard oil, jute, ghee, tobacco, rice and paddy were found to be taxed 6 pice on every rupee's worth purchased in one place and in another place the tax on the last two articles was one anna in the rupee. The duty on export was levied at the time of sale and the purchaser was furnished with a pass to cross the frontier. Smuggling was punished by the imposition of double duty. The subdivisional Officer considered that the export duty was on an average 7 per cent. The tax was not levied directly on imported goods. The trader had to pay taxes according to the size of shop or the extent of his transactions. The pedlar had to pay for a license at the cost of the goods. It was generally fixed ad valorem on the estimated value of his goods. It was to be decided by mutual understanding between pedlar and the contractor. Besides his license in cash, the pedlar had to pay toll in kind. Once he made the payment he was free to hawk his goods without any risk of interference.[23] The Subdivisional Officer of Sitamarhi in Muzaffarpur district remarked that there was no duty directly levied by the officers of the Nepalese Government. There were "Thekedars" for hats and bazaars in Nepalese territory who imposed heavy taxes on the traders. For cloth sold and grain purchased in Nepal 10 annas per hundred rupees worth of things was charged. Besides, there had been a road tax called "Dhoor Uraye" at the rate of two "Lohiya Paisa" per pack bullock and four "Lohiya Paisa" per cart load. The ghee was levied at the rate of $\frac{1}{2}$ annas per maund and four annas per cartload. The duty on salt was five seers per cart load and on honey, four annas per maund. The Sub-divisional Officer of Supaul in the Bhagalpur district reported that no imports or duties other than 'Batti' or 'Chunge' were levied in the interior of the sub-tarai. Since September 1888, the taxes except in hide was abolished.[24]

The Nepalese Government had no regular stations for the collection of taxes. In the seven districts of the eastern Tarai region (Morang, Saptari, Mahottari, Sarlahi, Bara, Parsa and Rautahat) customs duties and other taxes were collected through contract. The contractors (the farmers) had to pay a certain amount to the state within a stipulated time. In the above mentioned districts contract was granted to Dittha Singh Bir and Captain Bishnu Bir for a total sum of Rs 18,859 - 13 for the year 1885 to 1886.[25] Similar systems of contract (farming) were also found in different districts of the western Nepal tarai.

One of the peculiar features of the commercial taxation was that the articles exempted in one place were dutiable in other places. For instance, duties were collected on twenty or twenty-one items in other districts, but the schedule for Sheoraj district of Western Nepal contained only seventeen items. Items which were subjected to duty elsewhere could be exported freely from Sheoraj, while those that were dutiable here were abolished elsewhere.[26] Similarly, the rates of Sair and other duties on goods imported from India, were applicable only to trade conducted through the Kathmandu valley. The rates were different on goods imported from India through the Golas of eastern Nepal.[27]

The Nepalese Government published a list of articles that were exempted from customs duty along with the articles importation of which was prohibited within special permission or license, and also a list of articles importation of which was prohibited. The import of Cannon, Fire arms (gun, rifles, pistols, etc) of all kinds, explosives of all kinds, opium and wines was prohibited without special permission or license. The import of impure sugar, Government badges or medals studded with jewellery, biscuits other than K.P. Basu & Co.'s Hindu Biscuits, the sole right of importation of which was granted to Dr Ratna Das, electric materials of other than passed by Government Electric Department, Cigars or Cigarrettes other than approved by Government monopolist was prohibited. But all foodgrains, fruits, animals and vegetables were exempted from import duty.[28]

5.2 British Objections against the System of Taxation

The British Government raised serious objection to the system of commercial taxation in Nepal. The British Government considered it as a great impediment to the growth of Indo-Nepal trade. G. Ramsay, the British Resident in Nepal opposed it vigorously. According to him taxes imposed by Nepal greatly exceeded the amount fixed by the engagement of 1839.[29] Dr Daniel Wright, the British Residency Surgeon, wrote that the Government of Nepal imposed 12 to 14 per cent duty on British goods.[30] Markham Clement, an itinerant, remarked that the export and import duties levied by the Nepalese Government were ruinous to the Indo-Nepal and Tibet trade.[31]

Charles Girdlestone did not agree with the above statements regarding the system of taxation. He reported that some important sections of British Indian traders had informed him that there was no obstructiveness or undue taxation to complain against Nepal.[32] Similar view was also expressed by the Deputy Commissioner of Gonda. He clarified that there were no exactions imposed by the Nepalese authorities.[33] The Faizabad conference of 1880 did not agree that the duties levied by the Nepalese Government were exceptionally burdensome and the trade was hampered to a great extent. Upon enquiries, it was found that the duties were seldom heavy and in no case prohibitory.[34]

As regards the amount of the taxation Girdlestone argued that since there was no complaint about the irregularity of duties, the prevailing prices convinced him that not more than the published duties were charged. Further, he added that the import duties levied on merchandise by the Nepalese Government were justified on the same ground as those which justify the imperial duties levied by the British Government on the merchandise in India. These taxes were the same for the Nepalese as for the British subjects.[35]

Considering the rate of taxes in India, the taxes imposed by the Nepalese Government was seldom heavy. In 1859 the rate of customs duty in India was raised to 10 per cent. In 1864 it was lowered to 7½ per cent and in 1875 to 5 per cent.[36] According to the Deputy Commissioner of Kheri, Chungi (octrai) was levied in almost every town in India under the supervision of Municipality.[37] He had prepared the following tables to compare the ad valorem rates of the octrai levied in Nepal with those in the Indian town of Lucknow.[38]

Table 15 (a)

Comparison between the ad valorem Rates of octroi Levied on Exports in Nepal with those in an Indian Town

Articles	Exports from Nepal					
	Nepal			Lucknow		
	Rs	a	p	Rs	a	p
Spices	6	0	0	3	0	0
Edible grains	9	8	0	9	4	0
Oil seeds	Not known			4	9	10
Ghee	12	8	0	3	4	6
Wax	9	0	0	4	0	0
Country cloth	0	12	0	1	8	0

Table 15 (b)

Imports into Nepal

Artic'es	Nepal			Lucknow		
	Rs	a	p	Rs	a	p
Cotton	6	4	0	1	8	0
Sweetmeat	1	9	0	4	11	0
Spices	6	0	0	3	0	0

Contd.

Articles	Nepal			Lucknow		
	Rs	a	p	Rs	a	p
Edible grains	9	8	0	9	4	0
Salt	4	13	0	Not indicated		
Country cloth	0	12	0	1	8	0
European	3	2	0	1	8	0
Refined sugar	3	2	0	3	12	0
Unrefined sugar	4	13	0	1	7	2
Fruits	6	4	0	Not indicated		
Wheat	9	6	0	9	11	0
Tobacco	4	13	0	6	4	0
Fish	0	5	0	2	1	8
Metal	7	2	3	1	8	0
Ghee	12	8	0	3	4	6

When Girdlestone, the British Resident in Nepal was asked by the British Government to press the Nepalese Government to reduce the rate of taxation he refused to do so on the ground that the British Government had no right to interfere with or even to advise upon the commercial policy of Nepal and also because the British Government was itself a receiver of excessively high duties upon salt and opium. The truth was that the system of duties in Nepal was complicated only from the European point of view, because it was made up of several items of demand on one and the same thing.[39] The real objection of Girdlestone was against the system of farming taxation. In course of his discussion with the Nepalese Prime Minister, the British Resident put forward the problem arising out of the system of farming taxation. In his opinion, "Such a person (contractor or farmer) wants to make money quickly, and therefore is apt to demand more than the authorized tariff allows, and to cause oppression and vexation to traders by employing untrustworthy agents and servants. These evils are avoided if the Government work through its own responsible officials."[40] The Prime Minister agreed that there was oppression in the system of farming. He promised to remove the contract system slowly and replace it with 'amanat system' (collection of customs duties by government officials). The Commander in Chief, who was present at that time remarked that if there was oppression the courts were there to listen to their complaints.[41]

There were several courts in Nepal near the border to hear the complaints of the traders.[42] From time to time the Nepalese Government warned the contractor not to collect unauthorised duties. For instance, in 1882 the contractor of Sheoraj district of Western Nepal was punished according to the law when he was found taking unauthorised duties. His mistake was that he had collected the duties on the basis of the practice followed in other districts. He charged duties at 6 annas, 8 annas, 10 annas, 12 annas or 13½ annas per cartload and 1 anna per head load (tagi). He held up foodgrains purchased by Indian traders on the border until duties were paid. Because the contractor collected unauthorised duties at arbitrary rates in this manner, Indian merchants went back without purchasing any foodgrains in Sheoraj. Local Land-owners were, therefore, unable to sell their foodgrains and pay taxes to the Government. The complaint of Indian merchants was that since they had to pay customs duties on export they were unable to buy foodgrains. Therefore, they declared that they would make purchase only if the prices of the commodities were reduced. The landowners of the district requested the Nepalese Government to abolish customs duties on foodgrains and they assured that they would compensate the loss of revenue on a proportionate basis. Therefore the Government announced that a surcharge of 3½ paisa on each rupee of land tax should be collected in lieu of duties on the export of foodgrains. Section 6 of the revenue regulations for Sheoraj 'Mal' (Revenue Department) mentioned that new and unauthorised payment should not be collected.[43]

G. Ramsay, the British Resident in Nepal, pointed out that the merchandise, which could pass from the plain of India to Tibet for 6 to 8 per cent levy in 1864, had to pay from 12 to 14 per cent levy ten days later.[44] But an investigation made at the instance of the British Government was later to reveal that the duties levied by the Nepalese Government were not high. In fact they were in conformity with the levy imposed by the British Government in India.[45] On 26 December 1907 the Nepalese Government demanded that a rebate of customs duties should be given on all articles of equipment imported by Nepal from England for the troops. But the British Indian Government refused it with regret.[46] Similarly on 27 April 1908 British Indian Government requested the Nepalese

Government to revise the schedules showing the duties levied on articles imported into or exported from Nepal. But this request was postponed till the return of the Prime Minister from England.[47] On 14 September 1914, the Government of Nepal informed that some corrections had been made in the schedules of 1909 with an addition to a few items. But these schedules could not be applied to the bazars at Brahmadeo Mandi, Morang and Birgunj until after the expiry of the periods of contracts[48] under which they were working. The taxes were heavy only in the western part of Nepalese bazars. It was done to popularize the market. But these taxes were withdrawn by the Nepalese Government in 1896. The taxes were heavy in case of luxurious goods, but were light in the case of necessary items.[49]

In June 1836, the East India Company Government exempted all imports from Nepal from the payment of customs duties in India. The Government of Nepal, on the other hand, continued to collect duties on goods imported from India.[50] The Company Government had their own commercial interest to exempt the duties because there was no great demand of Indian goods in Nepal as compared with the Nepalese products. It wanted to capture the Nepalese market by abolishing commercial taxes on the Indo-Nepal border.

For the entire period of Indo-Nepal trade relations the question of customs duties remained unsettled. The Nepalese Government had no option but to impose taxes for the sake of revenue. The British Government also realised that "the Nepalese frontier tariff was imposed rather with reference to revenue than to interfere materially with trade."[51] Even then local duties levied on goods in transit among the hill districts, were abolished. A similar exaction in the Tarai in respect of goods displayed for sale at the fairs in different localities had been discontinued since 1914. Chungi (octroi) which had long been imposed upon the transport of goods within the Kathmandu Valley was also abolished.[52]

5.3. Trade Registration Centre

There was no customs house in the Indian districts all along the frontier of Nepal. Before 1875 no attempt was made by the

British Government to register the amount of trade traffic passing through the different sectors on the Indo-Nepal border. Although there were customs houses in most of the border districts on the Nepalese side, the Nepalese Government did not attempt to register its trade with British India.[53]

On 23 August 1875 the Bengal Government passed a resolution to sanction certain arrangements for the registration of traffic between Bengal and Nepal with effect from the first day of September. The decision for registration of inter-provincial traffic was taken at a conference at Allahabad. The Conference was attended by delegates from Bengal, North Western Provinces and Oudh, the Punjab and Central Provinces. The Collectors of Bhagalpur, Darbhanga, Muzaffarpur and Champaran were also consulted. The resolution of the Conference mentioned that hitherto there would be no organized attempt to register the amount of traffic between India and Nepal. It was also agreed that there was great difficulty in organizing a complete system of registration, as the boundary line was extensive and the trade found its way through numerous channels. The arrangements sanctioned were "experimental only and liable to modification."[54] It was also decided that a copy of daily returns of each registering station in prescribed proforma should be submitted every week by the registering clerk (Mohurir) to the district headquarters for the purpose of analysis and preparation of monthly returns. The clerks were instructed to register the names of the places and export and import of commodities The resolution added that nothing elaborate in this direction was required, but it was desirable to bring to the notice of the Government all the most important markets, and the amount of their traffic.[55]

On 28 August 1875 the British Indian Government approved the establishment of registration posts at Khandauli and Birpur in Bhagalpur district, Sitamarhi and Pupri in Muzaffarpur district; Jaynagar, Kamtaul and Madhubani in Darbhanga district and Katkana, Raxaul and Ghorasahan in Champaran district.[56] On 4 September 1875 registration posts were established at Amona, Sikti and Kalughat in Purnea district.[57] On 2 October 1875 the registration stations at Kunjulio, Ghoompahar, Adhikari and Naxalbari were ordered to register the frontier traffic between

Darjeeling and Eastern Nepal.[58] From 1 June 1885 the registration of traffic at Naxalbari was discontinued. It was replaced by the registration post at Siliguri. Later on three posts at Sukhiapokri, Kunjulia and Siliguri registered the traffic with Nepal. But after 1898 only two registration posts called Sukhiapokri and Kunjulia continued to register the trade with Nepal.[59]

There were 24 registration posts in the districts of Gorakhpur, Basti, Gonda, Kheri, Pilibhit and Kumaun adjoining Western frontier of Nepal. Five new posts were also established later on. These posts were Jhulaghat in Kumaun district, Sagarpur in Gonda district, Sohas in Basti district and Jogiabari and Narkulia in Gorakhapur district.[60]

All the above-mentioned registration stations were changed with the change of climate and diversification of trade routes and traffic. For instance in 1875 when the registration arrangements were first started, Bengal had 17 posts in 1882-83, and 34 posts in 1898-99. All these stations were kept open throughout the year. But Tribenighat in Champaran district was closed for two months (September to October), Naxalbari, Ghoompahar and Kunjulia for three months (16 June to 15 September),[61] Pathardewa for six months (1 June to 30 November), Sukhiapokri and Kunjulia for three months (16 June to 15 September), on account of rain.[62] Similarly the position of two posts situated in Kheri and Gorakhpur districts, was changed because of the extreme unhealthiness of climate. Tirkolia in Kheri district was shifted to Palia, Bahuar in Gorakhpur district to Baitulia.[63] The Palia registration centre was again transferred to Trikolia.[64] In 1883-84 owing to a change in the course of the river Sarda, the registration post at Brahmadeo was shifted to Tanakpur. The river having again changed its course, a great portion of the traffic was diverted to Mandiaghat.[65]

The main objective of registration was to guage the extent of the trade and to determine whether it was capable of increasing or not.[66] But the objective was not fully achieved. It was suggested that registration clerks should visit Nepalese hats and bazaars to register the import and export traffic. But neither a system of registration at the marts (bazaars) nor a system of frontier registration could be successful. Most of the commissioners of the divisions bordering Nepal in Bengal and North West Provinces and Oudh criticised the system of registration as "very imperfect", "completely untrustworthy", "inaccurate" and "complete failure".[67]

In 1878-79, there were 52 registration posts for a frontier of more than 700 miles, on an average one post for every $13\frac{1}{2}$ miles.[68] In 1877-78 there were 20 registration stations in the North Western Provinces over 330 miles of border.[69] The number of these stations was inadequate. There was every possibility of goods escaping registration. In most cases the traffic passed the frontier by hundreds of roads and footpaths were not controlled by the registration stations.

Charles Girdlestone did not rely on the statistics of trade supplied by registration stations, because they did not represent the actual amount of the traffic. The list of imports from Nepal omitted tea for which there was an increasing demand from Darjeeling and Kumaun. The supply of Chinese tea through Tibet decreased because of the bad relations between Nepal and Tibet.[70]

The traders did not want to expose portable and valuable goods such as coin, gold dust, silver and musk. The export of musk, silver gold and furs from Nepal and imports of coral and precious stones and personal clothing escaped registration. Much of the musk, which was highly valuable, was sent from Nepal by the British Residents' post and brocade and uniform entered Nepal by the same means. Some items generally found in the personal baggage of the travellers also escaped the notice of the registering clerks. The Sub-divisional Officers of Kishanganj reported that several elephants, horses and 20,000 pigs were taken to Nepal every year but these did not pass through the registration stations. Similarly large quantities of timber and musk were imported from Nepal but these were never registered. There were only three registration offices, while there were about 200 roads. Consequently everybody chose the easiest route for himself and would not take the trouble to pass by a circular route to have the articles registered.[71]

The Sub-divisional Officer of Madhubani reported that some merchants from Mirzapur attended the Janakpur fair in Nepal without registering their commodities. The export from Nepal such as grain, timber, ghee, oilseeds, firewood, dhup (incense wood) and bunkas (a fibrous grass used for ropes) were taken across the border avoiding the registering stations.[72]

It was also reported by the Deputy Commissioner of Darjeeling that the clerks in the registration stations of Darjeeling district had got confused with the classification and columns of the registration forms. Their entries were frequently incorrect and their figures had double meanings. He suggested that it was essential to appoint clerks familiar with the language spoken by the frontier traders and also Hindi.[73]

Newberry, the District Magistrate of Bhagalpur, reported that the people were against the system of registration. In most cases the traders refused to supply information to the registering clerks.[74] To the Commissioner of Bhagalpur division the unsuitability of police agency for trade enquiries became so obvious that he suggested the system of registration should be abandoned as far as possible. The sub-divisional officers and sub-deputies also agreed that it was difficult to collect statistics from half a million people scattered about in seven hundred villages. A single officer could not collect exhaustive information, even if he devoted all his time to the matter. The result would be equally untrustworthy even if he could confine himself to one bazaar only.[75]

The Indian traders of Muzaffarpur district avoided registration because they connected it with license-tax.[76] The sub-divisonal officer of Sitamarhi in Muzaffarpur district reported in 1879-80 that the falling off in the quantities of trade was due to the carelessness of the registration clerks. The clerks were careless in noting whether the traffic passing their registering posts was actually from Nepal or going to Nepal.[77] The problem was the same in Basti district. The registration of traffic in the district was vitiated by the unfitness, moral and mental, of the registration clerks.[78]

The value of timber in Nepal depended on size, length and quality.[79] But the registration clerks calculated the weight of timber and determined its value on the basis of guess. Hence the system of the valuation of timber was not correct.[80]

The salary of the registration clerks was quite low. They used to get $3\frac{1}{2}$ rupees per month.[81] Therefore they neglected to register the trade. There was not much supervision on them. In most cases, they trusted the traders and information given by them regarding the nature, value and quantity of goods that passed through their posts was accepted.

The annual expenditure of registration arrangement in the North Western Provinces was rupees 2,744 in 1877. The amount was not sufficient for the proper arrangement of registering stations and for increasing the wages of the registration clerks. Therefore, Charles Girdlestone suggested that the efficiency of the registration clerk should be increased by increasing their salaries. Better remuneration and close supervision would be the remedies for petty exactions from the traders.[82]

In spite of all these shortcomings, the system of registration had some utility. The statistical reports supplied by the registration clerks were not entirely baseless. The registration of the trade gave a fair idea of its fluctuations from year to year. The registration showed the volume and direction of exports and imports. In 1874, the special Committee on Statistics relating to India reported that the figures of the external trade of Oudh were "exact since they were collected by a number of registering clerks."[83]

REFERENCES

1. M.C. Regmi, "Sair Duties". *Regmi Research Series.* Kathmandu, 1 October 1979, Year 11, No. 10, p. 161.
2. The term used for import duty was "Chadhati Sair" and export was known as "Nimati Nikasi".

   Foreign Department, Genl. A. March 1882, No. 60, British Resident in Nepal to the Govt of India Foreign Department dated 14 February 1882, No. 13 p. (N.A.I.)

3. This estimate was based on the rate of about 7 2/3 per cent on the average of the known transactions for the four years 1871-72 to 1874-75. Foreign Department Rev. A. August 1877. No. 15.
4. Report on the Foreign Trade of the North Western Provinces and Oudh, during the Year 1877-78, N.W.P. and Oudh Govt. Allahabad, 1878, p. 11.
5. Revenue A. August 1877, No. 22.
6. *Ibid.*
7. *Ibid.*
8. M.C. Regmi, "Trade Outlets in Far Western Nepal". *Regmi Research Series.* 1 November, 1881, Year 13, No. 11.
9. Report on the Foreign trade of the Noth Western Provinces and Oudh. 1877-78. p. 10.
10. *Ibid.* p. 15.
11. Foreign Department, Revenue A. October 1879. No. 18. C.E.R. Girdlestone, the British Resident in Nepal to A. C. Lyall, Secretary to the Government of India. Foreign Department. dated 11 July 1879. No 24. p. (N.A.I.)
12. *Ibid.*
13. Report on the Foreign Trade of North Western Proxinces and Oudh 1877-78. The Nepalese then was double the length of the then of North-Western Provinces and Gudh. Cited in *Ibid.*
14. *Ibid.*
15. *Ibid.*
16. *Ibid.*
17. Rev. A. August 1877, No. 22.
18. *Ibid.*
19. Report of the external trade of Bengal with Nepal, Bhutan, Tibet, etc. for the year 1894-95. Calcutta, 1895, (N.A.I.)
20. Rev. A. August 1877, No. 22.
21. *Ibid.*
22. *Ibid.*
23. *Ibid.*
24. P.C. Rawat, "*Indo-Neqal Economic Relations*, Delhi 1974, pp 60-61.
25. M.C. Regmi, "Revenue from Customs and Pasturage in the Eastern Tarai Region". *Regmi Research Series*, April 1981, Year 13, No. p. 59.
26. *Ibid*, "Duties on Food Exports". *Regmi Research Series*, April 1984 Year 16, No. 1. p. 51.

27. *Ibid.* "Sair dutess", p. 161.

28. Ministry of External Affairs, Nepal. Register 1914, p. 241. a copy of which is also available in National Archives of India. New Delhi.

29. Foreign Department, Political A, August 1864, No. 51.

30. Daniel Wright, *op cit.* p. 28.

31. Markham Clements, *Journey of Thomas Monning to Lhasa.* First edition 1876, Reprint 1971, New Delhi, p. xcix.

32. Foreign Department, Political A, October 1879, No. 134.

33. Revenue A. August 1877, No. 16.

34. *Ibid.* Political A, July 1880, No. 296

35. *Ibid.* February 1875. No. 30. C.E.R. Girdlestone, British Resident in Nepal to H. Le Poer Wynne. Officiating Secretary, to the Government of India, dated 9 June 1874.

36. Memorandum on some of the Results of Indian Administration During the Past fifty years of British Rule in India, Calcutta. 1911. p. 31.

37. Revenue A. August 1877, No. 22.

38. *Ibid.*

39. *Ibid.*

40. Political A. October 1879, No. 136. Memorandum of Verbal Representation put in writing at the request of the Nepalese Prime Minister. (N.A.I.)

41. *Ibid.*

42. Foreign Department, Secret E, June 1893, Pros No. 389.

43. M.C. Regmi, "Duties on foodgrain". p. 52.

44. Foreign Department. Political A, February 1875, No. 30.

45. *Ibid.*

46. *Ibid.* External A, April 1908, Assistant Secretary to the Govt of India, Foreign Department to Major J. Manners Smith, British Resident in Nepal. dated March 1908, No. 914.

47. *Ibid*, May 1908, No. 104. Lieutenant Colonel F.W.P. Mac Donald, Officiating British Resident in Nepal to the Secretary to the Government of India, Foreign Department dated 6 May 198. No. 67.

48. Ministry of External Affairs, Nepal, Register. Letter of the Nepalese Prime Minister Chandra Shamsher to the British Resident in Nepal Colonel Manner Smith, dated 14 September 1914.

49. William Digby, *Nepal and India, A Friend in Need Friendship forgotten.* London, 1890.

50. M.C. Regmi, *op. cit.*

51. Foreign Department, Revenue A, February 1879. K.W. No. 2.
52. Sushila Tyagi, *Indo-Nepalese Relations (1858-1914)*. Delhi 1972. 229.
53. K.K. Adhikari, "A Brief Survey of Nepal's Trade with British India During the Latter Half of the Nineteenth Century". *Contribution to Nepalese Studies*. No. 1 February, 1975, p 187,
54. Revenue A, August 1877, No. 2. K.W.
55. *Ibid.*
56. *Ibid.*
57. *Ibid*, No. 8.
58. Progs. of the Bengal Government Gen. Mir, August 1876, File No. 190, S. No. 1-2. *Cited in Jahar Sen, op. cit.* p 8.
59. Report on the External Trade of Bengal with Nepal, Sikkim and Bhutan for 1884–85. p. 12. (N.A.I.).
60. Report on the trade of the North West Provinces and Oudh for the year ending 31 March 1879, p. 8. (N A I.).
61. Report on the External Trade of Bengal with Nepal, Sikkim and Bhutan for 1883-84. p. 14; for 1884-85, p. 12. (N.A.I.)
62. *Ibid* for 1893–94 p. 2: for 1894-95, p. 2; 1896–97, p. 2, 1898–99, p. 2; for 1898–99 p. 2.
63. Report on the Trade of North–Western Provinces and Oudh for the year ending 31 March 1879, p. 8. (N.A.I.)
64. Annual Report of Foreign Trade North-West Provinces and Oudh for the year ending 31 March 1881, p. 3. (N.A.I.)
65. *Ibid*, for the year ending 31 March 1885, p. 3.
66. Foreign Department, Political A. October 1879, No. 134, Girdlestone to Lyall, Secretary to the Government of India No. 22, p. dated 30 June 1879.
67. Jahar Sen, *Indo-Nepal Trade in the Nineteenth Century*. Calcutta, 1977 p. 88.
68. Foreign Department, Political A, December 1880, No. 38. Girdlestone to Lyall No. 32 p. dated 25 September 1880.
69. *Ibid*, October 1879, No. 124.
70. Foreign Department, Polical A, March 1880. Nos 228–306. K. W. No. 3. D. O. from Girdlestone to Lyall dated 28 December 1879. (N.A.I)
71. Jahar Sen, *op. cit.*, p. 90; Foreign Department, Political A, July 1880.
72. Annual General Report of Administration, Patna division for 1881-82.
73. Progs of the Bengal Government. Gen. Mis. August 1876. Colln 9–148 No. 212, dated Darjeeling 2 August 1876.

74. Progs. of the Bengal Government Gen. September 1878. File No. 62. S. No. 4–6. Cited in *Ibid.*
75. Progs of the Bengal Government. Gen. Mis. January 1886. File No. 15½. Cited in *Ibid.*
76. Annual General Administration Report of the Patna Division for 1879–80.
77. *Ibid.*
78. Gazetteer of th North West Provinces 1881, Vol. VI. p. 700.
79. Political A. October 1879. No. 134.
80. Jahar Sen, *op. cit.* pp. 92–93.
81. Foreign Department, Political A, October 1879. No. 132.
82. *Ibid.*
83. Foreign Department, Revenue A, August 1877. No. 3. Extract paragraph 6. From a report by Special Committee on Statistics relating to India. dated 10 December 1874. No. 73.

Currency, Market and Prices of Commodities

CHAPTER SIX

6.1 Circulation and mint of different types of coins

Both the Nepalese as well as the Indian currencies were in circulation in Nepal. However the Indian currencies were current only within the limited area of Kathmandu and in the tarai. It was not in circulation in mountains or hills and not at a distance of a few miles from the British Residency in the Kathmandu Valley.[1] Similarly, some of the coins minted in Nepal were in circulation in Indian districts adjoining the Nepalese border. Although official accounts were kept in Nepalese currency[2], the Nepalese Government valued Indian Currency much. For instance, there was a duty of 2½ per cent levied on the exportation of Indian currency from Kathmandu but there was no such charge on the export of Nepalese coins. In the tarai, people preferred Indian currencies. Specially in the western tarai of Nepal, the traders hesitated to accept Nepalese currency owing to the prevalence of a base counterfiet of copper coated with silver. In Golamandi and Banke they wanted payment either in Indian currency or in goods. In this regard, Captain A. Murray, Officiating Personal Assistant to the Chief Commissioner of Oudh, remarked, "The Nepalese will readily accept rupees in exchange for goods and our money is received into Darbar treasury, but the Nepal coinage is so debased and there is so much counterfeit coin, that merchants from British territories now refuse to receive payment other than in goods or rupees. Currency notes are not accepted in payment by the Nepalese."[3] The Officiating Deputy Conservator, Oudh Forest, was of the opinion that currency notes fetched rupees 99 per 100 notes of Calcutta and Northern Circle.There was plenty of evidence which proved that Nepalese and Indian counterfeit coins were minted and circulated in both countries. Indian Counterfeit coins were minted in the British Indian district of Gonda and in the Nepalese district of Butwal. In 1874, Jang Bahadur Rana, the Nepalese Prime Minister informed Girdlestone that he had Rs 450 British Indian Counterfeit coins in his Camp in the last cold weather and that he had two men in confinement charged with this offence[4]. In 1914, there were two establishments at Kanpur where Nepalese counterfeit coins were made.[5] British Indian coins were also not standard unit.[6] Indian currency notes were in slight demand on the Indo-Nepal border. Nepal made paper currency only in 1945-46.[7] There was a talk between the Nepalese and British Indian Governments regarding the circulation of Indian paper currency in Nepal, Consequently, in 1914 the Government of Nepal declared that paper currency note of India would be received only when the dues were heavy for the sale of timber. It was done for the convenience of the merchants and to remove the risk of carrying Indian currency from one place to another. The Nepalese treasurers were not allowed to make payment in I.C. notes. This could be done only when they were asked to collect I.C. notes and when amounts were small.[8]

In 1873, the British Indian Government proposed reciprocal arrangements for manufacture of coins. But this proposal was not accepted by the Nepalese Government. According to the Nepalese Prime Minister,"... if coins be struck according to the conditions of the Government of India, the old custom of this country would be put a stop to. The Nepalese Government is not able to agree to the proposed value of the coinage in the English language because as the Government of this country professes the Hindoo religion, it is proper that the Nagri Character should remain on its coins. Moreover, if the coins be manufactured as proposed, it will be necessary to shut the mint of this Government which will reflect slight and discredit on the Government of the country. The Nepalese Government and the people of the country prefer to have their old usages. The traders of this country, when trading in British India, receive British coins as legal tender."[9] He further added that the Nepalese Coinage was minted not only for the use of his country but also for Tibet.[10] The Prime Minister did not accept the proposal because it might have very bad effects on Nepal's commercial policy and her trade relations with other neighbouring countries especially Tibet. The Nepalese Government earned much profit out of the minting of coins for Tibet. The circulation of Nepalese coins in Tibet gave Nepal a strong position in the Tibetan economy.[11]

Minting of Coins : In 1866, there was a significant change in the history of Nepalese Taksal i.e. Mint. In that year minting machine was established and consequently handmade coins were replaced by machine made coins.[12] Jang Bahadur opened an office called Saraf Khana for the exchange of Nepalese and Indian rupees.[13]

Besides the Kathmandu Valley, there were several mints in the eastern parts of Nepal. The principal mints were located at Banglung, Beni, Wami Tansen, Samakot in the West[14] and Khika Maccha in the east.[15] In September 1876 Charles Girdlestone reported that Khika Maccha mint was the most famous of all the mints located in the eastern hills of Nepal.[16] One of the reasons for the establishment of mint outside the capital was to use mineral resources laying in other parts of the Kingdom.[17] Because of the difficult physiography and the system of transport, the Nepalese Government did not want to bring raw metals in the capital for minting coins.

Table 16

The amount of Nepalese Coins coined from 1872 to 1876.[18]

Years	Mohar rupee		Black pice		Gorakhpure pice		Thin or new pice			Purokalam	
	Rs	A	Rs	A	Rs	A	Rs	A	P	Rs	A
1872-73	276,900	9	47,021	8	257,832	11	58,669	2	3	1,662	8
1873-74	296,000	0	46,389	9	135,755	7	218,110	0	2	1,127	14
1874-75	105,400	0	35,700	3	194,028	8	132,800	0	0	280	0
1875-76	179,063	8	42.624	9	156,922	5	633,16	14	0	213	8
Total	857,365	8	171,735	13	744,538	15	123,224	1	1	3,283	14
Average	214,340		42,933		186.134		123,224				

There was no fixed policy as to the amount of coinage to be issued annually. It was primarily dependent upon the availability of metals and the demand for coinage.

Mohar rupees were coined in the Kathmandu Valley during the Malla period before the unification of modern Nepal. It was also called Mahendra Malli, named after a Malla King called Mahendra Malla. This silver coin was introduced by him[19] and remained in circulation even after the fall of the Walla dynasty. One Mohar rupee was worth 2 silver mohars each as the standard unit of account. A mohar rupee consisted of 16 annas or gandas, each worth 4 copper coins called paisa.[20] A mohar rupee was officially worth 64 paisa. However, its actual value was different in different parts of the country, depending mainly on the relative values of silver and copper.[21]

In 1876, the weight of a Mohar rupee was 96 Lals. A lal was less than a ratti which was current in India.[22] There was no fixed rate for exchanging mohar rupee with Indian currency. The exchange value of the mohari rupee with the Company's rupee varied from 119 to 122 for 100. The average value of the mohari rupee was equal to 13 annas 1 pice 1 1/3 dams of the Indian rupee.[23] A mohar had an intrinsic value of the Company's rupee 0-6-8 each. But sometimes it fetched as much as seven and a half and eight annas in India.[24] The mohar rupee bore the name of Gorakhnath and goddess Bhawani on the face, and that of the reigning King with date on the reverse.[25]

With the greater circulation of the Company's rupees in all parts of Nepal, the demand of the mohar rupees was less.Therefore fewer mohars were coined.[26]

The gold coins were also struck in a small quantity[27] in Nepalese mints. These coins were called asharfi. It had no legal tender[28] but was minted for giving presentation.[29] Colonel G. Ramsay reported, "gold coins are very rarely used in currency in Nepal, and in consequence of the small number coined they can be but little hoarded as a reserve for value. I am told that gold mohars are only coined in the Nepalese Mint in sufficient numbers to supply the requirements of the Sirdars and of the wealthier merchants of Kathmandu, who purchase them to offer as nuzzur to the King, the Minister, and other high functionaries, or to make up into gold ornaments. Some of the Sirdars occasionally receive a portion of their pay in gold, but only enough for these purposes."[30]

The gold coins had different denominations. These were called Duitole Asarfi 'Baklo', 'Patlo' (thin coin) or Majhawalo (middle coin) Suka, Suki, Ani, Adhani' Pai, Dam, Phoka Dam. These gold coins were not in general circulation. The Nepalese Prime Minister Chandra Shamsher informed that the smaller denominations were only minted on special occasions and for special purposes.[31] One Asarfi rupee was equivalent to Rs 20/- of the British[32] currency. However, their value generally fluctuated with the market price of gold.[33] G. Ramsay mentioned, "the double gold mohar ('Baklo Asarfi') is valued by the Durbar at Nepalese rupees 24, or British rupee 20, the single gold mohar is valued at Nepalese rupees 12, or British rupee 10, and so on; but single gold mohars can often be bought for British rupees 6-10-8, and sometimes they cost about British rupees 8-5-4 but rarely more than the last mentioned sum. The old Moorshedabad gold mohur is much coveted here, and costs from 21 to 22 British rupees, whilst those of a latter coinage can be bought for about 20 British rupees. The ordinary gold mohur is hardly known in Nipal."[34] Nepal earned silver partly from revenue collected in the Terai and partly from the imports of bullion from Tibet. British rupees were melted down to Nepalese currency.[35] The British Resident estimated that about 15 to 16 lakhs of British Indian currencies were annually brought from the Terai to Kathmandu, some portion of which was sent to the mint to be coined into Nepalese currency.[36] Similarly, Nepal imported five to eight thousand rupees worth of gold and about two thousand rupees worth of silver annually from Tibet. G. Ramsay remarked that the Nepalese Government purchased and brought gold from Tibet and India only when it was cheap and continued to mint the coin until the price of the metal had not risen.[37] In most cases, gold was imported from Tibet in the form of ornaments because gold ornaments brought into Nepal were not liable to tax.[38]

Black pice, Butwallya pice, Thin pice and Phook dam were some of the important copper coins that circulated in Nepal and adjoining Indian districts. The black pice was made at mints in east Nepal. It sold at 26½, 26 3/4, 27 gundas (107 pice), for a Company's rupees. The best known copper pice were made at Tansen, the headquarters of Palpa district in the Western hills of Nepal. The British Resident Girdlestone was of the opinion that for the trade with the Indian territory of Oudh like Basti and Gorkhpur, and Champaran, the coins made at Tansen played an important role. He further added that these coins almost displaced British pice which never gained a firm footing in that part of the border.[39] These coins were popularly known as Butwallya or Gorakhpuri[40] pice. In 1876, the average value of this copper coin 18 3/4 gundas (75 pice to the company's rupees.) The Tansen pice were square in shape, roughly cut by hand and with "an apology of stamp" on them, Copper was found in the lower hills of Nepal and was purified before it was coined.[41] Copper coins were generally manufactured in the vicinity of mines.[42] A copper coin called Phooka dam was used in market. It was a fraction of a Nepalese pice. Four Phooka dam was one pice. Black pice under the name of Lohiya was also in circulation in Indian districts of Muzaffarpur, Darbhanga, Bhagalpur and Purnea.[43] Before the introduction of this pice thin or new pice was prevalent.[44]

Some Indian Coinage such as the Patna rupee, the Kaldar rupee,[45] the Farrukhabadi rupee[46], the Sicca rupee[47], Lathsahi rupee[48] or the Kampani rupee, the Rikabi rupee[49] and Murshidabadi coins[50] were in circulation in Nepal. Among them, the Patna rupee was in widest circulation because the bulk of Nepal-India trade through Kathmandu Valley and the eastern tarai region was channelled through Patna. The actual market value of each of these Indian rupee units was different in terms of the mohar rupee. The exchange rate between Patna rupees officially fixed at 100 : 123 during the early years of the Rana regime.[51] According to the regulation promulgated by the Nepalese Prime Minister Chandra Shamsher (on March 22, 1908), the conversion was made at the rate of thirty gandas (120 paisa) for each Kampani rupee, and twenty-five gandas (100 paisa) for each mohar rupee.[52]

In 1865 a new copper currency—the thin new pice was introduced by Jang Bahadur in Nepal. Its rate in India in respect of the Indian rupee was 27 ganda[53]. In Champaran[54] and Tirhut, it had the same rate (27 gandas) instead of as formerly, 25 and 26 gandas[55]. The coinage had great influx in these two districts.[56] The Nepalese Prime Minister declared that the reason for introducing the new copper currency was the anticipated scarcity of old coinage. But the British Resident did not agree with the arguments because in his opinion the supply of the old pice was abundant. The Indian merchants were also suspicious of and dissatisfied with the new currency. They complained that neither the new silver nor the new copper currency would replace the old one. They argued that the new mohars (half rupee) were so soft that, if mixed with the old ones, they would soon be entirely defaced and useless.[57] But as a matter of fact they were not correct in their thinking. The new silver coinage was of the same average weight as the old one. The intrinsic value was also the same as that of the old one. The new copper pice was not more than half the weight of the old pice, but contained more than twice as much pure copper as the old one. The value of the old and new copper pice was put at par. Considering the complaint of the people against the proposed increased rate of the new coin, the relative value with the new mohar rupee (silver coin) of the new copper pice was fixed at 8 gandas instead of 11/, the old rate. The machine-made gold coin was also heavier and purer than the old one. The relative value of the new gold coin was 173 3/4 against 127 1/5 of the old one. The intrinsic values were found out by means of assay at Calcutta Mint.[58]

The Nepalese Government was quite conscious of the advantage it gained by the preference for Gorakhpuri pice in India and consequently made extentive issues of it During the scarcity of 1873-74 there was an extra-ordinary demand of this pice[59] in order to pay the labourers employed in relief work.The demand was quickly met by the Nepalese officials at Butwal in the Nepal Tarai.[60]

The Rikabi rupee of Lucknow, equal to 14 annas of Indian rupee was sometimes available at Butwal. In Kumaun, the Indian pice was current and from there it was freely taken to Doti in

Western Nepal. Jhardar pice, which was minted in Jaipur, was also used in the market of Pilibhit. The coin was on an average of the same value as the Indian pice. Bahraich merchants passed Indian pice into Nepal at the rate nine. Montgomery wrote that Nepal supplied copper currency to the whole tract of the plains between the Ganga and the hills, Munger and Pilibhit so that the adjoining market towns of northern India were virtually flooded with Nepali copper coins.[61]

The fluctuation in the value of the Indian currency as against the value of the Nepalese currency had been for a long time a source of great difficulty among all classes of people and especially business community. The solution of this problem was to use either Indian or Nepalese currency throughout the counrty,[62] but it was never done during the period under review.

Barter

Barter was common along the Indo-Nepal border. But it was mostly restricted to the exchange of local products such as dried fish, coarse sugar, earthen vessels and more rarely tobacco, cotton and salt for vegetables, rice and ghee. On 15 April 1876 the Deputy Commissioner of Gonda reported that Nepalese exchanged Tagans (horse) for European fabrics and country stuffs and dried fish.[63]

In some parts, especially on the frontier of Oudh, trade was conducted by the exchange of commodities on a money valuation without the intervention of coin. Similarly, in Kheri, barter was prevalent on the basis of money value of every article, though coins might not be actually used. For example, if the pieces of cloth were worth Rs. 200/-then ginger to that value would be exchanged. It was only when the products of the country were insufficient for such barter, the difference was paid in cash. In Bhagalpur one seer of salt was equal to three or four seers of rice, and one maund of potatoes to half maund of paddy. In the Nepalese district adjoining Bareilly salt, tobacco and coarse sugar were exchanged with Nepalese potatoes and other vegetables. One of the British documents mentions that the practice of bartering which formerly prevailed to a considerable extent in Nepalese market was still continuing. For instance, some of the articles such as gur (or molasses), tobacco and ghee were bartered in exchange for iron, dry ginger and salt. The officiating Deputy Commissioner of Oudh Forest also reported that great deal of Nepalese rice was bartered for other commodities. Some times iron, spices and musk from Nepal were bartered for salt, coloured clothes and piece goods.[64]

Credit and Payment of Debt

Ever since the time of King Ram Shah (1606-36) the Gorkhali rulers had set 10 per cent as the maximum annual interest that a creditor could charge from his debtor on loans. In case of default he was entitled to collect no more than double the amount of the principal in settlement of his claim. This rate of interest continued even after the enactment of the first legal code of the Kingdom of Nepal in 1854. The code clearly mentioned, "In case any person engaged in trade with Capital borrowed from a creditor stipulating in writing the payment of a stipulated share of the profits, he may recover the principal amount and profits as stipulated. But if he had stipulated payment of interest, not of profits, he shall be liable to pay only 10 per cent as interest."[65]

The British Indian Government made an enquiry with the British Officials of the frontier districts in India regarding the system of credit and payment of debt in Nepal. None of the Officers denied the fact that credit contracts were usually respected in Nepal and difficulty seldom arose between the contracting parties. Even when exportation of grain was prohibited on account of scarcity, such contracts were fulfilled. If the grain stipulated for could not be supplied, the money was returned with a small amount in kind by way of interest. In Purnea credit transactions were few and small.[66] The Collector of Bhagalpur wrote that there was no civil cases between the subjects of the two governments.[67] The Collector of Darbhanga stated that recovery was easier in Nepal than in India.[68] Similarly the Collectors of Champaran and Muzaffarpur reported that there was no difficulty in realizing debts or enforcing contracts in the Nepalese courts.[69] From Gorakhpur it was reported that there was no complaint regarding debts and suits were rarely filed by Indians in Nepalese Courts. But when a suit was filed the court immediately appropriated 10 per cent of the claim from the plaintiff and 5 per cent from the dependent. The orders of the Courts were executed in a summary manner.[70] Lumsden, the Collector, who had a long-standing connection with Gorakhpur, however, did not agree with the reports sent by the above-mentioned Collectors. He wrote that he had received repeated complaints from men engaged in trade with Nepal about the difficulty experienced in settling advances.[71] The report from Basti mentioned that debts were recovered with difficulty. The plaintiff had to deposit 25 per cent of the value of his claim before he was allowed a hearing by the Nepalese Court.[72] But the Assistant Collector of Pilibhit reported that the payment of debts was easily enforced in Nepal. If the plaintiff proved his case before the court his claim was realized from the sale of the defendants' property.[73] In this regard the civil code of 1854 stated, "In case any one has borrowed money from the government or from any individual, with or without a bond, he shall repay the loan from this wealth, or through the sale of his houses, lands, cattle, and other property. If he has no such property, he shall sign a bond stipulating repayment of the loan in instalments".[74] If the plaintiff did not prove his suit he had to pay twice the amount of the claim. A fee of rupees 5 from each party was demanded for the compromise settlement of a suit.[75]

The British Resident, Charles Girdlestone was fully satisfied with the judicial system of Nepal and the recovery of debts. In his testimony he wrote, "My own experience during a residency of four and a half years in Nepal is that there is no evasion in the Courts of Kathmandoo of the obligation incurred in 1839, by which the Nepalese Government enjoyed that 'British subjects shall hereafter be regarded as her own subjects in regard to access to the Courts of law, and that the causes of the former shall be heard and decided without denial or delay, according to the usages of Nepal'. I have also to remark that during this period I have never received from any British Official any reference concerning exactions or denial or miscarriage of justice in matters of trade as might have been expected from districts, Gorakhpore for instance, with respect to the traders of which the Collector now submits that difficulties exist ; I have never had a single complaint against the Durbar or any of its officials of oppression or restriction. I can only recall two occasions on which my good offices as the representative of the British Government have been invoked, and there were cases in which British subjects trading in the capital with Newar subjects of the Durbar wanted a settlement of accounts. In both cases the Durbar gave the necessary orders for the attainment of the petitioner's object, and saw that they were carried out. In one of the two cases in which the accounts were intricate and extensive, a special court composed of some of the highest officers in the country was entrusted with the duty of effecting the desired adjustment."[76]

The Nepalese Civil Code of 1854, used to give protection to the creditor only when the documents were not destroyed and eye witnesses were still alive. The Code mentioned, "Any dispute between two merchants in the course of business transactions, for which no bond has been signed, shall be settled on the basis of the accounts maintained by the two parties." At the same time it also included "'Any dispute between two merchants in the course of business transactions shall be settled on the basis of the documents in the possession of both, if they are still alive. If they are dead, and any person makes claim against their sons, it shall be settled on the basis of the accounts and records maintained by both parties, as well as the evidence of people who have knowledge of their business transactions. If no evidence or witnesses are available, the claim shall be dismissed."[77]

The Deputy Commissioner of Gonda informed that credit transactions were made to a limited extent, and in such cases the rate of interest was usually 2 annas in a rupee. Regarding the enforcement of the payment of debts in British and Nepalese courts, he did not find any evidence in which Nepalese traders appeared in Indian Courts.[78]

6.3. Market and Trade Centre

Trade Centre and markets[79] were developed as a result of the growth of Indo-Nepal trade. These markets were developed in the adjoining districts of both the countries. The most important trade centres and markets from western to eastern Nepal were Brahmadeo-Mandi, Gola-mandi, Nepalgunj, Butwal, Birjung,

Bijayapur and Ambarpur adjoining North Western Provinces and Bihar in India. Kathmandu, the capital of Nepal, was the Centre of entrepot trade.

Brahmadeo Mandi was the most important market place in the far western part of Nepal adjoining Indian border districts of Kumaun and Bareilly. The commodities produced in the region situated west of the Karnali river and east of the Mahakali river were sold at this mandi. There was state trading between Brahmadeo Mandi and Kumaun. The officials were instructed to purchase cardamom and wax on a monopoly basis. These commodities were brought by the people from hill areas to sell in the market.[80] The Nepalese traders were not allowed to cross the border to sell the commodities. Even the people living in the northern frontier of the country, such as Jumla, had to sell their birds and other articles only at Brahmadeo-Mandi.[81] Several thousands of rupees were spent to construct this market. Brick buildings were constructed[82] for opening shops. The market was on the bank of the Kali river which separated Indian border with Nepal in the far western frontier. There was a great anxiety in Nepal when the Nepalese Prime Minister was informed that the market at Brahmadeo Mandi on the British side would be closed and instead of it a new market would be established at Tanakpur. The proposed market was two miles away from the present market and was on the high bank of the Kali river. He was also informed that the ferry in the Kali river, which connected both the Mandies, in Nepal as well as India, would be stopped. The Nepalese Prime Minister requested the British Resident not to move the market from Brahmadeo to Tanakpur because it would cause great loss to the Government of Nepal. There would be loss of State revenue. The ferry tolls would also be lost.[83] In spite of the Nepalese request the Government of India decided to move the market, from Brahmadeo to Tanakpur. The cause of the removal, as stated by the Government of India was that the Kali river (Sarda) was dangerous for the safety of the market.[84] However, the reason did not satisfy the Government of Nepal.

On 19 September 1876, Charles Girdlestone, the British Resident reported that there was a permanent mart at Brahmadeo and two hundred shops on either side of British and Nepalese territory had been established. Communication was maintained by a number of small boats which were plying backwards and forwards all the day. Twenty thousand rupees had been collected by the Nepalese Government as duties at this mart in one season. He stated that the sum might be approximately taken to represent transactions of some two lakh rupees.[85]

The other local marts in this area were Katema, Sheopur, Muzaffarnagar, Puranpur, Kalinagar and Bhagwantpur on the British side and Dhaknabagh and Bilauri on the Nepalese side. There was a large annual fair held at Mandia Ghat on the right bank of the Kali (Sarda) river.[86]

Golamandi and Nepalgunj were the biggest marts in the western part of Nepal adjoining Awadh in India. These markets flourished only after 1860. when it was ceded by the British to the Government of Nepal. The Nepalese Government forced hill traders to sell their products only in these markets. After the sell, the British merchants were at liberty to despatch the articles according to their will. In 1876, there were fifty British subjects from Kheri, Barabanki, Sitapur, Lucknow, Kanpur, Shahjahanpur, Muradabad and Bareilly who had settled down as shop-keepers at Golamandi. In the same year, the number of British subjects who settled down permanently was about fifty-five at Nepalgunj in Banke district. More than one hundred merchants frequently visited the market for six months from November to May when trade was briskest. There were two kinds of British traders, one who kept shops permanently and the other itinerant dealers. The former had the right of transaction with the hillmen. But both of them did not stay for a longer period. They spent their time to despatch the commodities. The rent of the shops varied from Rupees 1-8 to Rupees 2-8 a month. If there were no shops available, the trader had to pay for the privilege of admission at the rate of Rupees 1-8 a year.[87]

The Nepalese traders were forbidden to cross the border for the purpose of trade and if they attempted to disobey the rule their goods were confiscated. If the traders faced any difficulty in selling their products, the Government officials were there to buy them sooner. It was the only way to check the Nepalese traders from crossing the border. The officials had money at their disposal for this purpose from the Government.[88]

The British Government raised objection to this system of market. It requested the Nepalese Government that its traders should not be compelled by the laws of Nepal to occupy shops in Nepalese markets, but they should be at liberty to make their own arrangements in purchasing and exporting articles of commerce from Nepal. According to it, many British subjects suffered hardship in the enforced occupation of shops. It created difficulties for those engaged in the trade which was against the interest of free trade. A man without shop could buy only the commodities which the occupants of shops had refused. Charles Girdlestone claimed that the British traders in Nepal without shops must have as good an opportunity of supplying their wants as the traders who occupied shops. It should be optional for the trader to have or not to have shop as his business might require.[89] But the Nepalese Government had no alternative except to enforce the law to popularise the market system.[90]

Successful efforts were made to develop these markets. A lot of money was spent in the construction of market at Nepalgunj. On December 1894, a project for the supply of water to Nepalgunj town had been approved. A total sum of Rs. 7,00 /- (Indian currency) had been sanctioned for the construction of water supply project on April 1895 and 1896 respectively.[91] Because of growing population, the demand for baked bricks and tile had been rising at Nepalgunj. On April 1897, Captain Khadga Bahadur Raimajhi Chhetri of Naya Muluk Ban Janch Goswara (Forest Inspection Office) reported that if bricks and tiles were supplied by the Government the revenue of State would increase from 800 to Rs 900 per year from Nepalgunj, Koilabas, Golaghat and Brahmadeo Mandi. In addition it would prevent the indiscriminate cutting of firewood from the local forests.[92]

R. Buck, the Director of Agriculture and Commerce, N.W. Provinces reported that Nepelase had established a series of marts.

The products and articles of Nepal and India were exchanged in these markets. As the Nepalese traders were forbidden to cross the frontier, Indian traders had to visit Nepalese markets to transact business. In many cases British subjects had settled on the Nepalese soil. But frequently North West Provinces merchants carried their articles of merchandise across the border of Nepal and returned with what they could not sell. This practice affected the returns of export and imports, since these articles which were returned unsold were entered both as export and imports.[93]

In November 1894, the Government of Nepal issued an order to the Naya Muluk Bandobasta Adda to shift the market of Golaghat (Golamandi) to Bardia district and construct a new market there. A sum of Rs 5,516 and 9 1/4 annas (Indian currency) was sanctioned for the construction of buildings at Rajapur. An additional sum of Rs 1,900 (Indian currency) was sanctioned in February 1897. Rs 12,000 was subsequently sanctioned for the renovation and construction of buildings and shops at Rajapur. Rs 6,745 was actually spent for this purpose.[94]

Captaingunj, Sisewa and Bahadurgunj were the chief marts in Deokhur district in Nepal. The Nepalese traders in this district secretly visited Indian markets. The most important Indian markets visited by the Nepalese were Tulsipur, Panchperia, Utrowla and Balrampur in Gonda district, Ekona, Bhinga, Matagunj and Naupara in Bahraich district, Biscohar in Basti district. The Nepalese traders also used to visit the great fair held at the shrine of Debi Patan near Tulsipur where they exchanged hill ponies for European and native piece goods and for dried fish.[95] But the number of the visitors was decreasing due to the restriction imposed by the Nepalese Government on traders.[96]

A great mart of Nepal between Arrah Naddi and Gandak was Butwal. There was small but improving trade between Indian districts and this town. Indian merchants brought cotton goods, coarse and fine, to sell in this market. These cotton goods were mostly manufactured at Tandah in Faizabad. The traders brought this article through Lalgunj or Basti in India. Cotton goods worth Rs 248,045 and Rs 285, 398 were brought in this town in the year

1873 and 1874 respectively. Besides Butwal, there were other markets in Nepalese territory. These were Taulihawa, Abiram, Bhagwanpur, Jogia, Sheorajpur, Gulabha, Kussahar and Batisi. Rice was the chief article sold in these markets. The local marts in Basti district in British territory adjoining the Nepalese district, were Bhojaha, Uska, Berdpur, Narkul, Mahana, Kakrowah, Mindehwal and Lotan. A fair was held annually at Pulta Devi near Birdpur early in the month of April. But only a few Nepalese traders brought spades to sell in this fair.[97]

The Nepalese markets adjoining Gorakhpur district, were Bharti, Hathbanwa, Palhi, Amanigunj. The local marts on the British side near the Nepalese frontier, were Nautanwa, Deoghat, Thunthibari, Nichloul, Mithanra, Bahwar, Baitanibya and further south were Pad rowna, Siswa, Dhani and Lar Bazar. The Nepalese frequently visited these markets. But they were too poor to visit all the markets established at far distant places. There were three soap factories in Lar Bazar in Gorakhpur district. There was practically no sale of this soap in this district : it was exported to Nepal. The main objective of establishing soap industry in this bazar was to import Kharimitti,[98] from Nepal and export soaps in return. In 1906, the total amount of Kharimitti imported was 2,369 maunds, and 2,150 maunds of soap were exported to Nepal. [99]

The chief markets in Bara and Parsa districts of Nepal were Chapkaiya, Barewah and Simraunghar. A fair was held twice, one early in February and other in March at Tribenighat on the Gandak river in Nepal. [100] Brass utensils and agricultural implements were sold in this fair. The Nepalese Prime Minister Bir Shamsher established another market called Birgunj.[101] As the name indicated the market was set up after his own name.

According to the regulations promulgated in the name of Birgunj Bazar Adda, the local traders were asked to sell their commodities only at Birgunj. In case they sold goods elsewhere, or exported them to India, without paying duties at Birgunj Bazar, the goods would be confiscated, and a fine of an equivalent amount imposed. The Birgunj Bazar Adda authorities were instructed to ooal consignments destined for the Kathmandu Valley and forward them to Chisapani, where duties were collected at fixed rates.[102] They were also instructed that the shops in Government owned buildings at Birgunj would be leased to the highest bidders. However, the Birgunj Bazar Adda was not able to discharge these functions properly. It was found that the traders diverted the consignments to other destinations in Nepal, or smuggled them to India, which were sealed by the Birgunj Bazar Adda at Birgunj and checked by Chure customs post. The traders could successfully evade payment because the customs duty on the consignment was collected only at Chisapani. There was, consequently, a wide gap between the amount of customs revenue assessed at Birgunj and the actual amount collected at Chisapani. Therefore arrangements were made for the collection of customs duties by the Birgunj Bazar Adda at Birgunj itself. The staff of the Birgunj Bazar Adda was expanded. A State Trading Agency was established at Birgunj. The agency was popularly known as Mahajani Adda. On January 1901, Birgunj Mal Adda was ordered to provide funds for the construction of an office for the newly-created Mahajani Adda in Birgunj. Accordingly, it released a total amount of Rs 7,500 in several instalments. The Birgunj Mal Adda (Birgunj Revenue Office) was ordered to provide Mahajani Adda with funds not exceeding Rs 41,665 every year on demand. The Mahajani Adda then requisitioned Rs 9,730. There was another trade agency known as Resham Kothi in Birgunj where raw silk was accumulated.[103]

The chief local marts in Champaran were Bettiah, Ramnagar, Sugauli, Matihari and Kutkenwa. Raxaul adjoining Birgunj was also developed as a market in Bihar.[104] Sugauli and Raxaul were the two important entrances of European and Indian goods into Nepal. These goods were carried directly to Kathmandu Valley. Kathmandu, the capital city of Nepal had direct contact with Calcutta and Patna. In January 1859, the Nepalese Government appointed a buying Agent in Calcutta for the purchase and supply of goods required by the government from time to time. He was instructed to purchase goods at the lowest available price. Money for this purpose was provided by the Government. The buying agent was instructed to maintain accurate accounts of such purchases, as well as of rents paid for the office, transportation charges, packing charges, etc. He was asked to obtain receipts while purchasing gold on behalf of the Government. The receipts should be obtained on the basis of the same weights and units that had been used at the time of the purchase. He was also warned by the Government that he would be punished according to law if he were proved to have debited amounts in excess of actual expenditure, or amounts which had actually not been disbursed.[105] Similarly, the Nepalese Government had set up Alainchi-Kothi (Cardamom Depot) in Patna to carry on trade with India.[106] It was found that several Nepalese gold and silver smiths visited Patna and settled there. They had no money except their tools. The Indian merchants gave them materials and paid them according to the quality of their work.[107]

The Nepalese Government had appointed a forwarding agent in India to forward goods purchased in Calcutta and in other parts of India by the Government, by the members of the royal family and Rana family, by other prominent persons, traders, etc. by railway to Patna on payment of brokerage. In January 1882, Biharilal, the forwarding agent, was instructed to charge brokerage (adhati dastur) at the usual rates without any increase in those rates. He was also asked to forward those goods to Patna or Motihari by railway and deliver them to the owner within the scheduled time. The agent was responsible for loss of any goods or consignments of which he had taken charge and for which he had been paid brokerage. No person was compelled to utilize his service if he preferred to bring his goods himself without paying brokerage to the agent. But on the other hand, no one was allowed to utilize the services of any other agent on payment of brokerage. The man would be penalised if he evaded the rule. The agent would be dismissed if he did not work in a satisfactory manner, increase the rate of brokerage, or fail to deliver goods to the owner in time. In addition, he would be held liable to pay compensation, and punished with a fine.[108]

Jang Bahadur, the first Rana Prime Minister of Nepal, also tried to develop market in Kathmandu and in other parts of the kingdom. He opened a retail shop in the city of Kathmandu.

G. Ramsay, the British Resident in Nepal, reported that ostensibly the shop belonged to Newar merchants but as it occupied a public building, a portion of Darbar, and the accounts were checked by the Government official, it was clear that the Prime Minister himself gained the profit. In fact it was done to control the price of the market, because, he thought his wives (Maharanees) and the people were charged exorbitant prices for all kinds of European articles. These articles were exposed for sale in a building in his own premises. Similar other shops were opened at different places in Kathmandu for the public.[109] The shopkeepers had English goods such as needles, tea pots, empty bottles, powders, and some calico with English mark in their shops. They had also various brass and other metal pots, strings of red silk or cotton and other valuables.[110]

Jang Bahadur tried his best to remove the practice of middleman between the producers and consumers. These middlemen were responsible for the increase of price of the articles of daily consumption. Jang Bahadur, therefore, issued an order to ban the system of middleman. He ordered that either the producers in the surrounding villages should bring the commodities in Kathmandu to sell or the consumers should visit the villages to buy the articles. Restriction was also imposed on small merchants who sent agents to the villages to collect the articles. G. Ramsay reported that this strange order had the opposite effect. Everything became dear as a result of this order.[111]

Jang Bahadur had a plan to establish large bazar at Beechakoh to be called Hayat Nagar. He wanted to erect stores, shops and barracks. He hoped that the British merchants would be encouraged to take resort in the market. But the British Resident doubted the success of his plan and reported to the British government that the intention of Jang Bahadur behind this plan was nothing but to expel the whole of British merchants from the Kathmandu Valley and expected to sell their goods at Beechakoh.[112] On the contrary, the intention of Jang Bahadur was to develop markets in the Tarai bordering India.

Jaleshower, Dhanukha and Janakpur were the three important markets[113] in Mahotari district of Nepal. Janakpur, the holy place of Ramayan, was popular for its annual fair. The fair Ramnavami was famous for cattle. Nepalese merchants freely visited Indian markets adjoining Mahotari district of Nepal. The local marts in British territory were Bairagania, Pachlakki, Majorgunj, Dyne Chapra, Bosahia, Monaha, Belanuchha Pakouni, Barahi, Sursand, Bhita and Madhawapur in Muzaffarpur district in India. There was an annual fair in Sitamadhi, Maniari and Marania. [114] Bairagania and Sursand were the great marts for Nepalese trade.[115] Bairagania, the terminus of the branch of the Bengal North Western Railway, was a large grain and oil-seed depot, where the dealers of the plains met the Nepalese hillmen, and the Nepal trade changed hands. [116] It was an important market for the frontier trade with Nepal. [117]

Siraha, Orahi, Sarsowr, Rampur and Hanumannagar in Saptari district were the important markets of eastern Nepal. Large annual fairs were held at Hanumannagar and Barachatra, Deodha, Lawkaha, Piprahi, Patauli, Khutowna in Darbhanga district and Kundowli, Bagjan, Panchpandaria, Silashpur and Birpur in Bhagalpur district, were the popular markets. [118] Madhuwani and Jayanagar were also prominent trade centres for Nepalese merchandise. Usually Nepalese traders used to bring their pack animals with the merchandise to the well known hat and bazaars on Indian border. Indian merchants would also take their own articles for export to the same places. Indian traders seldom visited interior places in Nepal. There was nothing like godown or store house where articles of export and import could be stored. After selling and purchasing the individual traders used to take away their merchandise offered by their counter-part. [119] "Meles" were the most popular for commercial transaction. Sonepur Mela in Bihar was the traditional trade fair where different kinds of European and Indian goods were exchanged with Nepalese dogs, forests products, curious and silver work. [120]

There were ten golas, six in Saptari and four in Morang districts. Vijayapur and Ambarpur were the two famous markets in these districts. Before 1858, the taxes on all the golas were collected under the ijara system (contract system). The Goladars created hardships. The traders were allowed to sell the commodities in India after paying customs duties only when they were permitted by the Goladars to do so. Due to lack of funds, they were not allowed to visit Indian markets nor would they like to procure the commodities. This system of monopoly was not favourable to the State revenue. Because of the difficulties created at the Golas some producers and traders used to make an attempt to smuggle cardamom and other commodities to India. It entailed loss of state revenue. After 1858, the Golas were operated under the Amanat system. Employees were deputed to different golas under the authority of the Commanding General for southern zone. He was directed to take cardamom and other commodities produced in the hill region for sale at Ambarpur and Vijayapur. The commodities would be weighed with weights bearing the royal seal and payment made at rates current from time to time. It was notified that the commodities of the smuggler would be confiscated if detected inside the frontiers of the kingdom. The proceeds would also be seized if the smugglers were apprehended even after the sale of the commodities across the frontiers. The traders were asked to sell cardamom and other commodities at the golas of His Majesty's Government. If they used force and smuggle commodities elsewhere, they would get punishment according to royal orders.[121]

This restriction did not continue for long. Nepalese traders were free to visit Indian markets after paying customs duties.

Markets were held at countless villages along the Indo-Nepal border for the exchange of rural produce and article of daily consumption.[122]

6.4 Prices of Commodities

From the rise of Jang Bahadur in 1846 to his death in 1877, the price of commodities rose to 200 per cent. Within fifteen years after his death the price index increased by 381 per cent. The price of commodities doubled in every ten years. Compared with other articles, the price of rice and paddy was increasing rapidly. For example, in 1875-76 6 pathi (48 lb) paddy cost one rupee whereas in 1888-89 only 1 pathi 4 mana(12 lb) paddy cost the same amount. In this way the price of 1 muri[123] (160 lb) paddy[124] increased by Rs. 3.5 to 13.33 in 1889.

On 19 September 1876 the British Resident in Nepal reported that the price of rice ranged, according to the season and places, from 64 to 10 seers per rupee.[125] The prices in the hills were always high as compared with the average rates in the plains.[126] The traders made profit by high prices rather than by large sales. According to the British Resident the Nepalese paddy was dearer than rice. The rice from the Nepalese tarai was three times dearer in Pilibhit than the rice from other British provinces. Regarding the prices of commodities imported from Nepal the Resident wrote, "Catechu, which is manufactured in large quantities on the Dhundwa hill, is found to be worth rupees 6 a maund in Gondah after payment of an ad valorem[127] duty of 13 per cent."[128] The prices of ghee was Rs 25 per maund in Kathmandu, Rs 20 at Sugauli and Calcutta, Rs 16 in Kumaun, Rs 12 in Gonda, as 27 in Gorakhpur and Rs 32-12 in Pilibhit. The price of borax was Rs 17 a maund in Kathmandu, Rs 8 in Kumaun, Rs 2-4 annas in Pilibhit and Rs 11 in Calcutta. The cost of large cardamom in the Kathmandu Valley was Rs 14 per maund.[129] But it was sold at Brahmadeo Mandi at the cost of Rs 30 per maund.[130] It was sold at the rate of Rs 23 per maund in Nepalgunj.[131] Smugglers smuggled 1 maund and 7½ seers of cardamom to Singahi in India and sold it at the rate of Rs 1 per seer.[132]

During 1874-75 the prices of gold was Rs 10 for 1 tola, of silver 12 annas per tola and of copper 2 annas per tola.[133] Among the cattle, elephant[134] was sold at the rate of Rs 25 per head, horse at Rs 7 per head, he-goat and ram at Re 1 per head. Among the sweetmeat peda, barfi, gulabjamun and jalebi were sold at the same price i.e. Re 1 anna 8 paise 3 per dharni. The price of balashahi and malpuwa was the same. Both of them cost Re 1 annas 4 per dharni. The swari was cheaper as it cost Re 1 per dharni.[135]

According to the sub-divisional offices of Madhubani, 13 seers of rice, 23 seers of paddy, 15 seers of millet, 13 seers of blackgrand (urad), 8 seers of flattened rice, 13 seers of potatoes, 12 seers of mustard, 14 seers of salt and 4 seers of oil were sold at the equal rate of Re 1 near Indo-Nepal border during 1888-90.[136]

Some British officials complained against the rising price of timber. The Assistant Collector of Pilibhit wrote, "the rate of timber in former times was Re 1 per log, and if a great many logs were taken 1 annas per log. When taken Oudh to this rate was raised to Rs 4 a log, and subsequently to Rs 5 and Rs 7. The rates are now according to measurement."[137] Gibbon, who had experience of Butwal forest over a period of twenty years, stated that for every hundred timbers sold a year by the Nepalese before the mutiny they did not then sell even a couple. He again complained that he had to pay Rs 25 for each of the logs 20 ft long and 24 to 28" in circumference. He believed that similar timbers were sold at Faizabad and Patna at cheaper rates.[138] Peppe, a British officer had to pay Rs 24 for a sal log 22 to 18 ft long and 12 to 15" in diameter at Taulihawa in Western Nepal.[139]

Table 17

Comparison between the new and old rate of timber sold during 1870-71 and 1875-76

Girth feet	Length feet	Old rate			New rate			Drawbacks[140]		
	Sal wood	Rs	A	P	Rs	A	P	Rs	A	P
4½	24 to 27	18	9	0	20	14	0	6	8	0
5	,,	22	7	0	25	3	0	7	4	0
6	,,	28	12	0	32	5	6	9	4	6
7	,,	50	7	6	56	12	0	16	5	0
4½	30 and 31	20	1	0	22	9	0	6	8	0
5½	,,	28	14	6	32	8	0	9	8	0
6½	,,	45	0	0	50	10	0	14	12	0
7	,,	52	3	9	58	11	3	16	14	0
5½	15 and 16	17	4	9	19	7	0	5	9	6
6	15 to 16	18	4	6	20	9	0	5	14	6
6¼	15 and 16	22	3	9	25	0	3	2	1	0
6¼	15 to 16	29	15	6	33	11	3	9	11	0
7	,,	31	14	0	35	14	0	10	5	0
7¼	,,	33	15	0	38	2	6	10	15	6
	Shisham wood									
3¼	24 to 27	10	13	3	12	2	6	3	15	0
4	,,	11	8	6	12	15	6	4	0	0
5¼	,,	21	9	0	24	4	0	8	8	0
6¼	,,	23	11	0	26	10	3	8	15	0

Sources : Revenue A. August 1877. No. 22.

The price of timber increased with the greater demand of timber in India. But the export of timber declined in course of time, "partly owing to the large felling of timber in a most extravagant and short sighted manner and partly owing to misconduct of some Indian traders."[141]

Timber was cut to any extent on payment of Rs 30 or more. But this practice was stopped in 1868 and the Nepalese Government employed its own officials to cut down timber and sold by auction at different Kathmahals[142] or Thinguri-mahal.[143] There were eighteen Kathmahals in the Tarai Region in Nepal at the end of the nineteenth century.[144] After 1877 timber was not sold to contractors in the forests. It was cut by the Nepalese officials and carted to the Kathmahal or Thingurimahal where it was sold by auction. Indian merchants were not allowed to cut timber in the forest.

REFERENCES

1. Foreign Department, Political A. April 1866. No. 170. Colonel George Ramsay, the British Resident in Nepal to D.R. Onslow, Secretary to the Currency Commission, the treasury, Calcutta. dated 5 April 1866. No. 20. (N.A.I.).

2. The official accounts were maintained in Mohar rupees, annas, pice and dams, the relative value of which was as follows :

   4 Dams = 1 Pice
   4 Pice = 1 Anna
   16 Annas = 1 Mohar rupee.

   The valuation before the introduction of silver coinage was 4 dams = 1pice; 4 pice = 1 ganda ; 24 ganda = 1 paisa rupee.

3. Foreign Department, Revenue A. August 1877. No. 13. Captain A. Murray, Officiating Personal Assistant to the Chief Commissioner of Oudh to T.H. Thorton, Officiating Secretary to the Government of India. Foreign Department. 13 May 1876. (N.A.I.)

4. *Ib'd.* Political B. October 1874.No.143.C.E.R. Girdlestone British Resident in Nepal to the Secretary to the Government of India in the Foreign Department at Fort William. 12 September 1874, No. 26p (N.A.I.)

5. Records of Foreign Ministry of Nepal. Chandra Shamsher Jang Bahadur Rana to Colonel Manner Smith, British Resident in Nepal. dated 15 May 1914, p. 71.
6. M.C. Regmi. *The State and Economic Surplus, Production, Trade and Resource Mobilization in Early 19th Century Nepal.* Varanasi, 1984, p. 224.
7. *Ibid.* "Introduction of Paper Currency". *Regmi Research Series.* Year 16, No. 3, March 1984. p. 47.
8. Records of Foreign Ministry of Nepal. Marich Man Singh, the Adviser of the Nepalese Prime Minister to Austa Man Singh, Officer of the Nepalese Government. Kathmandu. Dated 29 October 1914
9. Foreign Department, Financial A, April 1873. No. 2. An abstract translation of a memorandum of Prime Minister and Commander in Chief of Nepal to the C.E.R. Girdelstone the British Resident in Nepal. 15 march 1973 (Chaitra Sambat 1923). (N.A.I).
10. Mahendra Malla, Malla King of Nepal, who reigned in 1560 A.D., made a treaty with Tibet, by which he supplied the Nepalese currency and obtained silver and gold from Tibet to mint coinage. The Tibetans had no knowledge of smelting metals, and hence they had to depend on the Nepalese for minting their coins. This privilege continued to be the source of an extensive annual revenue to Nepal. After the fall of the Malla dynasty and conquest of Shah King Prithvi Narayan Shah in 1768 in the Kathmandu Valley Tibet refused to accept Nepalese currency. But this practice continued even during the Prime Ministership of Jang Bahadur Rana.

    E.H. Walsh, *The Coinage of Nepal*, Delhi, 1973, pp 16–17 ; Captain Samuel Turner, *Tibet, An Account of an Embassy to the Court of the Teshoo Lama in Tibet*, Delhi 1971, p 372.
11. The Nepalese Government made a profit of a lakh of rupees annually in exchange of silver coinage for Tibet. In exchange for his bullion the Tibetan merchant received Nepalese currency. The Nepalese Government derived a profit of twelve percent from the transaction, four per cent being charged on account of coinage and eight per cent arising from the alloy of the rupee.

    Colonel Kirkpatrick, *An Account of the Kingdom of Nepal.* London. 1801 p. 211.

    Ravuri Dhanalaxmi, *British Attitude to Nepal Relation with Tibet and China 1814-1914*, New Delhi, 1981, p 8 ; D.R. Regmi, *Medieval Nepal* op. cit. part II, Calcutta 1966, pp. 43–44 ; Leo Rose. *Nepal Strategy of Survival* Bombay 1971, pp. 14 ; Ramakant, *Nepal-China and India*, New Delhi 1976 p. 19.

12. Krishna Kant Adhikari, *Nepal under Jung Bahadur 1877.* (unpublished Thesis) Nagpur University, 1974, p. 440.

13. Hem Narayan Agrawal, *The Administrative System of Nepal.* New Delhi 1976, p. 12.

14. Adhikari, *op. cit.*

15. Revenue A, August 1877. No. 22.

16. *Ibid.*

17. Adhikari, *op. cit.* 348.

18. Nepal Residency. 10 August 1876, Nepal Residency Records. Sl. No. 32. F. No. 82-G of 1876. (N.A.I.)

19. E.H. Walsh, *op. cit.*, p. 16.

20. M.C. Regmi, *The State and Economic Surplus*, p. 223.

21. *Ibid.*

22. Nepal Residency. 10 August 1876. op. cit. ; 8 pice = 1 rattee ; 8 rattee = 1 masha ; 12 masha = 1 tola. cited from *Ibid.*

23. *Ibid.*

24. Revenue A, August 1877, No. 22.

25. Adhikari, *op. cit.*, p. 443.

26. Nepal Residency. 10 August 1876. *op. cit.*

27. Adhikari, *op. cit.* p. 444.

28. Nepal Residency. 10 August 1876, *op. cit.*

29. Foreign Department, Political A. April 1866. No.170. Colonel G. Ramsay, British Resident in Nepal to D.R. Onslow, Secretary to the Currency Commission, the treasury, Calcutta. dated 5 April 1866, No. 20.

30. E.H. Walsh, *op. cit.* 48.

31. Adhikari, *op. cit.*

32. E.H. Walsh, *op. cit.*

33. Political A. April 1866, No. 170.

34. *Ibid.*

35. *Ibid.*

36. *Ibid.*

37. *Ibid.*

38. *Ibid.* Revenue A, August 1877, No. 22.

39. Revenue A, August 1877, No. 22.

40. It was so called because the coin was minted on the model of those minted at Gorakhpur in India. See, M. C. Regmi, The State and Economic Surplus, ***op. cit.***, p. 24.

41. W. Brook Northey and C.J. Morris, *The Gurkhas—their manner, customs and country*. Delhi 1974, p. 85.

42. Revenue A, August, 1877. No. 22.

43. *Ibid.*

44. *Ibid.*

45. The term Kaldar first appeared in the Nepal-Company documents in the Anglo-Nepal trade treaty of 1835. See, Ludwig F. Stiller. S.J. "Currency Confusion". *Journal of the Tribhuvan University*, Vol. VIII, No. 1. November 1973, p. 4.

46. It was minted at Farukhabad. See, Adhikari, ***op. cit.***

47. It was Mughal currency. The Nepalese king Prithvi Narayan also issued this coin. It consisted of 16 annas and was confined to the Kathmandu Valley. See *Ibid.* p. 444.

48. The British coin issued from Calcutta was called Lath Sahi in Nepal. The term Lath'Shahi denoted the Governor General during British rule. Side by side with the Lath Sahi, Company rupee was also commonly circulated in Nepal. Probably the Lath-Sahi and Company's rupee were the same coins, only called by two different names. *Ibid.*

49. Rikabi rupee as its name suggests, was round in shape. *Ibid.*

50. The coin minted at Murshidabad. It was issued in the name of the titular Emperor Shah Alam in the nineteenth year of his reign. In 1913 the Nepalese Government had 20 or 30 lakhs of Murshidabadi coins which were not easily exchangeable in British India. Upon the request of Nepalese Government, British Government agreed to exchange their stock of Murshidabadi coins for current British Indian coins at the rate of one rupee a tola. The date of exchange was limited up to 1 July 1913. Foreign Departmrnt. Internal B, April 1913, No. 271. The Assistant Secretary to the Government of India in Foreign Department to Leiutenant Colonel H.L. Showers, British Resident in Nepal dated 7 April 1913. No. 727-1A. (N. A. I.)

51. M.C. Regmi, ***op. cit.*** p. 225; Devichandra Shresth ***op. cit.*** p. 10.

52. *Ibid. Reading in Nepal Economic History*, Varanasi 1979, p. 57.

53. Political A, April 1866, No. 170.

54. Two copper coins called Lobia and Gorakhpur pice were current in Champaran district. The latter were largely composed of copper and the former of iron. Both were called Dhebua. These were manufactured in Nepal

and United Provinces. They have no fixed value but varied according to the demand in the market and the season of the year. Generally 104 to 128 used to get the rupee but in 1907 their value rose as high as 90 to the rupee. L.S.S. O'Mullay, *Bihar, Orissa District Gazetteers,* Champaran. Patna 1938, pp. 103-4.

55. The British Resident in Nepal, Charles Girdlestone, argued that the thin or new pice were in circulation in Kathmandu and adjacent hill districts as far as Hetauda in the Tarai. These circulars and fairly stamped coins had an average value of 29¼ gandas (117pice) to the Company's rupee. Revenue A, August 1877, No. 27.

56. Foreign Department, Political A, June 1866, No. 177, Colonel G. Ramsay, the British Resident in Nepal to the Secretary to the Government of India in lhe Foreign Department, dated 13 June 1866, No. 16. (N.A.I.)

57. *Ibid.*

58. Adhikari, *op. cit.* pp. 440-41.

59. Revenue A, August 1877, No. 22.

60. *Ibid.*

61. Montgomery Martin, *The History, Antiquities. Topography and Statistic of Eastern India.* Vol. 2. reprint of 1828 ed, Delhi 1976, p. 119.

62. Barun Shamsher, ed., "From the Himalayan Height". *Nepal Guardian.* Kathmandu, n.d. p. 17.

63. Revenue A. August 1877. No. 16. The Deputy Commissioner of Gonda to the Commissioner of Faizabad Division. dated 15 April 1876, No. 964.

64. *Ibid.* The Officiating Deputy Conservator, Oudh Forests, Bahraich Division to the Conservator of Forest, Oudh. dated 4 March 1876. No. 196.

65. Ministry of Law and Justice, *Shri 5 Surendra Bikram Shahdeva ka Shasanakalma Baneko Muluki Aio.* (Legal Code enacted during the reign of King Surendra Bikram Shah Dev), Kathmandu, 2022 (1965), pp. 93-94.

66. Revenue A, August 1877, No. 22.

67. *Ibid.*

68. *Ibid.*

69. *Ibid.*

70. *Ibid.*

71. *Ibid.*

72. *Ibid.*

73. *Ibid.*

74. Ministry of Law and Justice, *op. cit.* p. 90.

75. *Ibid.*

76. Foreign Department. Revenue A, August 1877, No. 22.

77. Ministry of Law and Justice, *op. cit.* pp. 98-99.

78. Revenue A, August 1877, No. 16.

79. These markets were permanent as well as temporary. Permanent markets were usually called Mandi or Golas. Hat-Bazaars were temporary markets.

80. On May 1897, approximately 325maund of cardamom had been purchasd at a total cost of Rs 11,848. In addition approximately 1¼ maunds of cardamom was acquired in lieu of duty(Chungi),while ¼ maund was confiscated from smugglers. Unsold stocks from the previous years totalled 1½ maund worth Rs 49·49. From June to December 1896, eight maund of wax was purchased at a total cost of Rs 217-12, and approximately 1¼ maunds was collected as duty or confiscated from smugglers. Cited from Mahesha Chandra Regmi, "State Trading at Brahmadeo Mandi," *Regmi Research Series*, Kathmandu 1 October 1981. p. 145.

81. Debi Chandra Shrestha, "Brahmadeo-Mandi". *Nepal Economist* (Arthik Nepal) Vol. I, No. 3, June 1983, p. 25.

82. Nepal Residency Record. File No. 1972 of 1883. Abstract translation of memorandum from the Prime Minister and Commander in-Chief of Nepal to the British Resident in Nepal, dated 16 December 1883 (21 Aghan, Sambat 1940). (N.A.I.)

83. *Ibid.* Abstract translation of Memorandum from the officiating Prime Minister and Commander in-Chief of Nepal to the British President in Nepal. dated 18 April 1884 (Baisakh, Samvat 1941) Record No. D-45 III.

84. *Ibid.* No. 843 of 1885. The Commissioner, Kumaun Division to British Resident in Nepal. dated 21 May 1884.

85. Revenue A. August, 1877, No. 15p.

86. *Ibid.*

87. *Ibid.*

88. *Ibid.*

89. Foreign Department, Political A, December 1880. No.48. A memorandum from the British Resident in Nepal to the Prime Minister and Commander in Chief of Nepal, dated 16 August 1880.

90. *Ibid.* No. 49. A memorandum from the Prime Minister and Commander-in-Chief of Nepal to the British Resident in Nepal. dated 31 August 1880 (= 11 Bhadon, Sambat 1937).

91. M.C. Regmi, "Development Activities in the Naya Muluk". *Regmi Research Series*, Year 13, No. 5; May 1981, p. 73.

92. *Ibid.* p. 74.
93. Foreign Department, Revenue A. December 1877. No. 2. E. Buck, Director of Agriculture and Commerce. North Western Provinces to C. Robertson, Secretary to the Government of North Western Provinces. dated 1 November, 1877. No. T-187.
94. Regmi, *op. cit.* p. 73.
95. Foreign Department, Revenue A, August 1877 No. 15. The Deputy Commissioner of Bahraich to The Deputy Commissioner of Faizabad 13 December 1875. (N.A.I.)
96. *Ibid.*
97. Revenue A, August 1877. No. 22.
98. The principal ingredient in the soap was a light grey kind of earth called Kharimitti.
99. *Indian Trade Journal*, 2 May 1907, p. 234.
100. Revenue A. August 1877, No 22.
101. Mahesha Chandra Regmi, "Impact of Railway". *op. cit.*
102. *Ibid.* "Birgunj Bazar Adda". *Regmi Research Series.* Kathmandu, Year 13, No. 9, September 1, 1981, p. 135.
103. *Ibid.* pp. 36-37.
104. Revenue A, August 1877, No. 22.
105. Mahesha Chandra Regmi, 'The Calcutta Buying Agency'. *Regmi Research Series.* Kathmandu, Year 13, No. 8, 1 August 1981, p. 126.
106. *Ibid*, Cardamom Farming in Nepal, p. 54.
107. Surendra Gopal, '*Patna in the 19th Century* (*A Socio-cultural Profile*), Calcutta, 1983, p. 42.
108. Mahesha Chandra Regmi, "Appointment of Forwarding Agent in India". *Regmi Research Series.* Kathmandu, Year 13, No. 7, 1 July 1981, p. 128.
109. Foreign Department, Foreign Consultations, 26 August 1859, No. 211.
110. Francis Egerton, *Journal of Winter Tours in India with a visit to the Court of Nepal.* Two Volumes. Vol. I, London, 1852, p. 233.
111. Foreign consultations, 26 August 1859, No. 211.
112. *Ibid.*
113. Revenue A, August 1877, No. 22.
114. *Ibid.*
115. L.S.S.O' Malley, *Bengal District Gazetteers, Muzaffarpur.* Calcutta, 1907, p. 94.

116. *Ibid.* p. 138.

117. *Ibid.* p. 156.

118. Revenue A, August 1877, No. 22.

119. P. C. Roy Chaudhury, *Inside Bihar*, Calcutta, July 1962, p. 169.

120. Rawat, *op. cit.* p. 59.

121. Mahesha Chandra Regmi, 'The Golas of Eastern Nepal', *Regmi Research Ser es.* Kathmandu, Year 12, No. 5, 1 May 1980, p. 78.

122. W.W. Hunter, *The Indian Empire, Its peoples, History and Products.* London, 1892, p. 691.

123. The traditional dry measures are as follows :

    10 muthi = 1 mana
    8 mana = 1 pathi
    20 pathi = 1 muri

    1 muthi is handful.One mana is equal to half a seer or approximately equal to 1 lb. One muri is equal to 0 lb. The mana is the commonest measure used in the hilly regions of Nepal. But in the Tarai the measurement and weight are the same as in India. Mana consists of a brass vessel shaped like a cup, the bottom being bulbous and widest than the mouth. There is a stamped seal on the side showing that it is a certified measure. See British Ministry of Defence, *Nepal and the Gurkha*, London, 1965, p. 152.

124. Shreshtha, *op. cit.*, p. 12.

125. Revenue A. August 1877, No. 22.

126. Political A, February 1875, No. 30.

127. In the ad valorem system of Nepal the valuation depends on the market price both at the place of purchase and the place of sale. Revenue. A. August 1877. No. 22.

128. *Ibid*.

129. *Ibid.*

130. Regmi Research Series, *op, cit.* p. 145.

131. *Ibid.* p. 75.

132. *Ibid.*

133. Adhikari *op. cit.* p. 449.

134 Elephants were captured by the state through compulsory and unpaid labour and kept for sale at state operated establishments known as Hathisars. They possessed the exclusive right of sale and export, and elephants purchased by individuals from other sources were confiscated. Elephants

were captured while quite young and they were also sold according to height. Before 1829 import of elephant from India was banned. But after three years of experience the ban was abandoned. See Regmi, *The State Economic Surplus*. p. 198. Francis Hamilton *op. cit*. p. 63.

135. The system of weights in Nepal is as follows :

$4\frac{1}{2}$ tolas = 1 Kanuwa or Chatak

4 Kanuwa = 1 Pan

4 Pans = 1 seer

3 Seers = 1 Dharni.

136. P.C. Roy Chaudhury, *Bihar District Gazetteer*, Darbhanga, pp. 304.

137. Revenue, A. August 1877, No. 22.

138. *Ibid.*

139. *Ibid.*

140. According to British Resident drawback was for the cost of carriage to the depot. *Ibid.*

141. Report on the Administration of N.W. Provinces and Oudh for the year ending 31 March 1899. Allahabad, 1900. (Pattan Tata Library, Delhi (University.)

142. Kathmahal was an establishment for the export of timber of twelve main varieties, including sal and sisham with a diamater of more than three feet. See M.C. Regmi, "Kathmahal in the Tarai and Inner Tarai at the end of the 19th century". *Regmi Research Series*. Year 11, No. 10, October 1979. p. 160.

143. The export of timber of smaller sizes was handled by a separate establishment known as Thingurimahal. *Ibid.*

144. Kathmahals in the Tarai Region of Nepal.

Kathmahal	*District*
1. Kosi-Purwari	Morang
2. Kosi-Pachhuwari	Saptari
3. Kamala	Saptari
4. Bhanwarpura	Mahotari
5. Tinpatan	Sindhuli
6. Chhattauna	Rautahat
7. Jamuni	Bara
8. Chhapkaiya	Parsa
9. Reumadi	Chitaun
10. Tribeni	Butwal
11. Banganga	Butwal

Kathmahal	*District*
12. Dunduwa	Dang
13. Rapti	Banke
14. Babai	Bardia
15. Karnali	Kailali
16. Mohana	Kailali
17. Mahakali	Kanchanpur
18. Gusari	Kanchanpur

See *Ibid.*

Impact of Indo-Nepal Trade on Nepal

CHAPTER SEVEN

Indo-Nepal trade had a great impact on the politics, culture and economics of both the countries. The British felt more secure from Nepalese attack from the north during the Rana rule because they found the Nepalese more involved in trade than in anything else. The people in general had little to do with politics. For them it mattered little whether the individual or the group who wielded power in Kathmandu belonged to the Thapa or the Rana family. Hodgson was right when he said that the more the Nepalese became trade-minded and earned profit the less would be the possibility of war between India and Nepal. For instance, after the rise of Rana rule in Nepal, the Nepalese Government took more interest in trade than in war. Neither Nepal nor Britain had aggressive designs on the territories of each other and there was no basic conflict in their interests. Regulations promulgated by the Government of Nepal for different districts of the Tarai region before and after 1857 clearly indicate the changed situation. For example, throughout the late eighteenth and early nineteenth centuries, local authorities in the border districts were instructed, "If Chinese and English troops violate the borders and kill or loot our people, take appropriate steps to defend our territories. Refer the matter to us for instructions if there is time, and act according to such instructions. If not, take appropriate steps to defend our territories and repulse the enemy."[2] But after ten years, the same authorities were ordered to take steps to repel external aggression only with Kathmandu's approval.[3] It clearly shows that the Government of Nepal did not anticipate any threat to national security that might necessitate urgent action through local initiative. The Government was thereafter able to follow its policy of reorganizing the district administration as well as settlement in the Tarai region without any fear of external aggression.

Indo-Nepal trade paved the way for signing new treaties and engagements. It was necessary for both the Governments to maintain law and order to promote trade. This necessity compelled them to sign an extradition treaty in early 1855. The treaty required each Government to extradite criminals guilty of murder, attempt to murder, rape, maiming, thuggee, dacoity, highway robbery, poisoning, burglary, who escaped into its territories.[4] The British officials were forbidden to intrude into Nepali territory in pursuit of criminals, and the Nepali officials too were directed not to intrude into British Indian territory for such purposes.[5] Similarly the treaty of 1923 was also signed to safeguard the commercial interests of both the countries. Article VI of treaty reads, "No customs duty shall be levied at British Indian ports on goods imported on behalf of the Nepal Government for immediate transport to that country provided that a certificate from such authority as may from time to time be determined by the two Governments shall be presented at the time of importation to the Chief Customs Officer at the port of import setting forth that the goods are the property of the Nepali Government, are required for the public services of the Nepal Government, are not for the purpose of any State monopoly or State trade, and are being sent to Nepal under orders of the Nepal Government."[6]

The British Government also agreed to the grant in respect of all trade goods, imported at British Indian ports for immediate transmission to Kathmandu without breaking bulk en route, of a rebate of the full duty paid, provided that in accordance with arrangements already agreed to between the two Governments, such goods may break bulk for repacking at the port of entry under customs supervision in accordance with such rules as may from time to time be laid down in this behalf. The rebate might be claimed on the authority of a certificate signed by the said authority that the goods had arrived at Kathmandu with the customs seals unbroken and otherwise untampered with.[7]

Indo-Nepal Trade had some effects on the internal administration of Nepal. The Government had to open new offices and new posts for it. Jang Bahadur first of all opened muluki adda under a mulki subba for the general administration of the country.[8] Administration under the Ranas had two main functions : the collection of revenues and the maintenance of law and order, the latter primarily in order to facilitate the former.[9] Jang Bahadur introduced Moth Tahvil to deal with all the revenues. He also opened a forest office. Muluki Khana was established as the Government treasury. An accounts and audit office known as Kumari Chowk started by Prithvinarayan Shah, was retained by Jang Bahadur. The Kausi Tosakhana as the disbursement office was also retained. Munshi Khana as the foreign office started by Bhim Sen Thapa continued to function till the Rana period. All these offices were either loctated at the house of the Prime Minister at Thapathali or at the house of the persons who were associated with the administration.[10] Ranodip Singh introduced the royatwari system and established an efficient system for the collection of national revenue and audit of public accounts.[11] Similarly Chandra Shamsher also made many changes in the administrative system of the country. The old Kumari Chowk office was reorganized to have more sections in order to have stricter control over audit and accounts.[12] Rakam Bandobast Office was opened to investigate and report on different sources of revenue and to dispose of monopolies.[12] The Office of Banjanch Goswara and a number of chowkis of forest guards were established for the better administration of the forests.[13] Muluki Adda Report Niksari Phant and Kath Mahal Niksari Phant were also opened. The main function of the former was to receive reports from the districts about law and order, revenues, woods, forest, sale of timber, customs, etc. The latter dealt with the sale of timber, and forest products, their management and administration and exercised general control over Kathmahal hakims in the tarai.[14] Bazar adda, Bhansar adda, Taksal adda and lagat adda were opened to carry on Indo-Nepal trade effectively. The office which collected customs was called bazaar adda. The officer who was appointed for the collection of customs was called Bazaar Hakim. Chandra Shamsher opened bazaars in tarai districts. This office managed both bazaars and customs for the tarai only during the entire Rana period. Bhansar adda was the same as the bazaar adda. It administered customs and markets in hills and the valley. It was set up by Chandra Shamsher to increase the revenue of the State. Taksal adda was opened after the days of Prithvinarayan Shah. Bir Shamsher and Chandra Shamsher opened new sections and added more staff to it. The lagat adda maintained more staff to it. The lagat adda maintained a list of goods and articles and checked their estimates, prices, etc. This office was under the control of Kumari Chowk and the Commander in Chief of Nepal.[15]

With the expansion of Indo-Nepal trade, many agencies and institutions were established in Nepal and in some of the Indian towns. Singha Darbar Jinsi adda in Nepal[16] and the Calcutta buying agency[17] and Patna Illaychi Kothi in India were the prominent among them. Jinsi adda was opened by Chandra Shamsher to store articles and make their purchases from Calcutta and England. Ilaychi Kothi was situated near Jalan's fort in Patna on the bank of the Ganga. It imported illaychi (cardamom) from Nepal to Patna during the Rana period.[18] It also worked as a Nepalese consulate office. It dealt with the East India Company in Patna and kept liaison between Kathmandu, Patna and Calcutta.

In this way Rana Government built a strong administrative machinery to maintain peace and to exploit natural resources. It should, however, be noted that the Government under the Ranas functioned as an instrument to carry out the personal wishes and to serve the interests of the ruling Prime Minister. Its main objective was to exploit the country's resources to enhance the personal wealth of the Rana ruler and his family. The Rana family secured a monopoly of political power through which it controlled and exploited the nation's resources for its own benefit. However, in order to sustain that monopoly the Ranas had to share the economic benefits of their rule with the aristocracy and the bureaucracy. But later on some of the Ranas were deprived of these benefits.[19] They were dissatisfied with the ruling family. So they took active part in the revolution against the Rana Government. Some other sections of Nepalese society especially intellectuals and ordinary merchants were also against the Rana rule, because, they were not getting any kind of privilege. They started a campaign against the

Rana Government. Ultimately the Rana Prime Minister had to resign and his Government failed in 1951.

Indo-Nepal trade helped the people to settle down in each others's countries. As a result large number of people migrated from Nepal to India and vice versa. After 1860 the Rana rulers encouraged the hill people of Nepal to settle down in the tarai region. The main purpose behind it was to develop the region and exploit its natural resources. But unfortunately they did not settle in a hot and malarious region of the tarai ; instead, they preferred to migrate to India, Sikkim and Bhutan. As an alternative, the Rana rulers began to encourage the Indians to come over to the tarai. Then, a large number of Indians began to migrate to the tarai region. The number of traders was large among them.[20] They established matrimonial relationships with the Nepalese. The traders who settled in the valley and in the hill adopted the Nepalese way of life and culture. It created problems for the Nepalese Government as economic difficulties and unemployment increased and the Government was not able to solve these problems. Majur, the president of Rastriya Samaj Sudhar Sangathan (National Social Reform Forum of India) criticised the Indian Government for the massive influx of Indians into Nepal. He said "If you want to take over Nepal, march your army in, but for God's sake do not march your population."[21] Similarly the influx of Nepalese into India was also increasing day by day. It grew to such an extent that in 1900 just under a quarter of a million people of declared Nepalese origin were recorded in the Indian Census. This number had increased by over 30,000 in the period 1900 to 1911 with no increase in the Indian army recruitment. By the early 1930's about one Nepalese-born person in twenty was living in India.[22]

Indian as well as Nepalese traders profited greatly by the Indo-Nepal trade relations. However, they had to face a lot of difficulties to carry on this trade. They had to tolerate ihe hardships of nature and the fear of robberies on their way. The traders from hot plains had to visit Tibetan plateau and the traders from the snowy mountains had to travel to hot lands. They had to cross dense forests and malarious region of Nepal. Some of the traders had to lose their lives and some others reached the destination with much difficulty.

The Newars, Thakalis and Sherpas among the Nepalese and the Gosains, Iraqis, Musalmans, Baniyas and Marwaris from India were the prominent merchants who were most active in Indo-Nepal trade.

The Newars controlled the trade between India in the south and Tibet in the north.[23] They had been carrying on trade from the earliest times.[24] The Newars were the indigenous traders of the Kathmandu Valley who had spread all over the kingdom since the 15th century A.D. They settled in the remote corners of the hill for the sake of trade.[25] The spread of Newar traders and small manufacturers westwards from Kathmandu during the latter half of the nineteenth century, contributed significantly to the physical and economic growth of a number of settlements. Some of the towns of Western Nepal such as Tansen, Pokhara, Butwal and Bandipur grew as a result of the emigration of Newars from Kathmandu to these places. When the Newars of Bandipur took interest in commerce around 1870, operating as middlemen on the north-south trade route from Tibet to India (via Manang in the north), the town grew in size and importance. Since then the volume of trade between Nepal and India increased rapidly.[26] During the latter part of the nineteenth century Butwal, Tansen and Bandipur expended as major trading centres of West Central Nepal. Nepali merchants from Tansen, Butwal and elsewhere visited Lucknow and other Indian towns for the purchase of commodities.[27] These merchants took cash along with them for the purpose, having little in the way of exports from the hills to offer to Indian merchants. Bandipur merchants visited Indian towns with armed guards and coffers loaded with money to purchase manufactured goods there.[28]

The Newars in the Kathmandu Valley enjoyed monopoly in trade. They had great influence in the Nepalese Darbar. They were supported by the Rana Government for the growth of trade and commerce. For instance, Subba Dhurb Narayan, a Newar merchant was a close associate of Jang Bahadur Rana. He had commercial links with some of the Indian towns.[29] The Newars were also called Bhaju[30] for their profession as a trader. They occupied good position in the Royal Palace and in the administration.

Before the influx of Indian merchants to the Kathmandu Valley, the Newars were the sole agents for entrepot trade.[31] They had upper hand in Nepal-Tibet trade. They had several shops in Tibet.[32] However "as a rule the Newars do not settle permanently in Tibet, but make a stay of some five or six years if fairy successful in business, if not, their exile may be indefinitely prolonged."[33] There were about 3,000 Nepalese and a Nepalese Vakil (consul or resident) in Lhasa in 1877. They carried corn, oil, salt, tobacco, confectionary and other articles of domestic consumption to Tibet.[34]

The Newars, engaged in the Indo-Nepal and Nepal-Tibet trade were leading better life than the rest of other tribes. They built multi-storeyed houses crowded close together. They developed the architectural style of the pagoda. They founded the cities and villages in the Kathmandu Valley. The streets were paved with bricks. The settlement was divided into "toles", each of which was traditionally inhabited by members of a single caste. The high-caste as well as traders lived in the centre, the low-caste lived in the next ring, and the untouchables outside the boundaries of the town.[35]

The women of the traders were richly ornamented. Percy Brown described it as follows."In marked contrast to the somewhat common place garb of the men is the particularly striking costume of the women. This attire includes a brilliantly coloured jacket, opened so as to display another gaily-dyed garment underneath. But it is the voluminous cut of the lower portion of the costume which makes the Nepalese lady's presence so unusal."[36]

The Newar business men, who have a long history of trade and urban residence, also own farms, albeit often far away from their trading establishments. Since households can be quite large and involve joint families in some cases, it is possible for at least one male member of the household to spend most of his time away from 'home' running a business while his family or relatives run a farm with the help of hired labourers.[37]

Thakalis were the important trading communities of the north western frontier district of Nepal. They played a dominant role in the trans-Himalayan trade. In the second half of the nineteenth century and the early decades of the twentieth, prominent Thakalis were given customs contracts by the Nepalese Government which gave them control over the import trade in salt from Tibet. They held the position of 'Subba' for their contract. Tracks southwards used to become virtually impassable during the monsoon months whereas travel to Thak Khola from the north was easy ; on the other hand, the winter months were unsuitable for journeys to and from places further north, while to the south the tracks were passable. For the geographical reason the Thakalis had to store goods for transportation either northwords or southwards.[38]

Before 1959 the exchange of two commodities, salt and grain, was the main occupation of the Thakali traders. The two commodities were exchanged through Thak Khola in Mustang district adjoining Tibet in the north. The inhabitants of this place are still called Thakali. The salt collected from the salt lakes of Tibet was exchanged for grain grown mainly in the lower regions of Nepal. It was stored at the village of Tukche in the heart of Thak Khola until the growers of grain from the lower regions arrived with their produce to exchange it, or else the Thakalis themselves transported the salt to such centres of trade as Baglung and Pokhara. Besides salt and foodgrains, the Thakalis exchanged sugar, tea, spices, tobacco, cigarettes, paper, cotton and cloth for Tibetan wool, sheep and goats. The wool was generally sold in Indian markets while the sheep and goats were taken to the middle hills—or occasionally as far as the Tarai. The goods which the Thakalis took to Tibet and sold there to pay for their purchase of wool and cattle were partly Nepalese and partly Indian.[39]

Before 1860 no customs duty was levied by the Nepalese Government. But in 1860 the Government auctioned a customs contract including the monopoly of trade in Tibetan salt in Thak Khola. The first customs contractor paid an annual royalty of Rs. 44,500. From 1860 to 1932 the monopoly was the subject of keen competition, between big Thakali merchants and a few outsiders.[40]

After 1959 the trade of Thak Khola and the adjoining regions began to decline owing to the Chinese policy of restricting the type of goods to be exported from Tibet. The business activity of the great Thakali families brought them in the lower regions of Nepal. They started to settle down in the Pokhara Valley and in other adjoining areas. Most of the rich Thakalis had acquired houses and built up business in towns of the lower regions.[41]

Another cause of this drift was the opening of a motorable road joining Indian border near Bhairahawa to Pokhara in the hill which made Indian salt cheaper in the area which used to be served by the salt traders of the Thak Khola. The Thakalis living in Bhairahawa. Nepalese town in the Tarai, were the descendants of the subbas who were awarded trading contracts by the Nepalese Government in the late nineteenth and early twentieth centuries. These subbas who had the largest multi-enterprise business employed other Thakalis as representatives and Managers in that region. As a result of their emigration, Bhairahwa developed as a business. centre. Otherwise it was a small settlement as described by Landon in the late 1920. He mentions : "to the south, a few miles nearer India, is the unprogressive little village Bethri.[42] Here there is a brick court-house, a gaol, and a few few other official buildings. It is the residence of Bada Hakim. with two subas under him.A few sentries are detailed from Butwal to guard the Nepalese Government treasury there. Bethri is a fair example of many smaller towns in this district. Situated along the northern side of the tarai and in the danger zone, they act as centres of commerce without at the same time attracting any considerable number of inhabitants. During the summer the place is almost empty. Markets are held twice a year to which many villagers come in from over a wide area. They bring in large quantities of rice, pulses, vegetables and fruit, and barter them for the produce of the hills and of Tibet. The place is almost encircled by extensive jungles and a few mango groves close to the Kachari, or court-house, render the town picturesque. Still, as was once said of a famous bridge at Cambridge, Bathri is eminently a place of transit and not of lounge, and the small colony of permanent inhabitants in the reed houses pay a heavy toll in human life for the trading profits, considerable though these are. It is one of the places like Hetaura, of which the permanent existence, despite climatic defects, is secured by its position on the high road just where the under features of Himalayas burst up through the tarai."[43] But with the coming of the Thakali and other merchants from India and the Nepalese hills, the situation changed. The reed houses were replaced by brick buildings and seasonal markets changed into a permanent big town.

The Sherpas were the next important Nepalese traders after Thakalis who were engaged in Indo-Nepal and Trans-Himalayan trade. The pattern of the trade was the same as Thakalis. The difference lay in the geographical location viz. one in the east[44]and the other in the west. Like Thakalis, the Sherpas also brought salt, wool and sheep and sent foodgrains and other commodities. For geographical reasons Tibet did not grow enough foodgrains for her consumption, but produced abundant quantities of salt and wool. On the other hand. the hill region of Nepal had a surplus production of foodgrains, but lacked source of salt supply. The Sherpas traditionally functioned as middlemen in the exchange of the foodgrains of the hills and Tarai region for Tibetan salt and wool. Some commodities reexported by Sherpas were of Indian origin.

The involvement of the Sherpas in Indo-Nepal and Tibetan trade, had made them different from other tribes in the midhill region. As Furer-Haimendorf observes, "The Sherpas' favourable position as middlemen in the trade between Tibet and the lower-lying regions of Nepal enabled them to attain a standard of living far above that of most other Nepalese hill people, and in particular that of their southern neighbours, the purely agricultural Rais. Though the latter dwell in the country of milder climate and richer soil. they possess none of the luxury goods found in many of the more prosperous Sherpa houses and have nothing to match the cultural achievements of the cold-windswept highlands of Khumbu."[45]

The Sherpas started another profession when the Chinese Government closed Tibetan border for any kind of transactions. They took to mountaineering as their occupation. They became popular as soon as Tenzing Norgay reached the summit of Mount Everest with Sir Edmund Hillary[46] in 1953. They earn handsome money from this profession. It was trade which stimulated them to choose much work, because they learned mountaineering expeditions in course of their transactions with Tibet behind the big mountains.

Apart from these, some Brahmans, Chetris and Banjaras were also taking part in Indo-Nepal trade. Banjaras of Dolakha were active in entrepot trade.

The Muslims[47], Iraqi[48] and Marwaris[49] were the most notable among the Indian traders who were engaged in Indo-Nepal trade. The Muslims were migrants from Kashmir[50] and other parts of India. They were also called Churauti (bangle sellers) in the hills.[51] Some other Muslims were called Iraqi. These Iraqis had several shops in the Kathmandu valley. The Iraqi shops are still popular among the Nepalese women living in the Kathmandu valley. One of the markets and streets at the Capital is named after the Iraqis and is called Raqi Bazar and Raqi Sadak (street). The Marwaris[52] also made their fortunes in Nepal.[53]

The Nepalese Government acquired a considerable amount of revenue by imposing taxes on these merchants.[54] Certain reductions in taxes were made in favour of a class of merchants in Nepal known as the "Bathis Kothi" merchants. But who or what these "Bathis Kothi" merchants were,.was not known to anybody.[55] The Collector of Bhagalpur wrote that British subjects who had shops in Nepalese towns were never charged import duty on goods brought into Nepal for sale at their shops All they had to pay was a ground rent for these shops.[56] The Deputy Commissioner of Kheri, who had obtained most of his information from the traders themselves, remarked that there were two descriptions of traders from British territories. Those who rented shops from the authorities and resided in the Nepal marts for the whole of the trading season from January to May and those who merely lived long enough to make their sales and purchases. The former were alone permitted to trade with the hillmen. They were not only traders but also acted as brokers. There were no Nepalese shop-keepers and brokers. The only men from that country who frequented the marts were the hillmen (Parbatia) who like the itinerant dealers from these parts, stayed only long enough to buy and sell what they desired.[57]

Generally, there were two types of merchants : those who are concerned primarily with the purchase and exports of Nepalese goods, and others who were primarily concerned with importing Indian goods. Most merchants and traders were of Indian origin and by virtue of their ability to acquire larger resources, were able to restrict competition from potential Nepalese merchants. Most of their agricultural purchases were undertaken through agents who used to attend village and haat bazaars on their behalf. In order to assure reasonable supplies, merchants usually advanced preharvest loans to farmers against the value of crops, which the farmer was then bound to sell to the merchants.[58] This practice is still continuing in some parts of Nepal especially in the Tarai.[59]

The presence of Indian traders in large numbers was resented by local traders. The former had strong hold over business in the Kathmandu Valley and in other places, which was against the commercial interest of the local merchants. The Indian merchants were engaged in various economic activities and were also monopolizing the trade. This influx of Indian traders is still increasing day by day. According to the President of National Social Reform Forum of India, 80 per cent of Nepal's economy is controlled by the Indian business community. He expressed fear as to what would happen to Nepal if the present rate of Indian migration into Nepal continued for a few years more.[61]

For the security of the traders and mercantile classes the Nepalese Government had to establish several police posts (Chowkis) from the eastern to the western parts of Nepal. On 27 May 1893, the British Resident informed that there were several police chowkis all along the frontier from Mechi nadi to the Mahakali at a distance of three to six kos (approximately two miles). The Government also had to open district courts[62] to hear the complaints of the traders. The British Resident also supplied a long list of the courts[33] adjoining Indian districts.

With the growth of Indo-Nepal trade the use of foreign goods greatly increased among the Nepalese ruling elite and nobility. European cloth was preferred by the well-to-do people who lived in or near Nepal's capital. They imported it for their own consumption and also reexported a moderate amount to Lhasa in Tibet. The whole trade in luxurious goods was with the Kathmandu Valley where the consuming classes such as the nobility, the army and all the high officials lived.[64] The consumption of imported luxury goods and the surplus required for their maintenance also increased equally.[65] In the second half of the 19th century the Nepalese nobility and Rana family came in contact with European culture and acquired a taste for upper class western style of living. symbolised by beautiful palaces with cut class chandeliers, motor cars, watches, and so forth. Although some of these goods were purchased directly from Europe, many were acquired in India. Hence, they needed Indian currency to buy these luxury goods. They tapped a number of sources to obtain Indian coins for these purchases.[66] The most productive sources were land revenue and commerce.

Several palatial buildings were constructed in the Kathmandu Valley on the model of Western architecture. The residence of Prime Minister Jang Bahadur at Thapathali in Kathmandu had four or five stories with large, lofty, and ornamented public rooms containing pictures and carvings and other curies of Nepalese, Chinese and English manufacture.[67] The public reception rooms in the house of the lesser nobility were also built in the English style, with lofty ceilings and glass windows, the walls of which were ornamented with mirrors and pictures, and the floors covered with Brussles carpets. These rooms were also filled with the most curious medley of useful and ornamental articles of English and French furniture. Besides that, the buildings were furnished with steel fire-places with marble mantelpieces, sofas, couches, easy chairs, billiard tables, and four-posted beds, candelabras, pianos, organs, glassware, vases, etc.[68]

There were twenty to thirty palaces in Kathmandu built for the Rana family. All were built in European fashion.[69] The Narayanhiti Seto Darbar of Prime Minister Bir Shamsher was the first palace built in such style. Two members of the Rana family, Kishore Narsingh and Kumar Narsingh, were the architects of the later Rana palaces. These include the Kaiser Mahal, Bahadur Bhawan and Sital Niwas which were all built after the First World

War. The biggest palace built before the war was Singha Darbar. It was constructed in 1903 for the residence of Chandra Shamsher. The architects of this palace were the French. The palace had 7 inner court yards and some 1,600 rooms.[70]

Since the 1920's the Rana had had motor cars in Kathmandu even though there was no road connection from India to Nepal over high mountains. The motors were carried to Kathmandu on the backs of porters over the Himalayan foothills. The same process was adopted to carry other articles such as statues of Prime Minister, mirrors, chandeliers, town clocks, sofas, bathtubs, grand pianos, central heating apparatus and so on. The Rana family had furniture which was unknown during ancient and medieval times in Nepal. Their gardens were decorated with ponds and trees.[71] The construction of these palaces stimulated a demand for building materials and services of masons, carpenters and labourers.[72]

A significant portion of the income derived from commerce and land revenue was spent on imported luxuries.[73]

With the expansion of Indo-Nepal trade the Nepalese Government felt the need for employing more porters for the transportation of mail. There were two types of porterage service: Kagate hulak for the transportation of official mail, and thaple-hulak for the transportation of arms and ammunition, gifts and presents to the royal palace and such other goods as may be specified from time to time under the signature of the Prime Minister. At the same time the system of "Jhara" and "Rakam" were also becoming more acute. Both these systems were one or another form of unpaid or forced labour. These were a kind of labour taxes imposed on the porters. The porters working under Jhara system had no choice but to provide service without wages. But in the latter system the porters were allotted some rice land for their services. Jhara labour could be rounded up by force,[74] if necessary, but Rakam obligations needed sustained motivation. The people under rakam system enjoyed some facilities and privileges during the early years of the nineteenth century. They were exempted from the payment of homestead taxes and levies and got security of occupancy rights on their rice lands. The Brahmans of both Jaise and Upadhyaya were given such privileges for the transportation of mail. The enrolment of members of untouchable communities for this purpose was usually banned. In this way, discrimination was practised in labour taxation on the basis of caste status. Consequently, the burden of such obligation.[75] However, it should be noted that unpaid and forced labour was used only for Governmental requirements. In June 1809, the Nepalese Government declared that labour should be employed for private purposes only on payment of wages at the rate of 2 annas only. Government officials were required to pay wages at the rate of ten paisa daily if they exacted porterage services from the inhabitants of homesteads and villages assigned to them. But in 1888 a law was passed by which daily wage rate of four annas was abolished, and employees were required to pay only reasonable wages fixed through mutual consent.[76]

A large-scale migration of Nepalese labourers from hill areas to Bengal, Assam, Burma and elsewhere, was the result of their exploitation by wealthy merchants and rulers. It was a kind of economic loss to the country as Major Northey observed, "Another and not less important factor is the unauthorized recruitment, very often on a very large scale, of Nepalese for coal-mines, rubber planting, and work generally under conditions that can but be the reverse of beneficial to the hillman. Prompt measures are needed to prevent this immigration becoming a real menace to the future welfare and prosperity of the Nation."[77] However, it was beneficial to the Indian Government, because, the emigration of economically active labour force of Nepal contributed much to the development of Indian economy. The development of the coal-mining industry in the adjoining provinces of Bihar and Bengal, and of the tea industry in Bengal and Assam, during the third quarter of the nineteenth century created a big demand for unskilled labour which, to some extent, was met through Nepalese emigrants. They also contributed to the opening up of new areas for reclamation and settlement in India.[78]

Nepalese proceeded towards modernization as a result of the growth of trade and commerce. Western science and technology were adopted in the scheme of modernization. An electric supply plant was set up near Kathmandu under the direction of an English engineer. A telephone line of 74 miles was opened in 1915 between Kathmandu and Birganj.[79] The Government started to explore the natural resources of the country for exporting the maximum amount of commodities to India and elsewhere. Geological exploration was put in charge of an Indian minerologist. A department of forestry was created with the co-operation of the Indian Forest Department. The river irrigation projects were started with the assistance of British and Indian engineers. Bir Shamsher established a hospital for the first time in 1890. Chandra Shamsher opened eighteen hospitals and fourteen dispensaries. A bacteriological laboratory and an X-ray Unit were also set up. All the doctors and nurses in the hospitals were from Bengal. Later on they were replaced by Nepalese doctors trained in Indian medical colleges. A system of drainage was started and Kathmandu got sewers in 1899. For the supply of drinking water in Kathmandu, pipelines were laid in 1892. Although in a restricted manner, the Rana Prime Ministers opened some educational institutions. Jang Bahadur employed a few Englishmen and Bengalis as private tutors of his relatives. In 1880, a High English School was established for the first time in Kathmandu for the Rana family and the nobility. Chandra Shamsher established an intermediate college in his name in Kathmandu in 1919.[80] He granted scholarships to enable Nepalese students to study medicine and technology in India and abroad.[81] In this way the Rana Prime Ministers had initiated development projects in Nepal[82] only when the revenue of the country increased as a result of improvement in trade and commerce. The modernization of army became possible when the British Indian Government allowed Nepal to import arms and ammunition in accordance with Article V of the Anglo-Nepal treaty of 1923.[83] Prior to it, it was restricted by Indian Government.

The Indo-Nepal trade had some remarkable impact on the economic development of the country. The revenue of the country greatly increased with the export of commodities and the increased production of the land. In 1853, the revenue receipts of the state totalled Rs. 961,375 in different Indian rupee units, worth Rs. 1,182,491 in Nepalese currency at the official exchange rate of

100:123.[84] The amount increased in the later periods of the Rana rule. Nepal had an annual income of Rs 3 to 3½ crores, out of which, after deducting the minimum possible expenditure on administration, a huge amount went into the pocket of the Rana Prime Ministers. They had huge amounts of money in foreign banks in their personal accounts, and in the account of their wives and children.[85]

Very little was spent for the development of industry. The Rana did not encourage the establishment of new industrial enterprises in order to keep the country isolated from external liberal influences. The ruling class was not only afraid of technical innovation, but also feared changes in the values and aspirations of the common man. They thought that the development of industries would create conditions favourable to the formation of organizations which would lead to a new awareness among workers regarding the sharing of political power. Hence no efforts were made to start consumer goods industries that could have potentially exploited the national economy and purchasing the increased power of the people. The treaty of 1923 allowed for practically unrestricted import of British goods to Nepal. Naturally it had the effect of discouraging the establishment of new industries.[86] Naturally, the exports of Nepal consisted merely of raw materials. However, it had a very good effect on the southern side of the Nepalese border, viz. north India where industries flourished and exports boomed.[87]

REFERENCES

1. K. Majumdar, "British Impact on Nepal". *Bengal Past and Present,* January-June, 1971, p. 4.
2. M.C. Regmi, *Thatched Huts and Stucco Palaces : Peasants and Landlords in tbe 19th Century Nepal*, New Delhi, 1979, pp. 18-19.
3. *Ibid.*
4. Ramakant, *Indo-Nepalese Relations, 1816 to 1877.* New Delhi, 1968, pp. 373-374.

5. Regmi, *op. cit.*
6. A.S. Bhasin, *Documents on Nepal's Relations with India and China 1949-66.* New Delhi, 1970, p. 11.
7. *Ibid.*
8. Hem Narayan Agrawal, *The Administrative System of Nepali from Tradition to Modernity.* New Delhi, 1976, p. 11.
9. Piers Blaikie, John Cameron, David Seddon. *Nepal in Crisis : Growth and Stagnation at Periphery.* New Delhi, 1980, p. 32.
10. Agrawal, *op. cit.* p. 12.
11. Francis Tuker, *Gorkha : The Story of the Gurkhas of Nepal.* London, 1957, p. 168.
12 Agrawal, *op. cit.* pp. 19-20.
13. *Ibid.* p. 21.
14. *Ibid*, pp. 39-40.
15. *Ibid*, pp. 62-63, 64.
16. *Ibid*, p. 65.
17. M.C. Regmi, "The Calcutta Buying Agency". *Regmi Research Series.* Year 13, No. 68. August 1, 1981. p. 126.
18 M.C Regmi, "Sale of wax in Patna". *Regmi Research Series.* Year 15, No. 3, 1 March 1983, p. 37.
19. Chandra Shamsher divided the Rana family into A, B and C groups A class Ranas were born of wives who were of the similar castes as their husbands. B class were born of wives entitled by caste to every form of association with their husbands except eating of rice together and C class were wives of such caste status as were not permitted marriage. Only A class Ranas were worthy to be a Prime Minister. Chandra Shamsher put Jang's sons and grandsons in B class. The condition of C class Rana was worst. In 1934 all C class Ranas were exiled to India. Among them Subarna Shamsher and Mahavir Shamsher were the two most important persons who played very active part in the revoluation of 1950-51.
20. Ramakant and B.C. Upreti, "India Community in Nepal : A Study of the Indian Migrants". *Indian in South Asia* (ed.) I. J. Bahadur Singh. Delhi, 1984, p. 23.
21. *Ibid*, p. 5.
22. Blaikie, *op. cit.* p. 37.
23. G.H.D. Gimlette, *Nepal and the Nepalese*, London (n.d.) p. 79.
24. The Newars were the oldest living group not only in Nepal but in the whole of India. Their civilization goes back to a period older than

Mohanjodaro. Their contribution to art and commerce is famous all over Asia. The main occupation of all the Newars except Jyapus (farmer) was commerce and craft and industry. They had covered the whole country as traders. All the mechanics of the country were Newars, except a few workmen from the plains of India, employed by the Government in the public workshops and arsenals. See. Daniel Wright, *op. cit.* p. 46: D.R. Regmi, *op. cit.* pp. 11-19.

25. *Ibid.* pp. 172-73.
26. Blaikie, *op. cit.* p. 124.
27. M.C. Regmi, *A Study in Nepali Economic History, 1768-1845.* New Delhi, 1971.
28. Blaikie, *op. cit.* p. 125.
29. Political A, August 1864, No. 51.
30. Bhaju means trader and is appended to the name of every Newar, See, D.R. Regmi. *op. cit.* p. 19.
31. M.C. Regmi, *op. cit.* p. 24.
32. Alastair Lamb, *Britain & Chinese Central Asia : The Road to Lhasa 1767-1905.* London, 1960, p. 346.
33. Gimlette. *op. cit.* p. 80.
34. Wright, *op. cit.* p. 46.
35. Heinrich Seemann, *Nepal : Till Yesterday, A Forbidden Country.* 1973 reprint Delhi, 1978, p. 17.
36. Percy Brown, *Nepal Gurkha and Newars of Himalayan Valley* J. A. Hammarton, ed. *Tribes, Races & Culture of India and Neighbouring Countries.* 1856, reprinted Delhi 1984, p. 322.
37. Blaikie, *op. cit.* p. 245.
38. *Ibid.* p. 151.
39. *Ibid.*
40. Chistoph Von Furer—Haimendorf, *Himalayan Traders : Life in Highland Nepal.* London, 1975, p. 188.
41. Blaikie, *op. cit.* pp. 151-52.
42. Bhairahwa was called Bethri at that time. See Blaikie, *op. cit.* p. 125.
43. Landon *op. cit.* p. 363.
44. The Tibetan word Sher means East : and Sherpa accordingly means "an easterner". The word is commonly used to denote the Bhotiyas of North Eastern Nepal, but the real homeland of these people is Solu Khambu, near Tibeto—Nepalese frontier,. See, C. J. Morris, *The Gurkhas: An Ethnology*, 1933, reprint Delhi 1985, p. 125.
45. Furer Haimendorf. *op. cit.* p. 60.

46. Hillary took initiative for the development of the region inhabited by the Sherpas. With his efforts one hospital, a school, a number of bridges and a landing strip for planes were built at about 9,000 ft height. Seeman *op. cit.* n.p. 18.

47. The first Musalmans to arrive in Kathmandu were Kashmiri traders who came from Tibet during the rule of Ratna Malla in the late 15th and early 16th centuries. They were traders of rays, carpets, shawls and other woolen goods. They travelled back and forth from Kashmir to Lhasa via Ladakh. It is believed that a few of them were invited to Kathmandu by an envoy of Ratna Malla in Lhasa. Soon after that some more Musalmans entered into the western hills. During the 17th or 18th century other Musalmans were brought from India to Nepal in the service of some of the Chaubise rajas of Nepal to train soldiers in the use of firearms. Later on large numbers of Musalmans migrated from India into the Tarai area as agricultural labourers and into the hill as sellers of bangles, glass beads and leather goods during or after the Indian Mutiny of 1857. See, Dor Bahadur Bista, *People of Nepal*. Kathmandu, 1980, p. 150.

48. Kashmiri and Iraqi were the principal traders in article of European manufacture. See, Wright, *op. cit.*, p. 46.

49. During the Moghul period of Indian history (1529–1707) several Marwaris began to move outside their homeland (in Rajasthan). They participated in the long range trade and high finance of North India. See, Thomas A. Timberg, *The Marwaris : From Traders to Industrialists*. New Delhi, 1978, p. 41.

50. The Kashmiri merchants migrated to Tibet when the trade with their own land was not extensive. They were very important in the economy of Tibet. The native of Kashmir might be compared with the Jews in Europe or Armenians in the Turkish Empire, for their far flung commercial enterprises through the eastern Kingdoms of Asia. They carried on an extensive traffic between the distant parts of East Asia and Tibet. They had also agents in South east India and in Nepal. See, Schuler, *op. cit.* p. 61.

51. Bista, *op. cit.* p. 150.

52. The Indian Marwaris and Baniyas were given right to settle down permanently in Kathmandu for trade after 1740 A.D. See, Jain, *op. cit.* p. n. 9.

53. Most of the industries in Nepal, were set up by them. They have shares in all the commercial activities of Nepal even today.

54. Blaikie, *op. cit.* p. 149.

55. Report on the External trade of Bengal with Nepal, Sikkim and Bhutan for 1880-81.

56. *Ibid* for 1882-82.

57. Revenue A. August 1877, No. 14.

58. Report on the External Trade of Bengal with Nepal, Tibet etc.

59. Bista, *op. cit.* p. 130.

60. More recently the Nepalese Government has frequently declared its intention of limiting economic activity by Indian nationals in Nepal. But the measure taken by the Government to control 'foreign' tıaders is difficult to inforce, because some Indian merchants have both Nepalese as well as Indian citizenship and can therefore invest in industries and conduct business in both countries. Others have married Nepalese wives or arranged marriages between members of their families and Nepalese citizens so that profit can be given to their families in India. Some businessmen conduct business on behalf of Indian owners through Nepalese managers. See, Blaikie, *op. cit.* pp. 149-50.

61. Ramakant and B.C. Upreti, *op. cit.*

62. General E. June 1893, No. 35 Pros. Lieutenant Colonel H. Wylie, the officiating British Resident in Nepal to the Secretary to the Government of India. dated 27 May 1893, (N.A.I.)

63. All the Departments of the Government were run on military lines. All the civil and judicial functionaries bad military titles. District judges were given the title of Lieutenant. See, C.G. Bruce & W. Book Northey. "Nepal". *The Geographic Journal.* Vol. LXV. No. 4, April 1925, p. 289.

64. Narendra Krishna Sinha. ed. *The History of Bengal (1757-1905).* Calcutta, 1967, p. 363.

65. Blaikie, *op. cit.*

66. Gaige, *op. cit.* p. 43.

67. Daniel Wright described the palace as a "curiosity of Nepalese, Chinese and English manufacture, from a baby's frock to a reflecting telescope or an Erad's Piano." See, Wright, op. cit. p. 18.

68. Oldfield, *op. cit.* p. 107.

69. Seeman, *op. cit.* p. 68.

70. It was the biggest of all the palaces in Asia. From 1951 until the night of 9 July 1973, when a huge fire destroyed the whole complex within 48 hours, the palace served the Nepalese Government as its Secretariat. Only the front wing which was used for state receptions survived. See, *Ibid.*

71. *Ibid.*

72. M.C. Regmi, *Thatched Huts and Stucco Palaces.* p. 156.

73. *Ibid*, p. 157.

74. For example, orders were issued in 1803 to the headmen of several villages in Sindhupalchok district in the hill region east of the Kathmandu valley to round up labourers and assemble them in Chitwan for an elephant hunt. It was a normal practice throughout the nineteenth century. Most of the material for the construction of palaces was brought by the porters under Jhara system. See, M.C. Regmi, *The State & Economic Surplus*. footnote 56, p. 109.

75. Regmi, *op. cit.* p. 96-97.

76. *Ibid.*, p. 100.

77. Bruce and Northey, *op. cit.* p. 298.

78. Regmi, *op. cit.* pp. 134-35.

79. Majumdar, *op. cit.* p. 9.

80. *Ibid.*

81. Manindra Bhushan Bhaduri, "Bagchi-Levi in Nepal ; A Glimpse of Rana Rule in the Early Twenties". *Calcutta Review*. Vol CLXIV. 1 July, 1962 ; p. 32.

82. Shriman Narayan, *India and Nepal : An exercise in Open Diplomacy*. Delhi, 1971, p. 62.

83. Bhasin, *op. cit.*, pp. 10-11.

84. Regmi, *The State and Economic Surplus*, p. 135.

85. Agrawal, *op. cit.* pp. 127-28.

86. P.C. Lohini, "Industrial Policy : The Problem Child of History and Planning in Nepal". *Nepal in Perspective*. (Eds) Pashupati Shamsher J.B. Rana and Kamal P. Malla, Centre for Economic Development and Administration, Kathmandu 1973. p. 2.

87. The location of industries in Bihar adjoining the Nepal border was based on agricultural raw materials. Up to the mid 19th century, Bihar enjoyed a fair share in India's trade and manufacture in hydro, salt-petre, textile, opium, jute, rice, etc. Indian jute mills were mostly located in west Bengal, Bihar, Assam and Orissa. In 1910, there were 220 industries in U.P. adjoining western Nepal. See, S.C. Kuchhal, *The Industrial Economy of India*. Allahabad, 1965, p. 71, also see, T.N. Kapoor, *Industrial Development in the States of India*. Delhi 1967, pp. 93-95, 102.

Conclusion

During the period under review Indo-Nepal trade witnessed significant expansion and ramifications, and served as the pivot around which political, cultural and other relations between Nepal and British India revolved. This trade was subject to fluctuations from time to time, but the ups and downs were not always due to economic and commercial causes. Non-commercial factors frequently intruded affecting its nature and extent, altering its pattern, and the commodities involved in transactions between the two countries. The fluctuations were often linked with changing policies and attitudes of the Government of the two countries. This is particularly noticeable in the case of Nepalese Prime Ministers Their attitude towards this trade reflected change rather than continuity, which was often dictated by the motives of personal gains and occasionally by their whims and fancies. In one respect, however, there is a remarkable continuity and consistency in the attitudes of the various Rana Prime Ministers. They all harboured deep suspicions of British motives. Acutely aware of the Nepalese proverb "The tradesman brings the Bible, the Bible brings the bayonet", they were extremely reluctant to allow free access of British Indian traders into Nepal. They were not unaware of how British commercial activities in India ultimately paved the way for conquest and establishment of their rule in that country. Hence, penetration of British capital and enterprise into Nepal was never permitted by the Nepalese Government. Even commercial activities were to remain within specified limits prescribed through mutual agreements made from time to time. In order to keep the trade within reasonable bounds and in order not to let British goods swamp the Nepalese markets, the Nepalese Government pursued a carefully worked out policy of monopolies in respect of certain specified commodities, particularly timber which accounted for a sizable percentage of Nepalese exports. The policy of monopoly trade was also favoured because of the high profit derived from the lucrative Indo-Nepal trade in which senior civil and military officials were engaged. The rulers sold monopoly rights to merchants who remitted a share of their profit to the Prime Minister. The system of monopoly also served to divert the attention of the elite (Sardars, nobles, officers, intellectuals, etc.) from politics to commerce, which brought them handsome profits'. Fearful of political and territorial designs characteristic of British imperialism, the rulers of Nepal refused to be bequiled by the prospects of material prosperity dangled before them by the British. They preferred freedom of the country to enslavement and colonization as had happened in India.

Indo-Nepal trade, even within the parameters prescribed by the apprehensive Nepalese rulers. had enormous potentialities for benefiting the Nepalese people generally. But this was not allowed to happen, because commercial contacts between the two countries were bound to bring in certain political and ideological tendencies in Nepalese politics which were likely to undermine the firmly entrenched position of the Rana rulers. The thesis clearly demonstrates that the restrictions imposed on Indo-Nepal trade were partly dictated by the vested interests of the Nepalese ruling circles. Their stake was heavy in economically, socially and politically backward Nepal, which they sought to perpetuate.

The sluggish Indo-Nepal trade received a remarkable boost during the rule of Jang Bahadur Rana who had rendered valuable help to the British during the revolt of 1857. Thanks to his friendly attitude to the British, Indo-Nepal trade flourished during his rule. In fact it continued to grow rapidly during the entire period of the political supremacy of the Ranas. The period between 1858 and 1914 may be regarded as the golden age in Nepal's commercial annals, for she enjoyed a favourable balance of trade by virtue of her exports which far exceeded imports. It must, however, be remembered that the commercial policy of the different Rana Prime Ministers never made a sharp break with the traditional policy of isolation and of opposition to free trade, and to unrestricted British economic and commercial penetration into Nepal, which had ominous political implications. Whatever flexibility was seen and relaxation and liberalisation allowed in the rigid policy during the time of Ranodip Singh and Bir Shamsher was actuated by the motives of expediency, i.e., to seek British support to strengthen the autocratic stronghold of the Ranas. But even this was tempered by genuine anxiety that too intimate connection with the British would be detrimental to the interests of the country. No amount of British denial of hostile intentions could be able to disabuse them of the fear that the British wanted to conquer and annex Nepal. Hence their persistent policy was to keep the British at a safe distance.

It was only during the time of Chandra Shamsher that the British were able to enjoy an upper hand in Indo-Nepal trade relations. The strategic importance of Nepal came to be appreciated more clearly when the British suspected Franco-Russian designs on Himalayan regions. Coupled with the necessity of recruiting Gorkha soldiers, whose loyalty was beyond doubt, in the Indian army in view of growing nationalist movement in India, this brought the two countries closer, and expansion of trade and commerce followed as a matter of course.

Development of transport and communications and the proximity of the Tarai to British India also gave impetus to Indo-Nepal trade. A detailed analysis of the means of transport and communication, the different trade routes and the variety of commodities that passed through them provides a measure of the growth that Indo-Nepal trade witnessed during the period under review. A major factor in this growth was the opening of the Indian railways in the districts bordering Nepal. By the close of the 19th century railway lines were built to connect a number of towns on the Indo-Nepal border situated along important centres of trade in Nepal. Besides, the extension of the Indian railway system to market towns on the Indian side of the border gave a fillip to the growth of towns and markets on the Nepali side of the border as well. Nepalganj, Birganj and Biratnagar owe their growth to this factor. Newar merchants of Kathmandu and Muslim merchants from India owned several shops and commercial establishments in these towns and market places. The rivers and rivulets flowing from Nepal into India provided another important means for carrying commodities from Nepal to the adjoining Indian districts, such as Purnea, Bhagalpur, Darbhanga, Muzaffarpur, Champaran, Gorakhpur, Basti and Pilibhit. The Indian railway system did not entirely displace the river borne traffic, for water communication was much cheaper than road and rail communications. The Nepalese were not as enthusiastic as the British in developing roads. They regarded the hills as "their fortifications" and did not like them to be breached by constructing roads which would facilitate access of the enemy into the country. The road policy of the Nepalese Government, however, did not seriously hamper Indo-Nepal trade.

The Nepalese rulers were equally reluctant to allow the British to trade with Tibet through Nepal. Jang Bahadur and all his successors were extremely jealous of British attempts to open up Tibet for trade, fearing damage to Nepalese commercial interests in that country. A subject which aroused intense competition between the Nepalese and Indian traders was the entrepot trade with Tibet through Nepal. Since trade with Tibet was much more profitable for the Indians than that with Nepal, the British were keenly interested in developing this entrepot trade. But the Nepalese Government which had been enjoying extra-territorial rights in Tibet since 1856, did not yield to British pressure and refused to give up its privileged position in Lhasa.

Nepal enjoyed a favourable balance of trade on account of her large exports. Forest products predominated in the overall exports to British India. But these were replaced by foodgrains, especially rice, towards the end of the 19th century. It was mainly due to the growth of cultivation in the Tarai region and deforestation and conversion of forest land into cultivable area.

Timber and foodgrains constituted the principal items of export from Nepal in the 20th century. Imports into Nepal consisted mainly of salt, sugar, tobacco and cloth. Besides, luxury goods in substantial quantities were also imported for the use of the Rana family and the elite groups.

Slave traffic was an important feature of Indo-Nepal trade during our period of study. Slavery was legal in Nepal and poor people of northern India used to sell their children to Nepaelse official and gently. When efforts were made by the Nepalese Government to minimise the incidence of slave traffic people engaged in this trade took to smuggling to evade detection and punishment. The Government of India, which had abolished slavery long ago, did not find it easy to check this traffic on the frontier which was wide open. And it was not till 1924 that slavery was abolished in Nepal.

The system of commercial taxation and customs duties also occasioned friction between the Nepalese and the British Governments. The British had no case in demanding a reduction of of customs duties when the duties imposed by them were much heavier then those prevailing in Nepal. This was precisely the reason wny their Residents in Nepal refused to press the Nepalese authorities to accept the demand for reductions of duties. On the western frontier of Nepal, however, the British had no cause for complaint. There the Nepalese Government imposed high export duties on Nepalese traders and very light import duties on Indian traders. It was done in order to compel the Nepalese traders to sell their goods in Nepalese markets and to attract Indian traders to promote trade in the new underdeveloped and sparsely populated region. Commercial taxes and customs duties were an important source of revenue to the Nepalese Government.

Although the bulk of trade on the Indo-Nepal border was carried on through barter, money economy played some part in commercial transactions between the two countries. Along with Nepalese currency Indian currency was in circulation in Nepal. The ruling Rana family wanted as much Indian currency as possible in order to buy luxurious foreign goods from India. Land revenue was also collected in Indian currency.

Indo-Nepal trade had manifold impact on Nepal. It not only affected the economy of the country, but also its politics and culture. The growing commercial transactions between the two countries induced drastic changes in the administration of Nepal.

New offices were opened, old ones were reorganised and streamlined and new posts were created to cope with the ever-expanding commercial activities in the country. With trade the possibilities of cultural exchange between the two countries also opened and matrimonial relationships were established between several Nepalese and Indian families. Profits from commerce brought material comforts to a large number of Nepalese people, especially those living in the Tarai and the Kathmandu Valley. Prosperous trading communities built palatial building in western style, and their living standards improved markedly. Not only this, commercial contacts familiarised the Nepalese with modern science and technology, and contributed, albeit on a modest scale, to the modernization of those who were associated with trade and commerce in one way or another.

Indo-Nepal trade was also a valuable source of state revenue. The Rana Government received a lot of money derived from commercial taxes and monopolies. But unfortunately bulk of this money was not spent on the development of the country. Instead it went into the private coffers of the Rana rulers and was used for their personal comforts. Part of it they deposited in foreign banks in their own name. This mainly accounts for the lack of industry in Nepal. Thanks to her short-sighted rulers, Nepal remained an exporter of raw materials and importer of finished factory products from foreign countries throughout the period under review. The country remained economically and socially backward in spite of the growth of commerce which created pockets of affluence here and there.

Bibliography

Unpublished

Government Records, Documents and Secret Correspondence

Foreign Ministry, Nepal : Date and other details are given in footnotes.

Finance Ministry, Nepal : Date and other details are given in footnotes.

National Archives of India : Nepal Residency Records 1872-1914. Foreign Political Consultations 1858-1914, Foreign Secret Consultations 1859-1913, Foreign Department Proceedings, External Branch 1889-1908, Foreign Department Proceedings, General Branch 1870-1909, Foreign Department Proceedings, Internal Branch 1909-1913, Foreign Department Proceedings. Finance Branch 1870-1882, Foreign Department General, Miscellaneous 1870-1886.

Unpublished Thesises

Adhikari K.K : "Nepal under Jang Bahadur 1846-1877" University of Nagpur, 1974.

Ansari M.H. "Nepal in World Affairs" Vikram University. Ujjain. 1974.

Husain A. "British India's Relations with Kingdom of Nepal from 1857 to 1947". University of Minnesota. 1965.

Sharma N. :"Nepal Foreign Trade" University of Delhi. 1968.

Published Documents

Aitchison, C.U. *A Collection of Treaties, Engagements aud Sanads Relating to India and Neighbouring Countries*, 14 Vols. Calcutta 1863.

Bhasin, A.S. (ed): *Documents on Nepal's Relations with India and China 1949-66.* New Delhi 1970.

British Ministry of Defence : *Nepal and the Gurkha.* London 1965.

His Majesty's Government of Nepal, Ministry of Law and Justice : *Sri 5 Surendra Bikram Shah Devakashasan Baneka Muluki Ain.* (Legal Code enacted during the reign of King Surendra Bikram Shah Dev) Kathmandu 2022 V.S. (1965).

His Majesty's Government of Nepal and Asian Development Bank: *Nepal Agriculture Sector Strategy Study.* Vol. II. Kathmandu, December 1982.

Intelligence Branch Army Headquarters of India : *Frontier and Overseas Expedition from India.* (Volumes 7) reprint of 1857, ed. Delhi 1983.

Rajvamsi, Shankarman : *Shahkalin Aitihasik Chittipatra Sangraha.* (Collection of Documents of the Shah period) Vol. I. Department of Archaeology, Kathmandu, 2023 V.S. (1966).

Memorandum

Memorandum on some of the Results of Indian Administration: During the Fifty Years of British Rule in India. Calcutta 1911.

Reports and Gazetteers

Report on the Foreign Trade of North Western Provinces and Oudh During the Year 1877—78. N.W.P. and Oudh Government. Allahabad 1878.

Report on the Trade of the North Western Provinces and Oudh from 1879—85.

Annual Report on the Foreign Trade of the North Western Provinces and Oudh for the year ending 31 March 1880.

Report on the Administration of the North Western Provinces and Oudh for the year ending 31 March 1899. Allahabad 1900.

Annual General Report on Nepal for the year 1906—7.

Administrative Report of the Patna Division for the year 1872—73.

The General Administration Report of the Bhagalpur Division for the year 1881—82.

Annual General Report of the Patna Division for 1881—82.

Annual General Administration Report of the Patna Division for 1890—91.

Report on the External Trade of Bengal with Nepal, Sikkim, Bhutan and Tibet 1878—79 to 1913—14.

Conbeare, H.C. ed. : *Gazetteer of N.W. Provinces.* Vol. VI, Allahabad 1881.

Das, Arthur Jules ed. : *Bengal District Gazetteers, Darjeeling.* Alipur 1947.

District Gazetteers of U.P., Gorakhpur Vol. XXXI.

Gazetteer of North Western Provinces 1881. Vol. VI.

Hunter, W.W. ed., : *Statistical Account of Bengal, Tirhut and Champaran.* Vol. XIII, London 1877.

————, *Statistical Account of Bengal, Purnia.* Vol. XV. London 1877.

————, *Statistical Account of Bengal, Patna and Saran.* Vol. XI. London 1877.

————, *Statistical Account of Bengal, Bhagalpur.* Vol. XV. Calcutta 1877.

Imperial Gazetteer of India, Afghanistan and Nepal, Calcutta 1908.

O'Malley, L.S.S., ed. : *Bengal District Gazetteers, Champaran.* Calcutta 1907.

————, *Bengal District Gazetteers, Muzaffarpur*, Calcutta 1907.

————, *Bihar, Orissa District Gazetteers, Champaran,* Patna 1938.

————, *Bengal, Bihar, Orissa and Sikkim*, Delhi.

Nevill, H.R. ed. : *District Gazetteers of the United Provinces of Agra and Oudh.* Vol. XVIII. Allahabad 1909.

————, *District Gazetteers of the United Provinces, Basti.* Vol. XXXII. Calcutta 1907,

Roychaudhury P.C. *Bihar District Gazetteers, Darbhanga,* Patna 1964.

————, *Bihar District Gazetteers, Champaran.* Patna 1960.

Books

Acharya, Yagya, : *Nepal Ka Itihas,* Kathmandu (2039 V.S.) 1982.

Agrawal, Hem Narayan : *The Administrative System of Nepal,* New Delhi 1976.

Alexander, McLiesh, : *The Frontier People of India,* London 1931.

Ali, Shah Ikbal, : *Nepal : The Home of the Gods ;* London n.d.

Blaikie, Piers; Cameron, Joh and Seddon, David. : *Nepal in Crisis: Growth and Stagnation at Periphery,* New Delhi, 1980.

Banskota, N. P. : *Indo-Nepal Trade and Economic Relations,* Delhi 1981.

Bhoosan, B.S., : *The Development Experience of Nepal,* New Delhi 1979.

Bista, Dor Bahadur, : *People of Nepal.* Kathmandu 1980.

Burathokey J.B.S. and Malla U.M. : "The Physical Aspects of the Kingdom of Nepal". Seminar Paper on the Ecology of the Tropicai Highlands. Nepal National Commission for UNESCO, 1968.

Campbell A. : *Notes on the Agriculture and Rural Economy of the Valley of Nepaul.* Kathmandu 1837.

Camman, Schuyler : *Trade Through the Himalaya, the Early British Attempt to open Tibct.* Princeton 1951.

Covenagh, Orefeur, : *Rough Notes on the State of Nepal, Its Government, Army and Resources.* Calcutta 1951.

————, *Reminiscences of an Indian Official* London 1884.

Chaudhary, K.C., : *Anglo—Nepalese Relations from the Earliest Times of the British Rule in India Till the Gorkha War,* Calcutta 1960.

Dhanalaxmi, Ravuri : *British Attitude to Nepal's Relations with Tibet and China 1814—1914.* New Delhi 1981.

Digby, William, : *A Friend in Need* 1857, *Friendship Forgotten*. London 1890.

Diwakar R.R. : *Bihar Through the Age*. Patna 1959.

Egerton Francis : *Journal of Winter Tour in India with a visit to the court of Nepal*. Two Volumes, Vol. I, London 1852.

Furer-Haimendorf Chistoph von : *Himalayan Traders : Life in Highland Nepal*, London 1975.

Gimalette, G.H.D. : *Nepal and the Nepalese*. London (n.d.)

Gopal, Surendra : *Patna in the 19th century* (A Socio-Cultural Profile), Calcutta 1983.

Hammerton, J.A. ed, : *Tribes, Races and Culture of India & Neighbouring countries*. 1856 reprint Delhi 1984.

Hamilton, C.J. : *The Trade Relations between England and India (1600—1896)* 1919 reprint Delhi. 1975.

Hamilton, Francis, : *An Account of the Kingdom of Nepal* 1819 reprint, New Delhi 1971.

Hodgson, B.H. : *Essay on the Languages, Literature and Religion of Nepal and Tibet*. London, 1874 reprint New Delhi 1972.

Hunter, W.W., : *Brain Haughton Hodgson*. London 1896.

Hunter, W.W. :*The Indian Empire, Its People, History and Products*. December 1892. reprint New Delhi 1973.

Husain, Asad. :*British India's Relations with the Kingdom of Nepal 1857—1947*. London 1971.

Jain, M.S., : *The Emergence of a New Aristocracy in Nepal*. Agra 1972.

Kapoor, T.N. : *Industrial Development in the States of India*. Delhi 1967.

Kirkpatrick, William : *An Account of the Kingdom of Nepaul*. London 1801.

Kuchhal, S.C., : *The Industrial Economy of India*. Allahabad 1965.

Kumar, Satis : *Rana Polity in Nepal*. Bombay 1967.

Lamb, Alastiar : *Britain and Chinese Central Asia : The Road to Lhasa 1767—1905*. London, 1960.

Landon, Perceval : *Nepal.* : Vol. II. London, 1928.

Lohini, P.C., ; *'Industrial Policy : the Problem Child of History and Planning in Nepal'*, in Rana Pashupati Shamsher J.B. and Malla, Kamal Prakash (eds), *Nepal in Perspective.* CEDA, Kathmandu. 1973.

Mehra, Parshotam, : *The Younghusband Expedition*, Bombay 1968.

Majumdar, B.P. : *The Socio-Economic History of Northern India.* Calcutta 1960.

Majumdar, : Kanchanmoy *Anglo-Nepalese Relations in the Nineteenth Century*. Calcutta 1972.

———, *Political Relations between India and Nepal.* New Delhi 1973.

Markham R. Clement : *Narrative of the Mission of George Bogle to Tibet and of Journey of Thomas Manning to Lhasa.* London 1876.

Martin, Montgomery, : *The History, Antiquities, Topography and Statistic of Eastern India.* Vol. 2. reprint of 1828 ed. Delhi 1976.

Morris C.J. :*The Gurkhas : An Ethnology* 1933. reprint Delhi 1985.

Mridula, Abrol.:*British Relations with Frontier States (1863-1873).* New Delhi 1974.

Narayan, Shriman : *India and Nepal : An Exercise in Open Diplomacy.* Delhi 1971.

Nepali Chittaranjan : *General Bhimsen Thapa Ka Tatkalin Nepal.* Kathmandu (2013 V.S.), 1956.

Oldfield H. Ambrose : *Sketchas from Nepal.* Vol. II, London 1880, reprint Delhi 1974.

Premble, John : *The Invasion of Nepal*, Oxford 1971.

Ramakant *Indo-Nepalese Relations 1816—1877.* New Delhi 1968.

———, *Nepal, China and India.* New Delhi, 1976.

Ramakant and Upreti, B.C. : Indian Community in Nepal : A Study of the Indian Migrants. in I.J. Bahadur (ed.) *Indians in South Asia*. Delhi 1984.

Rana, Pashupati Shamsher : J.B. and Malla, Kamal Prakash (eds): *Nepal in Perspective*. Centre for Economic Development and Administration. Kathmandu, 1973.

Rawat, P.C. : *Indo-Nepalese Economic Relations*. New Delhi, 1974.

Regmi, D.R. : *Ancient Nepal*. Calcutta, 1969.

————, *Ancient and Medieval Nepal*. Kathmandu 1952.

————, *Inscriptions of Ancient Nepal*. New Delhi, 1983.

————, *Modern Nepal*. Calcutta 1960.

Regmi, M.C., : *A Study in Nepalese Economic History 1768—1846*. New Delhi 1971.

————, *Thatcted Huts and Stucco Palaces, Peasants and Landlords in 19th Century Nepal*. New Delhi 1978.

————, *The State and Economic Surplus : Production, Trade, and Resource Mobilization in Sarly 19th Century Nepal*. Varanasi 1984.

————, *Reading in Nepal Economic History*. Varanasi, 1979.

Roychaudhury, P.C. : *Inside Bihar*. Calcutta, July 1962.

Sanwal, B.D. : *Nepal and the East India Company*. Bombay 1965.

Seemann, Heinrich, : *Nepal : Till Yesterday, A Forbidden Country*, 1973, reprint Delhi 978.

Sen, Jahar : *Indo-Nepal Trade in the nineteenth Century*. Calcutta 1977.

Shah, K.T. : *Trade, Traffic and Transport in India*. Bombay 1923.

Shaha, Rishikesh, : *An Introduction to Nepal*. Kathmandu 1975.

————,*Essay in the Practice of Government in Nepal*. Delhi 1982.

Sharma, Balchandra.: *Nepal Ko Aitihasik Rup Rekha*. Banaras, 1976.

Sinha, N.K. (ed) : *The History of Bengal* 1757-1908. Calcutta 1967.

Shreshtha, B.P. *An Introduction to Nepalese Economy*. Kathmandu 1966.

Shrestha, Chandra B. and Sharma, Pitamber : *Physical Setting and Natural Resources, Availability and Prospect*, Nepals Economy —An Overview. Centre for Economic Development and Administration, Tribhuvan University, Kirtipur, Kathmandu, April 1980.

Shrestha, Devi Chandra (ed) : *Mabarg Niwaran* (Price Control Measure). Kathmandu (V.S. 2030), 1973.

Shreshtha, Saranhari, : *Modern Geography of Nepal.* Kathmandu 1972.

Singh, I.J. Bahadur (ed) : *Indians in South Asia.* Delhi 1984.

Srivastava, S.N., : *Harijans in India.* Lucknow, 1980.

Stiller, S.J., Ludwig F. : *Rise of the House of Gorkha : A Study in the Unification of Nepal* 1768-1786. Kathmandu 1975.

———, *Prithvinarayan Shah, in the Light of Dibya Updesh.* Kathmandu 1968.

Timberg Thomas A. : *The Marwaris : From Traders to Industrialist*, New Delhi 1978.

Tuker, Francis, : *Gorkha : The Story of the Gorkhas of Nepal.* London 1957.

Turner, Captain Samuel : *An Account of an Embassy to the Court of the Teshoo Lama in Tibet.* Delhi 1971.

Tyagi, Shushila : *Indo-Nepalese Relation 1858-1914.* Delhi, 1972.

Uprety, Prem R. : *Nepal Tibet Relations 1850-1930 : Years of Hopes, Challenge and Frustration.* Kathmandu 1980.

Vansittart, Eden. : *The Goorkhas.* 1890 reprint, Delhi 1980.

Wright, Daniel *Nepal, History of the Country and People.* 1877 reprint, Delhi 1983.

Walse, E.H. : *The Coinage of Nepal.* Delhi. 1973.

Articles

Acharya, Baburam. : Rajendra Vikram Shah Ko Shasan (Role of

Rajendra Vikram Shah). *Purnima.* Vol. 27 Kathmandu, 1972.

Acharya Harihar : "Uttari Sima Vyapar" (Northern Frontier Trade). Gorkhapatra 5 May 1980.

Adhikari Krishana Kant. : "A Brief Survey of Nepal's Trade with British India During the latter Half of the Nineteenth Century" *Contribution to Nepalese Studies.* Vol. 2. No. 1. February 1975.

Bhaduri,: "Bagchi—Levi in Nepal; A Glimpse of Rana Rule in the Early Twenties" *Calcutta Review.* Vol. CLXIV, 1 July 1962.

Gurung, Hark : "Geographic Foundations of Nepal" *The Himalayan Review.* Nepal Geographic Society, Kathmandu 1968.

Hodgron, Brain H. : "On the Native Method of Making the Paper, denominated in Hindusthan, Nipaleso". *Journal of Asiatic Society of Bengal.* Vol. I, No. 1. January 1832.

Jha, S.K. :"British India's policy towards Nepal." *Journal of Bihar Research Society.* Vol. IV, Pts 1-4.

Kachikian, Levon. : "The Ledger of the Merchant Hovhannes Joughyetri." *Journal of Asiatic Society.* Vol VIII, No. 3. Calcutta 1966

Katti, Vijay. : "Commodity and Geographic concentration in Indo-Nepalese Trade". *Foreign Trade Review.* (18) October-December 1983.

Manandhar, Triratna, : "Rana Kalin Parcha Estihar". *Voice of History.* Journal of History Instruction Committee. Vol. II. Kathmandu 1976.

Majumdar, Kanchanmoy. : "British Impact on Nepal" *Bengal Past and Present.* January-June. 1971.

Nepal, Gyanmani, : "Nepal Ko Dhan Videshi Bank ma". (Nepal's wealth in Foreign Bank). *Arthik Nepal* (Ed.) Devi Chandra Shrestha. Kathmandu, November 1982.

Northey W. Brook and Bruce C.G., : "Nepal". *The Geographical Journal* Vol. LXV. No. 4. April 1925.

Sen Jahar., : "The Tune of Timber in Indo-Nepal Relations". *Calcutta Historical Journal.* Vol. VII, No. 1, July-December 1982.

————,"Slave Trade on the Indo-Nepal Border in the Nineteenth-Century" *Kailash.* Kathmandu. January-February, 1973.

Shamsher, Barun (ed) : "From the Himalayan Height" *Nepal Guardian.* Kathmandu n. d.

Shrestha, Devi Chandra (ed) : "Brahmadeo-Mandi", *Arthik Nepal.* Vol. I, No. 3, Kathmandu, June 1983.

Stiller, S.J. Ludwig F., : "A Note on Himalayan Trade". *Journal of Tribhuvan University.* Vol. VII, No. 1. November 1972.

—————, "Currency Confusion". *Journal of Tribhuvan University.* Vol. VIII, No. 1, November 1973.

Regmi Research Series.